*Great Britain and the Creation
of the League of Nations*

Great Britain and the Creation
of the League of Nations

Strategy, Politics, and International
Organization, 1914–1919

by George W. Egerton

The University of North Carolina Press
Chapel Hill

Copyright © 1978 by
The University of North Carolina Press
All rights reserved
Manufactured in the United States of America
ISBN 0-8078-1320-6
Library of Congress Catalog Card Number 77-17897

Library of Congress Cataloging in Publication Data

Egerton, George W
    Great Britain and the creation of the League of
Nations.

    (Supplementary volumes to The papers of Woodrow
Wilson)
    Bibliography: p.
    Includes index.
    1. League of Nations—Great Britain.   2. Great
Britain—Foreign relations—1910–1936.   I. Title.
II. Series: Wilson, Woodrow, Pres. U. S., 1856–1924.
Papers : Supplementary volume.
JX1975.5.G7E37   341.22'41   77-17897
ISBN 0-8078-1320-6

For Mary Trevelyan
and
Friends at International Students House
London

Contents

Acknowledgments

The author wishes to express gratitude to the following persons and institutions for permission to use copyright material under their control: The Controller of Her Majesty's Stationery Office (Crown copyright material in the Public Record Office, London); the Marquess of Lothian (papers of Philip Kerr, 11th Marquess of Lothian); the Hon. Mrs. Butterwick and the Dowager Viscountess Davidson (papers of Lord Willoughby H. Dickinson); Captain Stephen Roskill, R.N. (papers of Lord Hankey); A. J. P. Taylor and the House of Lords Record Office (papers of Lloyd George); Audrey Davis, secretary, League of Nations Union (records of the League of Nations Union); Gordon Phillips, archivist and researcher, the *Times* (papers of Wickham Steed, Arthur Willert, and Lord Northcliffe); Yale University Library (papers of E. M. House and Sir William Wiseman); and Professor A. K. S. Lambton (papers of Lord Robert Cecil).

Agnes Headlam-Morley provided information on the career of her father; The Right Hon. Philip Noel-Baker kindly granted two interviews; the late Sir J. R. M. Butler discussed with me his role in the creation of the league and showed me papers in his possession; and Sir Dennis Proctor made G. Lowes Dickinson's autobiography available to me before its publication in 1973.

I am indebted to Harold I. Nelson, Michael G. Fry, James Barros, Henry R. Winkler, Lawrence E. Gelfand, Arthur Walworth, and Douglas Goold for comments on various stages and portions of the manuscript. A special debt is owed to Arthur Link.

Research for this book was made possible by funds from the Canada Council and support from the University of British Columbia.

Introduction

Recent years have seen a wealth of scholarly publication on British foreign policy of the late nineteenth and early twentieth centuries, a period during which British statesmen responded to manifold challenges to the security of the home islands and the overseas empire and which culminated in the Great War. The themes of imperial rivalries, naval competition, continental commitments, and dominion relations have been analyzed by historians in light of the copious documentation now available. The politics and diplomacy of the war years and peacemaking have attracted many students of British history. The result of this new scholarship has been a major enlargement of our knowledge about Britain's position and role in world politics of this period, as well as the domestic underpinnings of her foreign policy.

There are, of course, gaps in the historical record and there will always be room for revision and changing insight. One such gap concerns the question of international organization debated in wartime British politics and the role of the British government in the creation of the League of Nations. The American part in the creation of the league, particularly the dramatic role of President Wilson, has been amply chronicled by historians. There remain, however, important uncertainties concerning the British side of this venture, most specifically the role of Lloyd George and the coalition government that he headed. Can we accept the assertions of Lloyd George that he and his government were consistent in their devotion to the league and entitled to major credit for its creation?[1]

Ray Stannard Baker grouped Lloyd George with Clemenceau in the conspiracy of the old order against Wilson, the league, and the New Diplomacy.[2] Frank P. Walters, author of the standard history of the league and a minor British participant in 1919, argues that there were those in his government's military and diplomatic ranks who strongly opposed the project and that "Lloyd George as Prime Minister cared nothing about the idea of a League."[3] Lord Robert Cecil, leader of the British delegation on the League of Nations Commission at Paris, later argued that although the prime minister officially supported the league, his approval was always "chilly," and he regarded it "as of secondary importance."[4] Does Henry Winkler's conclusion from evidence available in 1952 still stand, that the covenant, projecting a limited league, can "safely be said to have reflected the official British position in many of its most important aspects"?[5]

This study, building upon recent scholarship and utilizing new documentation, will examine the wartime debate in Britain on the question of international organization, analyze the attitudes and policies of government leaders, and reassess the contribution of the British government to the creation of the League of Nations.

The analysis is placed in the context of the larger debate on British strategy that preceded the war and underlay much of the war-aims debate and planning for future peace and security. Most government leaders and advisors hoped to fashion a league of nations that would complement traditional British strategies, whether based on naval hegemony and imperial strength or on a continental commitment to uphold the European balance of power, and also facilitate Anglo-American cooperation in future world politics.

At the same time, the league idea, with its immediate origins in the nineteenth-century peace movement and the prewar politics of British radicalism and dissent, presented a direct challenge to traditional strategies and interests. For its proponents, the league project offered Britain the chance to surmount the inadequacies and dangers of her traditional strategies and lay the foundations for world peace and British security through a new strategy of liberal internationalism. Given President Wilson's championing of the New

Diplomacy, the league idea also suggested the alluring prospect of a lasting pax Anglo-Americana.

The challenge of the league idea to traditional strategies was doubly potent because, after 1917, the social and ideological consequences of the war made it impossible to divorce politics from war-aims declarations and strategic planning in what had become a revolutionary era. Because the war saw the rise of a powerful league of nations movement and wide-ranging popular commitment to the ideology of the New Diplomacy, it is necessary to place British debate on the league question in its broader social and strategic context. Not only did the league of nations movement see the realization of its immediate goal in the creation of the league at the Paris peace conference, but the ideas of wartime dissenters and proleaguers had a powerful impact on the political attitudes and values of postwar British society. The League of Nations trilogy of "collective security," arbitration, and disarmament had an irresistible effect on the domestic underpinnings of interwar British foreign policy. There is much to be said for A. J. P. Taylor's suggestion that the dissent of one generation tends to become the orthodoxy of the next.[6] The infusion of mass politics into strategic planning, however, vastly complicated the task of formulating British foreign and defense policies in a period that witnessed the denigration of both power calculations and traditional strategies in favor of collective security through the league.

Finally, in studying the creation of the League of Nations from the British side, and in analyzing the intense debate on the question that occurred within the government and in British society, it is hoped that what follows will make a significant contribution to the history of international organization in the twentieth century.

Great Britain and the Creation
of the League of Nations

War and Liberalism: The Birth of the League of Nations Idea

The years preceding the outbreak of the Great War had witnessed an intense strategic debate in Britain as naval, military, diplomatic, and political leaders attempted to reshape foreign and defense policies to meet the challenges of the Edwardian period.[1] The prewar debate had clarified the major strategic options open to Britain as an island empire centered off the European continent: a continental military strategy of alignment with a European bloc to preserve the balance of power and protect national security if war came; or a naval imperial strategy of aloofness from continental entanglements and reliance on the navy and the empire to protect national and imperial interests. Theoretically, these two strategies could have been integrated, but institutional divisions and traditional rivalries prevented such integration before the war. Given the newly acquired influence of the Foreign Office and the General Staff, British foreign and defense policy under Sir Edward Grey's foreign secretaryship proceeded on the basis of a continental military strategy, without subordinating the admiralty to this policy in strategic planning.[2]

The British declaration of war on Germany, 4 August 1914, and the dispatch of the British Expeditionary Force to fight alongside France saw the logic of the continental strategy work itself out in military intervention. Grey's parliamentary war speech of 3 August reflected the European focus of the Foreign Office and the General Staff by emphasizing the commitment to France and the vital British interests in protecting Belgium, preserving the balance of power and preventing all of Western Europe from "falling under the domination of a single Power."[3] The advocates of an imperial naval strategy would have to bide their time until the costs of a continental strategy became apparent.

Beyond the strategic choices of August 1914, the very decision to intervene in the war precipitated a major political crisis within the ruling Liberal party. Reversion to the barbarism of war presented radicals, pacifists, and the Left with a stunning blow to all their hopes for peace and progress. The cohesion of the Liberal cabinet was constantly in danger through this final crisis as Lloyd George and other radicals pondered the opportunities and risks of dissent.[4] Outside the government during the final days of peace, radicals and Labourites frantically attempted to organize a neutrality committee and a neutrality league to oppose British intervention, while the radical press thundered away on the same theme.[5] Only the invasion of Belgium enabled the prime minister, Asquith, and Grey to convert the cabinet to the cause of war. Soon patriotism, nationalism, and the call to blood swept the nation, but the conversion of the Liberal party caused misgivings and bewilderment, particularly for those liberals and radicals who were true believers in Christian pacifism or the humanist, rationalist, and progressivist tenets of liberal ideology.

One attempt to assuage the shock to the liberal credo and smooth the transition to war was to legitimize the conflict as a struggle for justice and righteousness. Here again the invasion of Belgium was central. Asquith lost no time in identifying the ideals that inspired the Allied cause. On 6 August, the prime minister disclosed to Parliament and the country his belief that no nation had ever entered into a great controversy with a clearer conscience and a stronger conviction of the virtue of its cause. Britain was fighting to protect the integrity of small nations, to ensure respect for international obligations, and to defend "principles vital to the civilization of the world."[6] In the hysteria of the first days of war, others picked up the theme of righteous war and went far beyond Asquith in enthusiasm. Dr. John Clifford appealed to free churchmen to

join the battle—"a battle of moral ideals and ideas against im-
moral; of spiritual forces against material . . . a fight for the human
soul to freedom, independence and self-control against an arrogant,
autocratic, swaggering and cruel military caste."[7] For H. G. Wells,
"Never was war so righteous as against Germany now."[8] Wells
went on to expound themes of "The War That Will End War,"
urging liberals to seize the opportunities for reshaping the world as
war now threw the ancient structures of Europe into the cauldron
of change:

> Let us redraw the map of Europe boldly as we mean it to be
> redrawn, and let us replan society as we mean it to be con-
> structed. Now is the opportunity to do fundamental things that
> will otherwise not get done for hundreds of years. If Liberals
> throughout the world—and in this matter the liberalism of
> America is a stupendous possibility—will insist upon a world
> Conference at the end of this conflict, if they refuse all partial
> settlements and merely European solutions, they may redraw
> every frontier, may reduce a thousand chafing conflicts of race
> and language and government to a minimum and set up a Peace
> League that will control the globe. The world will be ripe for it.[9]

The themes of righteous war, the evil enemy, and the millennial
possibilities of the future deeply appealed to the liberal conscience.
These themes, however, had little appeal to the radical intelligentsia,
whose attempts to resist the drift to war had all resulted in futility.
Although the appeal to war cut sharply into the ranks of radicalism,
leaders of new radical thought could find some solace in explaining
the war within the framework of their prewar critique of government foreign policy and the diplomatic system. Had not radicals
warned against the dangers of the arms race, imperialism, secret
diplomacy, the alliance system, and the government's dedication to
the balance of power?[10] In the early weeks of the fighting, largely
on the initiative of Arthur Ponsonby, a group of radical leaders
joined with dissident Labourites, who also refused to be swept
along with the prowar tide, to form the Union of Democratic Control.[11] The founding group included Ponsonby, Charles Trevelyan,
E. D. Morel, John Hobson, H. N. Brailsford, Norman Angell, and
Ramsay MacDonald. Rejecting the dogma of German and Austrian

responsibility for causing the war, the union was anxious to combat the idea that total victory over the enemy was the only path to a lasting peace. To put the foundation for a lasting peace before the public, the union published a program of four "Cardinal Points" in September 1914. These points stipulated the following:

> 1. No Province shall be transferred from one Government to another without the consent, by plebiscite or otherwise, of the population of such Province.
> 2. No Treaty, Arrangement, or Undertaking shall be entered upon in the name of Great Britain without the sanction of Parliament. Adequate machinery for ensuring democratic control of foreign policy shall be created.
> 3. The Foreign Policy of Great Britain shall not be aimed at creating Alliances for the purpose of maintaining the Balance of Power, but shall be directed to concerted action between the Powers, and the setting up of an International Council, whose deliberations and decisions shall be public, with such machinery for securing international agreement as shall be the guarantee of an abiding peace.
> 4. Great Britain shall propose as part of the Peace settlement a plan for the drastic reduction, by consent, of the armaments of all the belligerent Powers, and to facilitate that policy shall attempt to secure the general nationalization of the manufacture of armaments, and the control of the export of armaments by one country to another.[12]

From this beginning the UDC organized an educational campaign to enlighten British opinion on the type of program that would be necessary for a durable peace. Naturally, its program met with the hostility of fervent nationalists, who simply labeled dissenters defeatist or pro-German.[13] The government and prowar liberalism similarly had no use for the union. The union consciously directed its propaganda and program to the Left, and, although the Labour party remained solidly prowar and deaf to dissent through the first two years of the war, the UDC program met with a sympathetic reception from the Independent Labour party. In fact, the experience of the UDC in the early war period facilitated the movement of the more advanced radicals from liberalism to Labour. Later, when labor began questioning the war effort, the UDC program provided the principal inspiration for Labour party declarations on war aims and peace policy. Although the going was initially difficult for the UDC, by the end of 1915 over fifty branches had been established, and with the affiliation of many labor groups, the UDC could claim a membership of 300,000.[14] First in the field with a coherent peace program, through its publications and monthly magazine, the UDC did much to lay the conceptual foundation for the subsequent rhetoric and ideology of the New Diplomacy.

While the theme of international organization or an international council to guarantee peace had served as the third point of the UDC program, the major energies of the UDC concentrated on the other points of the program, particularly the central theme of democratic control of foreign policy. Another section of British liberalism would assume chief responsibility for developing and propagating the theme of a league of nations. Schemes for international organization had a long history by 1914. Nearly all major wars of modern history had been followed by projects for perpetual peace. The idea of a peace league had been thoroughly canvassed in the nineteenth-century peace movement, along with such themes as arbitration, international law, and disarmament.[15] As the role of governments generally expanded and as more technical and social cooperation became necessary across national boundaries, the idea of international organization received increasing attention and support. The outbreak of European war naturally revived interest in this idea.

There were many scattered references to the idea of a peace league in the early weeks of the war, but the major credit for the initial development of the league of nations idea must go to G. Lowes Dickinson. Dickinson, a classics scholar and Fellow of Kings College, Cambridge, had, even before the war, developed an interest in political philosophy and international relations.[16] His prewar political writing envisioned a world in harmony and peace where the human spirit could develop freely and fully, a vision shared by the peace movement and many radicals. In 1908 Dickinson projected this vision through the auto-character of Geoffrey Vivian:

> I see the time approaching when the nations of the world, laying aside their political animosities, will be knitted together in the peaceful rivalry of trade; when those barriers of nationality which belong to the infancy of the race will melt and dissolve in the sunshine of science and art; when the roar of the cannon will yield to the softer murmur of the loom, and the apron of the artisan, the blouse of the peasant be more honourable than the scarlet of the soldier; when the cosmopolitan armies of trade will replace the military of death; when that which God has joined together will no longer be sundered by the ignorance, the folly, the wickedness of man; when the labour and the invention of one will become the heritage of all; and the peoples of the earth meet no longer on the field of battle, but by their chosen delegates, as in the vision of our greatest poet, in the 'Parliament of man, the Federation of the World.'[17]

The war came as a shattering blow to this world view. Dickinson wrote despairingly to a friend: "One's whole life has been trying to establish and spread reason, and suddenly, the gulf opens and one finds the world is ruled by force and wishes to be so."[18] Dickinson's faith in the power of reason, however, soon revived, and he decided to concentrate on reforming the international system and working for the creation of a league of nations. In September he published probably the first systematic wartime scheme for a "permanent League of Nations of Europe." The main feature of this plan was the institution of a general system of compulsory arbitration. A central council open to all states would control the armed forces of members and ensure enforcement of arbitral awards. The council would deliberate openly and function under direct popular control.[19]

Though Dickinson joined the UDC in November, after hesitation and misgivings about its tactics, the league idea remained his principal political passion. In September and October he brought together a group of liberal educators, politicians, and journalists to discuss the idea.[20] Although Hobson and Ponsonby were included in the original circle, the group and its program remained quite distinct from the UDC. Soon known as the Bryce group after Lord Bryce joined and became its chairman, the group also included Sir Willoughby H. Dickinson, a Liberal M.P., churchman, and prominent member of the prewar peace movement; Richard Cross, a Quaker convert and business manager for the *Nation*; and Graham Wallas, a political theorist at the new London School of Economics.[21] The group exchanged ideas on possible schemes for postwar international organization, and detailed plans were submitted by G. Lowes Dickinson, Bryce, Hobson, Ponsonby, and W. H. Dickinson.[22] A synthesis of the various schemes was drawn up by Cross, secretary of the group, and circulated to members. Further discussion during the winter of 1914–15 resulted in the printing of *Proposals for the Avoidance of War* for private circulation among the group and a wider circle of liberal academics, journalists, and politicians. This scheme, although not published until later in the war, served as a basis for communication and discussion with similarly motivated individuals and groups in Britain and America.

The *Proposals* suggested a system, set up after the war by a treaty among the six European great powers, the United States, Japan, and all other European powers willing to join, for the peaceful settlement of international disputes. The scheme divided international disputes into two categories—justiciable and nonjusticiable. Signatory powers would agree to refer all justiciable disputes to the Permanent Court of Arbitration at The Hague or to another arbitral tribunal and to accept and give effect to the award of such a tribunal. Justiciable disputes were those "disputes as to the interpretation of a treaty, as to any question of international law, as to the existence of any fact which, if established, would constitute a breach of any international obligation, or as to the nature and extent of the reparation to be made for any such breach."

In the case of nonjusticiable disputes, the parties would agree to refer the matter to a permanent council of conciliation. The council would consist of members appointed for a fixed term of years, the great powers each appointing three and other powers at least one. The council, after considering the dispute, would publish a report containing recommendations for an amicable settlement and could frame suggestions for a limitation or reduction of armaments. Because members of the council would be persons of distinction and would not represent governments directly, their decisions presumably would be objective and unprejudiced.

Signatory powers would agree not to resort to hostilities against one another until twelve months after the submission of a dispute to either an arbitral tribunal or the council of conciliation, or until six months after a report published by either body. If a signatory power refused to submit a dispute to consideration by the council or tribunal, or resorted to hostilities before the expiration of the prescribed period of delay, the other signatories undertook to "support the Power so attacked by such concerted measures, diplomatic, economic or forcible, as, in the judgment of the majority of them, are most effective and appropriate to the circumstances of the case." Finally, if any signatory power, having submitted a dispute to the council, failed to follow the recommendations of the council, the other powers would consider what collective action, if any, to take.

The *Proposals*, while advocating a "real and radical advance" in the organization of international relations, avoided anything so utopian as to preclude practical acceptance and implementation. Therefore, no attempt was made to construct a world-state or even a European federation. No international police force or international executive was contemplated; all action by members of the union would be taken as sovereign states acting through their ordinary diplomatic and governmental machinery; the council was specifically denied executive power. The plan involved three essential obligations: to submit disputes to peaceful settlement; to refrain from hostilities while the dispute was being investigated; and to mobilize collective resistance against any power that acted contrary to the first two obligations. Attention was drawn to the potential effectiveness of a collective economic sanction, the hope being that some nations, including the United States, might be more willing and able to employ this weapon than actual armed force. While the scheme might not make war impossible, "the enforced period of delay, the consideration by an impartial Council, and the publicity given to its recommendations would be likely to prevent war by rallying the public opinion of the world in favour of peace," and, if war did break out, it was much more likely to be restricted.[23]

The Bryce plan obviously owed much to prewar radicalism and the peace movement. The themes of arbitration, conciliation, disarmament, and publicity were all good radical-liberal principles. Only the theme of collective economic or military action by peaceful nations to ensure peaceful procedures in the resolution of disputes departed from prewar radicalism. This theme, however, quickly assumed critical importance in the wartime league of nations movement. The Bryce group advanced it only after strenuous debate that revealed grave misgivings and opposition on the part of several members, as will be shown.

The Bryce group remained a loosely organized discussion circle. The *Proposals* served as a bridge to further discussion and did not represent an agreed upon policy or program of the group.[24] Nor did the group try to propagate the idea of a peace league. In May 1915, however, another group proceeded to draw up a definite program and soon began to organize a movement on behalf of the league of nations idea. On 4 February 1915 twenty to thirty people interested in a peace league met in the London home of Walter Rea.[25] Discussion centered on an article by Aneurin Williams, "Proposals for a League of Peace and Mutual Protection Among Nations," published in the November 1914 issue of the *Contemporary Review*.[26] The group met at the Rea home again on 10 March, this time as the Union of States Society. A provisional committee was set up to work on a possible program for the society. Members of this committee included Aneurin Williams, W. H. Dickinson, G. Lowes Dickinson, F. N. Keen, Raymond Unwin, and Mr. and Mrs. A. W. Claremont.[27]

By May the committee had reached agreement on a program. On 3 May 1915 a general meeting adopted this program as the constitutional basis of the League of Nations Society. Lord Shaw of Dunfermline agreed to act as president of the new society, and W. H. Dickinson, Ernest Rhys, and Aneurin Williams were appointed respectively as chairman of the executive, treasurer, and secretary. Through 1915 the League of Nations Society privately circulated its program in liberal circles and by November had attracted a membership of 148.[28] The first general meeting of the society, held

29 November 1915, adopted the following points as the "Objects of the Society":

> 1. That a Treaty shall be made as soon as possible whereby as many States as are willing shall form a League binding themselves to use peaceful methods for dealing with all disputes arising among them.
>
> 2. That such methods shall be as follows:
>
> (a) All disputes arising out of questions of international law or the Interpretation of Treaties shall be referred to the Hague Court of Arbitration, or some other Judicial Tribunal, whose decisions shall be final and shall be carried into effect by the parties concerned.
>
> (b) All other disputes shall be referred to and investigated and reported upon by a Council of Inquiry and Conciliation: the Council to be representative of the States which form the League.
>
> 3. That the States which are members of the League shall unite in any action necessary for insuring that every member shall abide by the terms of the Treaty.
>
> 4. That the States which are members of the League shall make provision for Mutual Defence, diplomatic, economic, or military, in the event of any of them being attacked by a State, not a member of the League, which refuses to submit the case to an appropriate Tribunal or Council.
>
> 5. That any civilized State desiring to join the League shall be admitted to membership.[29]

The program reflected close links in membership and thinking with the Bryce group. The division of international disputes into judicial and nonjudicial categories followed the Bryce pattern. The insistence that the council of inquiry and conciliation be composed of state representatives marked a more conservative approach than the independent council suggested in the Bryce *Proposals*. On the other hand the society's provisions for mutual defense were stated in much more explicit terms than in the *Proposals*. Both plans, however, approached the question of international organization in terms involving minimal changes in the existing international system. Both groups realized that schemes promoting real world government stood no chance of adoption. The two groups shared a common faith in a system of collective economic or military measures to protect peaceful members and compel resort to peaceful methods of resolving international disputes.

Through the first two years of the war, members of the League of Nations Society carried on a "quiet but not ineffective" program of education on behalf of the league idea.[30] During 1916 membership grew to about four hundred.[31] Members were drawn mainly from the well-educated and well-connected sections of middle-class liberalism. Academics, publicists, lawyers, educators joined with Liberal politicians in providing the leadership of the society. Later, liberal churchmen added their support. Pacifists, although sympathetic to the idea of a peace league, remained estranged from any program involving forceful sanctions.[32] Generally, the liberals of the society were moderates, more sympathetic to the Asquith-Grey brand of liberalism than the radicals. Therefore, the UDC and the society tended to go their separate ways despite some overlap in membership. Members of the society were loath to criticize the government and anxious not to be identified as pacifists or proponents of a negotiated peace. Nevertheless, the quiet work carried on by the society often encountered public suspicion and hostility.[33] Given the absorption of the nation in the war effort, society members were content to continue a low-key approach rather than launch a major campaign. Not until early 1917 did circumstances encourage the organization of a real league of nations movement.

In America, a group with objectives similar to the League of Nations Society had formed, largely on the initiative of Hamilton Holt, a leader of the New York Peace Society and editor of the *Independent*. In the spring of 1915, Holt joined with a group of prominent Republicans, including former President William Howard Taft, Harvard President Lawrence Lowell, and former American ambassador to Belgium, Theodore Marburg. Together, they formed the League to Enforce Peace.[34] Its program argued for American participation in a league of nations with the following commitments:

> First: All justiciable questions arising between the signatory powers, not settled by negotiation, shall, subject to the limitations of treaties, be submitted to a judicial tribunal for hearing

and judgment, both upon the merits and upon any issue as to its jurisdiction of the question.

Second: All other questions arising between the signatories and not settled by negotiation, shall be submitted to a Council of Conciliation for hearing, consideration and recommendation.

Third: The signatory powers shall jointly use forthwith both their economic and military forces against any one of their number that goes to war, or commits acts of hostility against another of the signatories before any question arising shall be submitted as provided in the foregoing.

Fourth: Conferences between the signatory powers shall be held from time to time to formulate and codify rules of international law, which, unless some signatory shall signify its dissent within a stated period, shall thereafter govern in the decisions of the Judicial Tribunal mentioned in Article One.[35]

Considering American neutrality, leaders of the League to Enforce Peace had more freedom to propound its schemes than did their British colleagues. The organization launched a vigorous and wide-reaching campaign on behalf of the league idea, establishing branches in many urban centers and drawing major support, particularly in the eastern states.[36] Although its leadership was largely Republican, important Democrats joined in the cause. Most important, President Wilson chose the forum of the first National Congress of the League to Enforce Peace in May 1916 to announce his public commitment to the league cause.

While the League to Enforce Peace and the League of Nations Society were concerned with laying the foundations for a popular league of nations movement, the British Fabian Society published the first full-scale wartime examination of questions related to international organization. Early in January 1915, the Fabian Society engaged Leonard Woolf to research the question and draft a comprehensive report.[37] After several months of intensive study and a conference organized by the Fabians in May with Hobson, G. Lowes Dickinson, Cross, and Unwin, Woolf submitted his report in June. He and Sidney Webb then drafted a detailed scheme for an international authority to be established after the war.[38] Woolf's report and the Fabian scheme were published successively as special supplements to the *New Statesman* on 10 and 17 July 1915.[39]

The major portions of Woolf's report analyzed the development of international legal and political practices and institutions, identified the outstanding problems, and suggested possible solutions. Woolf was optimistic that if the jurisdictions of a proposed international court and international conference were clearly defined, the thorny problems of national sovereignty and the principle of unanimity, which in the past had often paralyzed diplomatic conferences, could be avoided.

Generally, Woolf's report and the scheme published 17 July in the *New Statesman* followed the structure of the Bryce *Proposals*, including the key feature of sanctions to enforce the jurisdiction of the proposed institutions. Beyond this the Fabian plan outlined in detail the structure, jurisdiction, and procedures for an international high court and international conference. The plan particularly emphasized the development of international law, as legislated by the conference and applied by the court. The Fabian scheme also provided for a permanent international secretariat. This body would be at the service of the international council for communication, research, transcription of council proceedings, translation, and preparation of an official gazette. Included in the official gazette would be the publication of all treaties registered with the international court. No treaties would be considered valid until such registration had occurred. The secretariat would also administer the finances of the court and council.

After publication of the 17 July scheme, Woolf, still under the auspices of the Fabian Society, continued working on questions related to international organization. He examined international relations in their broadest sense—relations between peoples of different nations involving a whole spectrum of activities and interests that often had little to do with official interstate relations. Woolf provided one of the earliest comprehensive presentations of what would now be called a "functionalist" approach to international organization. The results of his research were published in 1916, together with his earlier report and the Fabian scheme, under the title *International Government.* From a detailed description and analysis of the wide-ranging institutions and forms of international cooperation that had evolved through the nineteenth century to serve definite international needs in communications, trade, finance, labor, science, art, health, and crime, Woolf concluded that the nucleus of international government had developed. The prevailing "legal, political, and diplomatic theories of the independence and sovereignty of States" were "false." Nations had a greater interest in international cooperation than in conflict, and the history of the growth of internationalism had shown that nations could cooperate without losing their independence. If governments could be brought to realize this, and if the skeletal structures of international cooperation could be developed into a true international government, Woolf speculated that a whole new era in the history of society might open. Functional international cooperation, then, along with the international court and council, seemed to Woolf the most encouraging foundation upon which to erect a structure for lasting peace.[40]

The studies by Woolf and the Fabian scheme provided the public with the earliest and most rigorous examination of the question of international organization. Woolf had provided a wealth of information, had identified many of the important issues, and had suggested detailed and far-reaching solutions. Woolf's material reached a wide audience and was studied carefully by members of the Foreign Office. The Fabian ideas had an important influence on those who ultimately prepared the British case on the league question for the Paris Peace Conference.[41]

Woolf's proposals, though radical, followed the Fabian pattern of building from existing foundations—a type of "gas and water internationalism." Other leaders of British leftist thought went far beyond Woolf in elaborating plans for full-scale international government. Schemes proposed by John Hobson and H. N. Brailsford insisted on endowing a league of nations with major authority and power in international legislative, executive, and judicial fields.[42] Such authority was essential if the league were to bring necessary change in international conditions and address the basic economic and nationality problems that in Hobson's and Brailsford's analyses lay at the root of international conflict. Their proposals incorporated an uneasy synthesis of classical liberal economic and political theory with extensive economic planning and control on a world scale. These proposals, particularly Brailsford's, were read extensively in leftist circles, and some of the ideas—those on colonial administration and protection of minorities, for example—contributed to the League of Nations Covenant. H. G. Wells also lent his enthusiasm and imagination to the problem of world government, publishing several far-reaching plans during the war and attracting a wide readership[43]

While those on the Left wished to expand the league idea far beyond Woolf's proposals, opinion on the conservative side of the British political spectrum, if not totally skeptical of, or hostile to, the league concept, called for much more modest beginnings. They advocated building upon the traditions of the Concert of Europe and the model of the British Empire. Philip Kerr, editor of the *Round Table* and a leader of the Round Table group—a group inspired by Lord Milner and devoted to the ideals of the British Commonwealth and the cause of imperial consolidation—argued that any postwar improvement of the international system should concentrate on arranging a regularized conference of statesmen from all the great powers, with a constitution to guide its procedures and guarantee the right to bring even the most controversial questions forward for discussion. Such a concert would be purely voluntary and, like the British Commonwealth, promote a partnership of nations cooperating freely for the common good. It would not attempt to create an international parliament; nor would it exercise legislative, executive, or judicial funtions. Although such an arrangement could not ensure or enforce peace, it could reduce the likelihood of war by promoting international understanding and cooperation.[44]

Leaders of the major proleague groups were aware of the dangers of ruining their cause by attempting too much. Plans for real international government, therefore, received little support in the mainstream of the league of nations movement. At the same time, leaders of the movement believed that more was possible and necessary than a mere revival of the Concert of Europe. By 1916, despite differences in their proposed schemes, the Bryce group, the League of Nations Society, the Fabians, and the League to Enforce Peace agreed on the basic framework of their approach. The leading plans contained three cardinal features. First, they stipulated certain benign principles and procedures of international behavior, which all member states would pledge to observe. These procedures generally involved the submission of judicable disputes to an international court and all other disputes to an international council. Members would agree to a moratorium on all warlike actions while a dispute was being considered. Second, the plans suggested permanent institutions—an international council and court, for example—to resolve disputes and promote cooperation. Finally, each scheme included plans for collective economic or military action by members to ensure peaceful procedures in resolving disputes, to punish any aggression, and to provide security for peace-loving members.

With this third theme—the plan to use collective force in the interests of peace and security—the early wartime plans advanced most radically beyond the prewar peace movement. The idea of collective action to enforce treaties and maintain peace was not new. The concept had figured in the peace schemes of Dubois, Sully, the Abbé de Saint Pierre, Rousseau, Pitt, and many others. Several European treaties had included plans for collective enforcement of their terms, and the idea of a general treaty of guarantee, or *alliance solidaire*, was debated extensively during the Congress of Vienna. The nineteenth-century peace movement periodically wrestled with the question of sanctions to uphold respect for international law and to provide security against aggression.[45] But the issue of sanctions always encountered the opposition of British pacifists who, on religious and moral grounds, resisted all suggestions for using force in the cause of peace.

After the turn of the century, however, the idea of internationally organized force to preserve peace was publicized by several well-known figures. Alfred Nobel, after attending several peace congresses, decried the idealism of the peace movement and its failure to face the realities of power. He concluded that "the only true solution would be a convention under which all the governments would bind themselves to defend collectively any country that was attacked."[46] In 1904 Andrew Carnegie suggested to the thirteenth Universal Peace Congress that if Britain, France, Germany, and America, with such other powers as would certainly join them, were to take a collective position, prepared, if defied, to enforce a peace settlement, the first offender, were there one, being firmly dealt with, "war would at one fell sweep be banished from the earth."[47] The most famous of all prewar pronouncements in favor of enforced peace came from Theodore Roosevelt in his acceptance address for the 1910 Nobel Peace Prize. Roosevelt contended that "it would be a master stroke if those great powers honestly bent on peace would form a League of Peace, not only to keep the peace among themselves, but to prevent, by force, if necessary, its being broken by others."[48]

The theme propounded by Nobel, Carnegie, and Roosevelt, however, had little immediate impact on contemporary peace thought. It took the outbreak of world war to destroy the facile optimism of the peace movement. The paralysis of the diplomatic system and the impotence of the peace movement during the crisis leading to war demonstrated that plans for arbitration and disarmament were not enough if war was to be eradicated. The war forced the nonpacifist, liberal-radical stream of the peace movement to face squarely the issue of power in international relations. The result was a widespread conversion to the collectivist theme suggested by Roosevelt and the others—that the power of peace-loving members of the international community must be organized in the cause of peace and security. The Bryce group, the Fabians, the League of Nations Society, and the League to Enforce Peace emphasized the need for a system of collective economic and, if necessary, military sanctions that would compel nations to abide by principles of international behavior and provide security against aggression. The League of Nations Society specifically argued that without sanctions, "the League would become a farce; there would be no security against aggressive States."[49]

The idea of an agreement to make war to preserve peace,

however, did not go unchallenged in the early debate on plans for a league of nations. Nationalists and most conservatives viewed any suggestion of interference with national sovereignty—political, economic, or military—as, at best, impractical and, at worst, treasonable.[50] And the idea of force in any form, collective or otherwise, remained unacceptable to absolute pacifists. Important radicals and laborites challenged the collective theory on pragmatic and moral grounds. Debate within the Bryce group illustrated a fundamental cleavage on the issue of making war to protect peace. Arthur Ponsonby put the case against collective force in the most cogent terms. First, Ponsonby argued, a collective obligation to declare war in certain contingencies would make armaments the basis of the whole project and "substitute fear for moral obligation." A system of joint armed action, furthermore, would mean the perpetuation of high armaments expenditure, the building of all-powerful navies by Britain and America, and a renewed balance-of-power struggle between league members and those outside. The requirement to intervene in all disputes would tend to universalize all wars, not localize them. To Ponsonby, collective force meant endorsing in a new form "the old fallacy *si vis pacem para bellum.*" Ponsonby, moreover, doubted that the threat of collective action against an aggressor would provide an effective deterrent. Referring to the coming of war in August 1914, he argued that wars did not usually arise from the action of an isolated agressor. Rather, they arose for complex reasons and involved a clash of rival power groupings, which no collective agreements could prevent. Ponsonby, following the UDC line, pointed to parliamentary control, abolition of secret diplomacy, disarmament, and growth of enlightened public opinion as the surest way to lasting peace. To create a collective military system "under the cloak of organized international hypocrisy" would be taking the wrong road and would make the whole scheme worthless.[51]

Ponsonby's arguments were generally shared by the UDC and their labor allies, and it was primarily the issue of collective force that divided the union from the league of nations movement.[52] Opposition to the idea of sanctions was overwhelmed, however, and the advocates of collective force triumphed in the league movement. Lawrence Lowell, president of Harvard and a leader of the League to Enforce Peace, dramatically summarized the case for collective force in a letter to G. Lowes Dickinson:

> We feel that the only thing that will prevent war is the certainty that the country going to war will have to meet the world in arms, and we believe that any country which is fully convinced that if it commits acts of hostility towards another before submitting the question in dispute to arbitration it will have to fight all the world, will never commit such acts of hostility, and hence that such a universal war will never be needed. On the other hand, we believe that an agreement among the nations for talking over what shall be done will have no effect upon a country that is determined to go to war—that it will simply result in a lot of diplomatic talk no more effective than the diplomatic correspondence among neutrals which now always precedes a war. . . . It seems to me that the repressive or punitive action provided for by any league must be automatic if it is to be effective and that the only automatic action that would be really effective is an agreement for universal war; and such an agreement, if genuine, would never need to be carried into execution.[53]

Bryce emerged from the debate over collective force in a dilemma. In a note of 9 January 1915, he admitted he did not expect any scheme involving armed coercion to be accepted by the powers and doubted, if they did accept it, they would carry out their obligations loyally when there was a conflict with national interests. Still, he felt a scheme for armed coercion ought to be proposed as a proper remedy, "else the whole thing will seem pointless and ineffective."[54]

In planning for common defense against aggression, the wartime proleague groups sowed an idea that took deep root in the soil of twentieth-century peace thought—the idea of collective security. Although the term "collective security" was not used commonly until the mid 1930s, the integral features of such a system were developed in the early wartime debate on a league of nations.[55] The fundamental idea of collective security was that the combined power of the peace-loving members of the international community was nearly always vastly superior to the power of any aggressor states. But the power of the peace-loving states was divided and disorganized, allowing aggressive states to pick off their victims one by one. The solution, organizing the total power of peace-loving states through economic and military sanctions against any and all potential aggression, would theoretically deter any aggressive behavior and compel resort to peaceful methods of resolving disputes. If any party did commit an aggressive act, the collective power of the peaceful international community would mobilize to protect the aggrieved party and punish the aggression. The system assumed that collective interest in preserving peace would always override separate national interests. Later, proponents of collective security argued that peace was indivisible—a threat to one nation, however remote, was a threat to the security of all. If all peaceful nations were willing to defend the peace collectively they would then be able to enjoy the resulting collective security.

Advocates of collective defense portrayed their plans as the nearest possible approach, in prevailing circumstances, to an international police force. An analogy was made with the evolution of law and justice in British history and in the early American West. Just as a rough and ready system of law and justice had been administered by means of the principle of the "hue and cry" in Britain and the posse in the American West, so on the international plane peace-loving nations could now band together on an ad hoc basis to protect themselves and mete out justice. Furthermore, just as a fully developed system of justice and law enforcement grew out of the "hue and cry" and the posse, so also would provisions for ad hoc collective defense grow into a more fully developed system of international justice.[56]

Whatever difficulties arose in plans for collective enforcement of peace, advocates brushed these aside in light of the great benefits that such a system promised to bring. Plans for enforced peace, as developed by various proleague groups, inspired extremely successful propaganda. On the surface the schemes appeared simple, plausible, and, above all, necessary to a world experiencing cataclysmic disaster. President Wilson's endorsement immeasurably advanced the idea of collective security. For the duration of the war, as the league movement grew and as plans for international organization proliferated, the idea of enforced peace increasingly provided a central theme for debate on the league question. A tremendously appealing and potent myth had been introduced into the history of twentieth-century international relations.

The idea of a league to preserve peace, then, had been reborn in the response of British liberalism to the outbreak of general war. The ideas and schemes of the prewar peace movement and British radicalism provided the foundation of plans for a league of nations. Many of the same divisions that weakened the prewar peace movement, however, reemerged to complicate planning for a league. The absolute pacifists remained estranged and opposed to any projects ultimately based on forceful coercion.[57] The radicals and laborites of the UDC, while favoring the creation of an international council to replace the balance of power, remained committed to the prewar radical critique of government foreign policy, a program more negative than positive in nature. The true proponents of the league of nations idea were the middle-class liberals of the Bryce group and the League of Nations Society. A major question for proleaguers was whether the appeal of liberal internationalism could be broadened to attract the support of British labor and the sympathy of conservatives who saw the specter of revolution behind the war.

One constant theme expressed from the beginning of wartime planning for a league of nations was that America might be persuaded to participate, or that President Wilson might head a liberal program to reform the international system. In fact, the idea of a league of nations quickly assumed a central role in wartime Anglo-American relations. It was in this context that the British government first expressed interest in the league idea, and the first detailed official British studies of the league idea were undertaken largely in response to American pressures.

2   War and Diplomacy: Grey
and the League Idea, 1914–1916

The first few months of fighting found the British government fully absorbed in the war effort. After the initial maneuvering
and the crucial frustration of the Schlieffen plan, the fighting quickly
settled into the pattern of trench warfare and bloody attrition along
the western front. If anything, the invasion of Belgium and the
desperate attempts to establish a military equilibrium to stem the
German advance confirmed the wisdom of a continental strategy of
intervention. Those favoring a naval strategy of initial aloofness
from the continental struggle made no headway in August 1914,
and the next year saw a further strengthening of western strategy as
"easterners" discredited themselves in the mismanaged Dardanelles
operation. The strategy of fighting flowed directly from prewar
strategic planning, but the appalling costs were totally unforeseen.

Those who proposed schemes for a league of nations to prevent
wars were reluctant to push their ideas in the early stages of the
war. They were hopeful, nevertheless, that leaders of the Liberal
government would respond favorably to their program. Asquith,
speaking in Dublin on 25 September, gave them some encouragement when he called for a return to Gladstone's idea of public right
and concert in European relations and suggested the creation of "a
real European partnership based on the recognition of equal right,
and established and enforced by a common will."[1] Asquith later
claimed that the "germ of the League of Nations" lay in these
remarks.[2]

Grey, however, appeared as the most sympathetic government figure in the eyes of liberal proleaguers. Grey's foreign policy had been vilified by extreme radicals, but he had always presented an image of conciliation and morality to moderate radicals and liberals. He had won back the support of many radicals by his efforts on behalf of the Concert of Europe and peace during the Balkan wars, and his role in the final crisis leading to war drew the support of all but hard-core dissenters.

In March 1914 Grey had argued that "fear will haunt our gates, until we have organized an international system of security and order."[3] The frustration of all attempts to convene an international conference in the final crisis led Grey to sympathize personally with the league idea, and through 1915 he established informal contact with leaders of the proleague movement in Britain and the United States. Grey's sympathy for the league idea, however, somewhat like his sympathy for prewar radical themes, remained fully subordinated to his conception of national interests. From the beginning Grey handled the league idea in this context, perceiving that the idea might be useful in cultivating the friendship of the American government, upon whose benevolent neutrality Britain quickly became dependent. Two letters of late 1914 to Theodore Roosevelt illustrate the direction of Grey's thought. He suggested that, had America been willing to support the sanctity of treaties on the eve of war, Germany might have been halted and militarism destroyed. There might have followed an agreement among the European great powers to refrain from attacking each other, limit their armaments, and submit disputes to arbitration. Under such an agreement, if any power refused arbitration, "the others would join forces against it." Grey expressed his sympathy for Roosevelt's suggestion of an international *posse commitatus* of neutrals to preserve peace and argued that in the future the moribund Hague conventions should be replaced with new provisions "only on the condition that those becoming parties to them bind themselves to uphold them by force if need be."[4]

Grey exchanged similar ideas with Colonel House, President Wilson's closest political and diplomatic advisor. Prior to the war, the British foreign secretary had discussed plans for disarmament and peace with House. When Grey now learned that the colonel was pursuing the possibility of American mediation to end the war and suggesting that a system of mutual guarantees might help establish future peace, security, and disarmament, a response followed swiftly. Through Spring-Rice, British ambassador to Washington, Grey advised the Americans that, while no peace negotiations could be undertaken before Germany's evacuation and restoration of Belgium and the humbling of Prussian militarism, a negotiated peace might be possible if the United States were prepared to join the European great powers in a mutual security system and "to join in repressing by force whoever broke the treaty."[5] Otherwise, they saw no hope for a durable peace "without exhaustion of one side or the other."[6]

House initially responded that America could not become an active party to an agreement binding members to enforce observance of treaties.[7] Nevertheless, the colonel's mission to Europe in the early months of 1915 gave Grey an opportunity to pursue these ideas further.[8] Upon arriving in London, House was queried on the possibility of American participation in "some general guaranty for world-wide peace."[9] House hedged on any general commitment and instead suggested further elaboration of rules, along the lines of The Hague conventions, to protect the rights of neutrals in wartime. When pressed by Grey, however, he held out the possibility of a "second convention" to establish a postwar peace-keeping system. Grey responded by portraying this possibility as "one of the great hopes for the future." The foreign secretary led House to believe that the British government would be willing "to make great concessions in that convention in regard to the future of shipping, commerce, etc., during periods of war."[10]

While traveling to Berlin with these suggestions in mind, House elaborated a plan to protect the freedom of the seas that included an association of nations formed to enforce neutral maritime and commercial rights. The Germans gave House's suggestions a warm reception. In further correspondence, however, House found Grey willing to consider such proposals only in the broader context of a postwar league of nations that would provide general security on land as well as sea. Grey advised House that any plan for the free-dom of the seas that allowed German commerce "to go free upon the sea in time of war, while she remains free to make war on other nations at will, is not a fair proposition."[11]

The German sinking of the *Lusitania*, 7 March 1915, made fur-ther peace talk very difficult, and House, failing to advance projects for American mediation, returned to America. Grey had made it clear that the price of any American intervention to arrange a nego-tiated peace was a definite American commitment to enforce the settlement and to participate in arrangements for preventing future aggression. Though they kept the Americans at bay for the present, the ideas advanced by Grey had established an important bridge in Anglo-American relations. Moreover, Grey had made an excellent impression on House.[12]

Through 1915, as German-American relations deteriorated starkly in the wake of the *Lusitania* sinking, Grey kept the line to House open, suggesting that involvement in the war on the Allied side would guarantee America a decisive voice in the debate on final peace conditions.[13] The idea of a league of nations to keep peace formed a constant theme in Grey's correspondence with the colonel. Grey summarized his views on the lesson to be learned from the outbreak of war in a letter to House, 10 August 1915:

> My own mind revolves more and more about the point that the refusal of a Conference was the fatal step that decided peace or war last year, and about the moral to be drawn from it: which is that the pearl of great price, if it can be found, would be some League of Nations that could be relied on to insist that disputes between any two nations must be settled by the arbitration, mediation, or conference of others. International Law has hith-erto had no sanction. The lesson of this war is that the Powers must bind themselves to give it a sanction.[14]

When, in a letter of 3 September, House asked Grey whether the president could make peace proposals "upon the broad basis of the elimination of militarism and navalism and a return, as near as possible to the status quo," Grey replied on 22 September, posing a series of crucial questions:

How much are the United States prepared to do in this direction? Would the President propose that there should be a League
of Nations binding themselves to side against any Power which
broke a treaty; which broke certain rules of warfare on sea or
land (such rules would, of course, have to be drawn up after this
war); or which refused, in case of dispute, to adopt some other
method of settlement than that of war? . . . I cannot say which
Governments would be prepared to accept such a proposal, but
I am sure that the Government of the United States is the only
Government that would make it with effect.[15]

Grey's letter arrived just as House and Wilson were recon-
sidering plans for mediation in the war. After discussions with the
president, House replied to Grey, suggesting an elaborate plan for
American mediation in secret collaboration with Britain and the
Allies. If the Central Powers proved obdurate, House promised that
"it would probably be necessary for us to join the Allies and force
the issue."[16] For the colonel this represented a major offer, "practically to ensure a victory to the Allies," but Grey's response, cabled
9 November, merely asked if the proposal meant that the United
States was ready to join a league of nations, as outlined in his
22 September letter, and guarantee the peace settlement.[17]

House pressed the wisdom of supporting Grey's proposals upon
the president, but subsequent correspondence between Grey and
House, leading to House's return to Europe in January 1916, revealed that the two sides were pursuing different objectives. The
Americans placed major priority on mediation to end the war,
offering the inducement of contributing to a postwar peace league
on the precondition that mediation was sought. Grey continued to
be skeptical about mediation and, while encouraging ideas for a
peace league, insisted that the Americans prove themselves in earnest by making firm promises to uphold the peace in the future. On
11 November 1915 Grey wrote to House, pointing out the difficulty
of Allied commitment to the American plan "without knowing
what it was, and knowing that the United States was prepared to
intervene and make good if they accepted."[18] Subsequently, difficulties resulting from British use of armed merchantmen in sinking
submarines and mounting American protests on blockade tactics

amplified Allied suspicions concerning Wilson's sympathies.

When House returned to Europe in January 1916, his instructions from Wilson were to sound out both belligerent camps on the possibilities of peace based on a military and naval disarmament and a league of nations to prevent aggression and maintain the absolute freedom of the seas. If either side agreed to discuss peace on these terms, Wilson's instructions asserted that "it will clearly be our duty to use our utmost moral force to oblige the other to parley, and I do not see how they could stand in the opinion of the world if they refused."[19] In private discussions with British leaders, House received some encouragement from Lloyd George, and Grey was willing to consider the question of the freedom of the seas, provided the United States would "join in a general covenant to sustain it."[20] Grey and Balfour, first lord of the admiralty, were more interested, however, in learning how far Wilson would be willing to enter into an agreement concerning European affairs. House explained that the president would "not be willing to do this at all," but would favor agreement on "broad questions touching the interests and future of every nation."[21]

House's principal concern, however, was to ascertain the possibility of an American mediation. In Berlin he quickly discovered that German war aims were so extensive as to preclude accommodation with the Allied powers. Returning to London, House nevertheless continued to press British leaders for eventual American mediation. Though the British clearly preferred American military intervention to mediation, after extensive *pourparler* and a 14 February dinner with Asquith, Grey, Lloyd George, Balfour, and Reading, lord chief justice, an agreement was reached concerning a possible American peace initiative. This agreement, formalized in the House-Grey memorandum of 22 February 1916, stipulated that President Wilson, upon hearing from the Allies, would propose a peace conference. Should Germany refuse, "the United States would probably enter the war against Germany." If such a conference failed to secure a peace not unfavorable to the Allies, "the United States would leave the Conference as a belligerent on the side of the Allies."[22]

House returned to America believing the agreement reached

in London heralded an imminent American initiative to end the war. After a briefing by House, Wilson enthusiastically endorsed the House-Grey memorandum. On 8 March a telegram informed Grey of the president's approval, subject only to the addition of the word "probably" to qualify American belligerency on the Allied side should the proposed conference fail to result in a satisfactory peace.[23] The colonel's reception in England, however, had led him to exaggerate the sympathy of British leaders for his proposals. In London the American offer was studied intensively by the War Committee on 21 March in light of the strategic prospects of Britain and her allies.[24] Grey argued the expediency of discussing Wilson's offer with the French if the war were likely to continue deadlocked in six months, when Britain's financial position would be worse, or if Russia faced possible defeat. The Conservatives and military leaders, however, strongly opposed seeking Wilson's mediation in a negotiated peace, and Asquith expressed doubts that Wilson's political position was strong enough to carry through on his offer. The War Committee, therefore, decided "that no action should at present be taken in regard to Colonel House's proposals." Grey subsequently wrote House that the current German offensive against Verdun made it impossible for Britain to take the initiative at this time in urging a peace conference on France.[25]

The colonel's hopes died slowly, however, and the amelioration of German-American relations, attendant upon the Sussex pledge in early May, prompted House to make further appeals to Grey. On 10 May he cabled the foreign secretary that Wilson was willing publicly to commit the United States to a league of nations as outlined in Grey's 22 September 1915 letter if, at the same time, the president could announce his intention to call a peace conference.[26] Grey's 12 May reply intimated that Allied opinion considered mediation or a peace conference, under present circumstances, "premature."[27] Personally, Grey sympathized with the president's aspirations and thought that "his proposals as regards a league of nations may be of the greatest service to humanity," but the foreign secretary clearly questioned the wisdom of linking the league idea with the immediate summoning of a peace conference. A bitterly disappointed

House confided to his diary that for two years Grey had agreed that everything depended on United States willingness to take her part in world affairs. "Now that we indicate willingness to do so, he halts, stammers and questions."[28] Further urgent entreaties from House failed to move Grey or the War Committee as plans for the Somme offensive were now well underway.[29]

Repeatedly frustrated by the Allied powers in his desire to act as peacemaker Wilson nevertheless resolved to enunciate unilaterally American policies concerning the war and the nation's future role in international relations. The result was Wilson's famous speech of 27 May 1916 to the League to Enforce Peace. Wilson stated that, although the causes and objects of the war did not concern America, the destructive effects on neutral rights and trade had involved America deeply and made her anxious to bring hostilities to an end. Wilson laid down certain principles for a settlement that would secure a permanent peace. First, each people should be free to choose the sovereignty under which it desired to live. Second, the rights of small nations were to be as sacred as those of great powers. Third, the whole world had a right to be free from aggression. If a settlement based on such guidelines could be achieved, the president promised American participation in future guarantees of peace. The speech culminated in the call for a "universal association of the nations to maintain the inviolate security of the highway of the seas for the common good and unhindered use of all the nations of the world, and to prevent any war begun either contrary to treaty covenants or without warning and full submission of the causes to the opinion of the world—a virtual guarantee of territorial integrity and political independence."[30]

The president's endorsement of the league idea was greeted warmly by proleague groups in Britain and America as a signal contribution to the advancement of their cause. Official Allied response to the president's speech, however, was cool and brought American mediation no closer. Particularly resented was Wilson's propensity to moralize on the conduct of international relations from a position of profitable neutrality while the Allies saw themselves involved in a life and death struggle to uphold many of the principles that

Wilson talked of so freely. Wilson's reference to the war and his assertion that "with its causes and objects we are not concerned" undid any sympathy the speech might have evoked from the Allies. At the same time, Spring-Rice repeated his warnings to Grey to put no faith in Wilson's offers. The speech was motivated by political factors in an election year, Spring-Rice warned, and, in any event, the president had no constitutional authority to commit America to a peace-keeping system without Congressional approval.[31]

For the duration of 1916, as the British increased blockade pressures on Germany, interfered with American mails, and published a blacklist of American firms dealing with the enemy, Anglo-American relations dramatically deteriorated. After the harsh repression of the Easter uprising, the question of Ireland once again embittered transatlantic relations. The president bitterly resented the refusal of the Allies to encourage his mediation, and he gradually developed strong suspicions concerning the real nature of Allied war aims. Grey remained strongly sympathetic to the idea of a postwar league of nations, as his correspondence with members of the League to Enforce Peace and other proleague groups shows. He publicly encouraged the league idea in two major press interviews.[32] He always made clear, however, that his views on this question were personal and unofficial. Grey never submitted his views on the idea to the cabinet for consideration, and he repeatedly turned aside suggestions that he publicly and officially endorse the league idea to elicit neutral sympathy.[33]

Writing to House in August 1916, Grey summarized his own position and explained why his country had failed to respond to the president's overtures. First, the president's statement of indifference to the causes and objects of the war, his insistence on the freedom of the seas as a principal responsibility for any league of nations, and his omission of any reference to observing rules of warfare on land as well as sea—all acted as great obstacles to a warm response in Britain. Furthermore, American determination to keep out of the war at all costs, despite such outrages as the violation of Belgium and the sinking of the *Lusitania*, made people wonder whether the

United States could ever be depended upon to uphold treaties and agreements by force, even with a league of nations. Yet, in Grey's opinion, "unless the United States is a member of the League of Nations and a member that could be depended upon to intervene, the peace of the world would be no more secure in future than it was in 1914." The foreign secretary asserted that he had gone as far in public endorsement of the league idea as was possible for "a man who has colleagues and allies to consider." He expressed disappointment with the lack of public response to his statements in America but held out promise of future support in Britain for the league idea once the present critical stage of the war had passed successfully. The letter concluded by advising House that neither Britain nor her allies were likely to consider peace "as long as the military situation continues to improve in their favour, or there is good prospect of its doing so."[34] This letter effectively ended any hopes that the Americans still held for intervention along the lines of the 22 February agreement.

Grey knew that his cabinet colleagues had mixed views on the league idea. Haldane, before his exclusion from the coalition formed in May 1915, circulated a memorandum to the cabinet that advised very serious consideration of the league idea. The lord chancellor argued that, while it was necessary to defeat German militarism, no territorial or economic penalties in an eventual peace settlement could prevent German revival and attempt at revenge. Furthermore, possible shifts in the relations of the Allies and the new menace of submarine and aircraft presented particular dangers to British security. Haldane argued that it was "vital to the interests of England" to negotiate with the great powers, including the leading neutrals, some arrangement that would ensure peaceful settlement of international disputes. The memorandum closely followed the scheme put forward in the Bryce *Proposals* and recommended collective diplomatic, economic, and, if necessary, military pressure to secure observance of agreements. Haldane suggested that formal arrangements be kept to a minimum to ensure members' sovereignty and attract American participation. The lord chancellor argued that a return to prewar conditions could ensure neither world peace nor British security after the war.[35]

In response to Haldane's memorandum, Kitchener, the secretary for war, circulated a hostile rejoinder, belittling the lord chancellor's "hopes for the advent of the millennium" and predicting that great power rivalries would continue after the war.[36] Balfour, however, provided the first systematic governmental critique of the league idea. In a cabinet memorandum circulated in January 1916, during House's second mission, the first lord of the admiralty analyzed the possibilities of an Anti-War Federation led by America to prevent aggression. How would such a peace league operate? Two approaches—a universal territorial guarantee and a system of compulsory arbitration—appeared to Balfour to offer insuperable difficulties. The former would freeze the territorial status quo while the latter would founder on the difficulties of meting out and enforcing impartial justice on complex international disputes. Balfour favored more "modest" and "practical" provisions for referring disputes to a "conference of the Powers." Such a conference could accomplish infinite good in compelling powers to confer, but it could not compel nations to agree. The first lord wondered whether the league should be bound to enforce the majority opinion of the conference against an intractable power like Germany and, if not, whether the league could be an effective instrument. To Balfour, these questions were easier asked than answered, particularly since the pacific and democratic nations making up the league would face great problems in acting quickly and resolutely. Despite these difficulties, Balfour hoped that America would abandon her traditional isolation and join in the attempt to prevent the recurrence of war.[37]

The league idea received further official attention in May 1916 when House renewed the pressure for American mediation, now that Wilson was ready to announce his willingness to see America participate in a league of nations. Balfour suggested letting the president know that his hopes for a peace league could best be furthered by active American intervention in the war. If American mediation induced an inconclusive or disastrous peace, plans for any great international scheme would be ruined.[38] Hankey, powerful secretary to the War Committee, bitterly attacked the whole concept of a league of nations. In a memorandum of 25 May, Hankey argued that the security provided by all such schemes would be "wholly fictitious" and give rise to dangerous illusions, particularly in Britain. With their traditional respect for law and the sanctity of international treaties, the British people would be especially prone to entrust their security to an international peace-keeping body. In the immediate postwar generation, given the universal exhaustion and longing for peace, the new international system would, no doubt, appear to work well. With this lever in the hands of "enthusiasts for social reform and the anti-war and disarmament people," Hankey feared the nation would be persuaded "to go to sleep so far as its military preparations go, and to divert its energies in other directions of greater immediate benefit to the human race."[39]

The Germans, their allies, and possibly the Russians, however, would fall prey to no such illusions. Rather, Hankey felt, these countries would use the new peace system as a shield behind which to build up a renewed preponderance of power. At the appropriate moment they would strike—either paralyzing the deliberations of an international council or flatly refusing to submit a dispute to it on the grounds of national honor. What possible faith, then, could be placed in collective international action to coerce Germany? In Hankey's view, the nations of the world would either divide on the merits of the dispute or be too frightened or self-centered to act politically, economically, or militarily against Germany. Furthermore, Hankey argued that no help could be counted upon from America, which could never be depended upon to take part in European affairs. According to Hankey, Americans were "so cosmopolitan and so wedded to the almighty dollar that they [could] not be judged even by the comparatively low standard of other nations in regard to questions of national honour." Even if America did cooperate, it would do so halfheartedly, since nations fight well only "when their vital interests are concerned" and not over "abstract principles or justice." In any event, war waged by an international police composed of a variety of armies, halfhearted in their commitment, was not likely to be very effective against a nation inspired by a national cause.

Hankey concluded that no advantages were likely to accrue to Britain or the world from the adoption of proposed peace schemes. Inevitably, these schemes would result in failure, "and the longer that failure is postponed the more certain it is that this country will have been lulled to sleep." The nation, rather, should continue to look to its own defenses as the sure guarantee of its security.[40]

Asquith, from time to time, expressed remote sympathy for the league idea,[41] but in the first comprehensive review of British war aims initiated by the prime minister at the end of August 1916, the idea of a league of nations received little attention.[42] The memoranda produced for this review projected peace terms that would guarantee British security in terms of traditional strategies. The General Staff concluded that the principal bases of peace should be the maintenance of the European balance of power, the independence of the Low Countries, and British maritime supremacy.[43] An admiralty memorandum underlined the importance of the latter strategy and argued strongly against basing British security in any significant way upon international agreements.[44] Memoranda from the Foreign Office and Balfour, dealing with the question of postwar territorial arrangements, expressed paramount concern for a continued European balance of power between the Allies and a potentially formidable Germany.[45] Both envisioned Britain's continued participation in a postwar alliance with France and Belgium.

None of these memoranda expressed any hope that a league of nations would fundamentally change the international system. The Foreign Office memorandum made this clear when it addressed itself to the question of future armaments reductions. The creation of a league of nations, "prepared to use force against any nation that breaks away from the observance of international law," might be a factor in facilitating reduced armaments. But the authors of the memorandum professed to be under no illusion that such an instrument could be effective until German militarism had been crushed and nations had learned, by a slow and difficult process, to subordinate their national interests to the benefit of the international community. The memorandum, however, pointed to the hopeful signs that America might abandon its traditional isolation and adhere to a postwar peace system, thereby allowing "a repetition of Canning's attempt to bring in the New World to redress the balance of the Old." The authors concluded, "If America could be persuaded to associate itself to such a League of Nations, a weight and influence might be secured for its decisions that would materially promote the object for which it had been created."[46]

If the debate on war aims illustrated that the league idea had made little impact on traditional strategic thinking, the idea did attract a new and highly placed convert in the fall of 1916. For some time Lord Robert Cecil, parliamentary undersecretary of state for foreign affairs and a member of the cabinet as minister for blockade since February 1916, had shown a growing interest in plans for future peace-keeping. In August he had argued before a Cambridge audience that some attempt must be made after the war to rescue Europe from "international anarchy."[47] In September he drafted "Memorandum on Proposals for Diminishing the Occasion of Future Wars." Outlining the suffering and destruction resulting from the war, the threat to the fabric of European civilization, and the probability of serious and numerous postwar disputes, Cecil urgently advocated a substitute for war as a means of settling international disputes. Neither the destruction of German militarism nor a territorial settlement based on nationality would guarantee peace. Ruling out a system of compulsory arbitration as involving too many objections, Cecil argued that the same objections did not apply to a regularized and mandatory conference system. Following the proposals advocated by several proleague groups, Cecil suggested that certain peaceful procedures for settling international disputes be compulsory before there was any resort to hostilities. He agreed that a system of sanctions was necessary to ensure resort to peaceful procedures and to protect law-abiding members. From his experience Cecil was optimistic that the blockade was a potent sanction "which could exert considerable pressure on a recalcitrant

Power without causing excessive risk to the Powers using it." If overwhelming naval and financial power could be combined in a peace system, "no modern State could ultimately resist its pressure." Moreover, Cecil was hopeful that, although America could not be expected to participate in European affairs, she might be willing to "join in organized economic action to preserve peace."

With these preliminary remarks, Cecil proceeded with "Proposals for Maintenance of Future Peace." First, high contracting powers would agree to maintain the postwar territorial settlement for five years. At the end of this period, or whenever any high contracting power so demanded, a conference of the powers would be called to consider and carry out necessary or desirable territorial changes. As part of the peace treaties, the powers would agree to submit any international dispute to a conference, which would be convened immediately in time of crisis. No action could be taken by any power until the conference had considered the matter and had come to a decision or had failed to reach a decision after a period of three months. Any decision reached by the conference would be enforced by all the high contracting powers as if it were one of the articles of the peace treaty. Each of the parties would agree to uphold the treaty, "if necessary by force of arms." If any power violated the provisions of the treaty or resorted to force without previous submission of the dispute to a conference, the other powers agreed to subject the offending power to a collective commercial and financial blockade. Cecil concluded the memorandum by specifying certain provisions necessary to make the blockade effective.[48]

As Cecil later pointed out in his autobiography, the drafting of this memorandum initiated a new phase in his public career.[49] A younger son of Salisbury, Cecil was one of "the three C's" in the Conservative party, although behind Curzon and Austen Chamberlain in rank and influence. His espousal of the league cause derived from a variety of sources. There was first the powerful influence of his father whose attachment to the ideal of the Concert of Europe and hope for an eventual international constitution to promote lasting peace and prosperity had an enduring effect on Cecil's thought.[50] Second, the moral and religious influence of his family led Cecil to view the cause of peace as "the cause of Christianity."[51] Equally important, Cecil's deep conservatism, and his premonition of what war was doing to the traditional values and social structure of Europe, led him to sympathize with schemes for preventing war.[52] If peace and order were to be sustained in the future, the international system must be reformed. At the same time, Cecil was never a good party man. As a free trader, Cecil's interest in liberal foreign policy themes had been deepened by his admiration for the principles and personality of Grey, his chief at the Foreign Office.[53] That the league project was a liberal idea mainly supported by liberals did not prevent Cecil from becoming a liberal internationalist for essentially conservative reasons. Cecil became passionately committed to the league of nations program and, after the war, devoted the remainder of his long life to the furtherance of international peace, often at great cost to his own career as a Conservative politician.

Cecil's proposals were not printed for the cabinet until May 1917, but they were circulated in the Foreign Office in October 1916 and occasioned a lengthy and detailed criticism by Sir Eyre Crowe, head of the Foreign Office Contraband Department. Crowe provided perhaps the most systematic and perceptive wartime analysis of the many difficulties schemes like Cecil's would face in practice. First, there was the problem of membership. If a league of nations plan projected a universal territorial guarantee, it was difficult to see how any state could be excluded from participation. But, as The Hague conferences had illustrated, such a grouping would be cumbersome, easily obstructed, and "feeble as an engine of development and well-directed efforts towards progress." Moreover, there was the questionable viability of a territorial guarantee itself. Would most nations be willing to participate in such a guarantee? Even if they did, what would ensure that they would loyally fulfill their obligations? Crowe asserted that the strength behind a collective guarantee was not something automatic or absolute. Rather, such strength depended on how the powers grouped themselves on any particular territorial dispute. Usually, nations divided on the desirability and justice of a territorial settlement. Whether or not they resisted or supported changes in the territorial status quo was decided in light of their own national interests and "the respective weights in the balance of power." When a combination of powers commanded a preponderance of force, there could be "no certainty that an effort on its part to alter the territorial settlement for its own benefit will be actively resisted by the rest of the world."

Obviously, however, an indefinite maintenance of a territorial status quo was both impossible and undesirable. Crowe therefore considered how plans like Cecil's could arrange peaceful territorial changes and also deal with nonterritorial international disputes. Crowe believed Cecil had rightly excluded compulsory arbitration as impracticable. Yet, Crowe wondered what an international conference, limited to unanimous decisions, could do when faced with international disputes involving vital national interests where no compromise was possible. Crowe argued that in such cases a conference of powers was futile unless the powers abandoned their roles as impartial mediators and formed a military coalition against an aggressive party to deter war. Again, as in the past, power calculations would determine the issue.

Crowe then described the realistic functions of a system of general conferences. These conferences could help stimulate cooperation among nations to create the strongest possible combination of forces against disturbances of the peace. They could facilitate compromise and allow time for resourceful diplomacy. Furthermore, as nations became accustomed to bringing quarrels before a conference "in which all are heard and none are coerced," the chances were better for peaceful settlement. Clearly, however, Crowe felt a system of conferences by itself offered no automatic solution.

Crowe's memorandum specifically dealt with "the one dominant principle" that he felt all schemes like Cecil's were based upon —the principle of the sanction, the certainty that force would be applied to restrain evil doers. Crowe clearly illustrated the ineffectiveness of any system based solely on economic sanctions and not backed up by military force. Military forces at the disposal of a league of powers, however, would have to possess actual military preponderance to be effective. Theoretical, ad hoc, international forces, divided by geography, nationality, and language, without common leadership and strategic preparation, offered no basis for security in Crowe's opinion. Crowe's conclusions illustrate his consistent attachment to the balance of power as an abiding principle in British strategy and international relations:

> The balance of power reappears as the fundamental problem. To prevent the possibility of any one State or group of States pursuing, through war and bloodshed, a policy of aggression and domination, nothing will serve but adequate force. Arbitrations and conferences have their uses, and serve their limited purposes. Their utility is likely to grow steadily with the development of modern political thought. But it is a necessary and preliminary condition of the proper functioning of general conferences as the guarantors of peace, that the community of nations has effectively organized force for the defence of the right. Whether and how this can be done, is primarily a military question.[54]

Cecil's interest in the league idea was motivated in large part by his reaction as a Conservative to the devastation of war. By early winter 1916, with the failure of the Somme offensive, the defeat of Rumania, and strains in both the French and Russian armies, Allied prospects looked alarmingly grim. Britain faced a mounting peril from German submarine warfare, which threatened to sever the nation's life lines. Added to all this was the growing hostility of the American government at a time when Britain's dependence on the United States for finance and supply was critical. It was known that Wilson, campaigning for reelection, was once again anxious to promote mediation and an end to the war. Lloyd George had temporarily thwarted hopes for a peace appeal in late September by his dramatic call for a fight "to the finish . . . to a knock out" and his assertion that Britain would tolerate no outside intervention.[55] Lloyd George, however, had spoken without consulting Grey or the prime minister, and, in its last month in office, the Asquith government witnessed an urgent debate on war strategy.[56]

Former Conservative Foreign Secretary Lord Lansdowne posed the crucial question of whether the strategic situation justified prolonging a struggle that was "slowly, but surely, killing off the best of the male population of these islands."[57] Full of tory misgivings about the social consequences of continued warfare on such a scale, Lansdowne argued that those who needlessly prolonged the war were as guilty as those who had provoked it and that no movement favoring an exchange of views about the possibility of peace should be discouraged. Grey also joined the doubters at this stage urging reconsideration of American mediation along the lines of the agreement with House of the previous February if military advisors could no longer guarantee defeat of Germany.[58]

With talk of a negotiated peace once again in the air, the attention of the Asquith coalition was quickly diverted to the domestic crisis that led to the demise of the government. The prime minister's laxness in managing the war and his tactical miscalculations in the December political crisis resulted in a new coalition headed by Lloyd George, 7 December, supported by the Conservative party under Bonar Law and resolved to fight the war with full determination and efficiency. The departure of Asquith and Grey, coupled with Haldane's earlier exit, meant that the liberal imperialists who had shown most support in the cabinet for the league idea were now out of power.[59] Only Cecil remained in the new government to defend the league cause.

By the end of 1916, then, the idea of a league of nations had attracted wide-ranging attention within official British circles and had played a central role in Anglo-American relations through the first two years of the war. Grey had skillfully used the league idea to cement a liberal entente with neutral America, manage the American desire for mediation, and, in the House-Grey agreement, provide a plan to fall back on if the Allies' strategic situation became desperate. The idea of a peace league had been scrutinized by political and military leaders in light of traditional British interests and strategies. The skepticism expressed by Balfour and the hostility of Kitchener and Hankey illustrated that the league project would have to surmount serious obstacles if it hoped to achieve official endorsement. The idea of a peace league resting on collective guarantees challenged traditional British strategies—particularly the penchant for a free hand, the historic attachment to the balance of power, and the reliance on naval hegemony. At the same time British diplomatic traditions favored the adjustment of international disputes by the methods of the European concert, and the league idea held out definite promise for progress along these lines. Haldane, Grey, and Cecil stressed this aspect of the idea, as had Balfour and even Crowe. Furthermore, the fact that Wilson had embraced the league cause not only encouraged the proleaguers, but also added a fascinating new dimension to the idea for British officials. Grey, looking beyond the war, saw the league idea as a means of establishing an Atlantic partnership and a new world balance of power.

Wilson's public commitment to the league idea did not lead, as he had hoped, to a British acceptance of mediation. Nevertheless, Wilson once again forced the Allied governments to review their war aims and the possibilities of the league idea at the end of 1916.

3 War and Ideology: The League of Nations Movement, 1917

The new Lloyd George coalition, which came to power on 7 December 1916, represented those who shared the prime minister's determination to fight the war "to a knock-out." One of the first tasks confronting the new government, however, was to respond to peace notes from both Germany and America. The German note of 12 December was dismissed contemptuously by Britain and France as a political maneuver. But Wilson's note of 18 December demanded careful handling, given the vital dependence of the Allies on American finance and supply. After reelection, fearing a new German submarine offensive, Wilson had determined to test the possibilities of peace. His note called for the clarification of the real war and peace objectives of the belligerents. As stated publicly, these objectives appeared very similar. Furthermore, both sides had expressed interest in a league of nations to ensure peace. Wilson promised that the American people and government were "ready, and even eager" to cooperate fully in this project when the war was over.[1]

In preparing a suitable response to Wilson, Cecil and Balfour, now foreign secretary, advised expressing warm sympathy with the president's desire for a league of nations while asking for more specific assurances that the American government "had the will and the power to give armed support to the decisions of any such league."[2] In addition, Wilson was to be made aware that the league project was dependent upon, and not a substitute for, a satisfactory peace.

The joint Allied reply to Wilson of 10 January 1917 was designed essentially as war propaganda and "an appeal to democracy." It set forth a program of war aims that involved a definite defeat of Germany and restoration of a European balance of power. The Allies, however, for the first time went on record as associating themselves "wholeheartedly with the plan of creating a League of Nations to ensure peace and justice throughout the world," and which could provide the sanctions necessary to assure the observance of international agreements.[3] A supplementary note by Balfour to Spring-Rice, which was to be sent to Wilson and published, amplified the British insistence that Wilson realize the necessity of buttressing future international law with definite sanctions.[4] The president's efforts, therefore, were deftly turned aside, as Balfour followed Grey in instructing the Americans on the price to be paid for a league or a negotiated peace.

Not only was the new government determined to bring more vigor to the war effort, it was also anxious to harness more fully the potential of the dominions. In fact, the Lloyd George government included a heavy representation from the imperialist strain of British politics. The new War Cabinet included two empire proconsuls, Curzon and Milner, and several leading Milnerites and members of the Round Table were given influential posts in government service. Philip Kerr left the editorship of the *Round Table* to serve in Lloyd George's personal secretariat—the Garden Suburb—as an advisor on imperial and foreign affairs, while Amery and Mark Sykes joined Hankey's War Cabinet secretariat.[5] Did this new infusion of imperialists into government service signal corresponding changes in the strategy of the war, in the formulation of war aims, and in the structure of imperial relations?

The latter question received a partial answer with the convening of the Imperial War Conference in the spring of 1917. For some time Milnerites had been pressing for a wartime imperial conference to coordinate the imperial contribution to the war effort. Milner had hoped that the common experience of war would forge a consolidated empire, while the Round Table group, led by Curtis, had been circulating elaborate proposals for imperial integration.[6] The creation of the Imperial War Cabinet represented partial fulfillment of Milner's ideal, and the discussion of war aims within this new institution gave the imperialists an opportunity to map out an imperial program for the future. Amery and Curzon pressed for war aims that placed priority on providing for the security of the empire in India and Africa, safeguarding the strategic areas of the Middle East, and satisfying the desire of the southern dominions to annex nearby German colonies.[7] Along with the imperial interests underlying the deliberations of the Imperial War Cabinet and its subcommittees there was a corresponding willingness to contemplate peace terms that left Germany strong in Europe, although stripped of her overseas colonies. This plan, of course, clashed with both the western strategy of the generals and the Foreign Office's concern for the future European balance of power. The imperial strategy also overlooked the war aims of Britain's European allies and the potential opposition of liberalism and the Left to a program of traditional imperialism. Lloyd George made it clear to the Imperial War Cabinet that the recommendations put forward at this time were accepted only as loose indications of objectives to be pursued in the eventual peacemaking.[8]

The results of the 1917 imperial conference, then, were ambiguous with regard to imperialists' hopes. Although the experiment of the Imperial War Cabinet was well received by dominion leaders, discussion of the future constitutional structure of the empire was postponed to a special postwar session. The formula projected for such a future conference—"full recognition of the Dominions as autonomous nations of an Imperial Commonwealth"—illustrated that the war had done more to stimulate dominion nationalism than imperial sentiment.[9] All in all, the forces of imperialism made little headway in mapping future strategy for Britain. They lacked a coherent program and could do little to alter the western strategy of the military, which concentrated on Europe. Later, the logic of the imperialist position led Milner, particularly after the collapse of Russia, to contemplate the possibility of a peace that left Germany strong in Europe, with Britain relying on its imperial power.[10]

The league of nations question, meanwhile, received important attention in the Imperial War Cabinet's study of war aims. In preparing the agenda for the imperial meetings, Hankey suggested three possible policy alternatives on future international organization. The first alternative involved aiming at "some sort of international organization, such as a league to enforce peace." If the plans for "enforced peace" were too radical a departure from traditional patterns, the government could attempt to construct "a league of the character of the Concert of Europe formed after 1815." Finally, there remained the alternative of simply reverting to "something in the nature of a balance of power."[11] In his survey of minimal peace terms before the first session of the Imperial War Cabinet, Lloyd George referred to the public discussion on peace leagues and argued that "there is no doubt at all that we should endeavour to establish a league of that kind,"[12] but only after Germany had been defeated and made to serve as an example and a warning to future potential aggressors.

The league question was referred to a committee established to consider economic and nonterritorial objectives. This committee, led by Milner, acknowledged the necessity of devising means that would tend to diminish the chance of war, but it concluded

> ... that any too comprehensive or ambitious project to ensure world peace might prove not only impracticable, but harmful. The proposal which seems to promise the best results proceeds along the path of consultation and conference for composing differences which cannot otherwise be adjusted. The Treaty of Peace should provide that none of the parties who are signatories to the Treaty should resort to arms against one another without previous submission of their dispute to a Conference of the Powers. The Committee think that the details of such a scheme should be discussed with our Allies and especially with the United States of America, before the conclusion of the war.[13]

When this report was considered by the Imperial War Cabinet on 26 April, the prime minister expressed the opinion that the committee "had rather thrown cold water on the idea of a League of Nations." He also pointed out that the committee had failed to deal with the issue of disarmament and the question of possible sanctions by which the decisions of a league or disarmament agreements could be enforced. Sensitive as always to the political implications of an issue, Lloyd George argued that there would be "a great disappointment if it were thought that nothing could be done in these directions after the war."

As the debate continued, Cecil pointed out that there were two principal alternatives concerning the question of a league: "an International Court of Arbitration or a system of International Conference and Consultation." Cecil agreed that "matters affecting the vital interests of the British Empire" could not be dealt with by any international authority. However, he believed a great deal could be accomplished if the habit of conferences and consultations could be "firmly established." Milner supported Cecil and suggested that failure on the part of any power to submit a dispute to the consideration of a conference should be a cause of war for all powers who were party to a league treaty. However, Milner felt the conference could not act as a court, binding the participating nations to enforce its decisions. Borden, the Canadian prime minister, expressed some doubt that any treaty could provide much protection and argued that the real basis of peace must lie in world public opinion. He stressed the importance of Anglo-American agreement, which "could do more than anything else to maintain the peace of the world."[14]

On 1 May when the debate on the league idea was resumed, both Milner and Cecil argued that the most that could be done was to make a conference mandatory in time of crisis. Cecil suggested a clause in the final peace treaty that would require a conference and a three-month delay if a serious dispute threatened the peace. Each of the signatories would enforce this agreement by severing "all financial and commercial intercourse from an offending Power."[15] There followed a discussion on the nature of possible sanctions, but the cabinet avoided reaching any decision in this thorny issue. Generally, debate in the Imperial War Cabinet illustrated that, although the league idea now merited important governmental consideration, Cecil's position was supported only by a minority in the cabinet, and proleaguers had an uphill task if they wished to convert the government to their cause.[16]

For the first two years of the war, proleague groups had purposefully restricted their activity to developing and refining their program and lobbying in limited circles. These groups felt that to do more was untimely and counterproductive until more progress had been made in the war effort.[17] Above all, there was a desire to keep the league idea separate from the cry for a negotiated peace. By early 1917, however, many of those involved in the league cause felt that circumstances had changed sufficiently to make it both possible and necessary to undertake extensive propaganda on behalf of the league idea. Wilson's endorsement had made the league idea respectable.[18] Furthermore, the political complexion of the new government, with Asquith and Grey gone, made it seem more urgent to stir up public support behind the league idea.[19] Finally, knowledge of the grim statistics from the battles of 1916, with more of the same to come in 1917, made the British public more receptive to plans for permanent peace.

The League of Nations Society, therefore, organized a large public meeting for 14 May 1917 in Central Hall, Westminster. Bryce, who chaired the meeting, was able to obtain a distinguished list of speakers and an overflow crowd attended. General Smuts, the South African member of the War Cabinet, agreed to deliver the principal speech and, after introducing a resolution in favor of forming "a union of free nations for the preservation of permanent peace," Smuts put forward the case for a new postwar international system. He cautioned that the subject would be a difficult one— "scraps of paper" and elaborate plans for institutions would not be enough without a fundamental change in public attitudes. A "good peace" was an absolute prerequisite. A mere "patchwork compromise between conflicting interests" would surely fail. Despite these difficulties, Smuts was still optimistic. The war and its threat to civilization had brought the visionaries and the realists together. The most fruitful path lay in the creation of a league for discussion and consultation on vital issues. Such a league must also make some provision for a sanction which, as a last resort, would ensure recourse to peaceful procedures. Moreover, it would be futile to try to prevent wars if nations remained armed to the teeth. In any event, it was now "time for action," and Smuts recommended the formation of an Anglo-American committee to explore the matter thoroughly.[20] Smuts's address was followed by brief speeches from the Archbishop of Canterbury, Lord Buckmaster, and Lord Hugh Cecil.[21] The meeting unanimously adopted Smuts's resolution.

Following this meeting, the League of Nations Society launched a campaign of education and propaganda. The league cause was put before the public in an ever-mounting stream of reports, pamphlets, articles, and books, for the most part published under society auspices.[22] The details of the various schemes often differed, but there was full agreement about the desired goal—a league of nations that would compel resort to peaceful settlement of international disputes.[23] G. Lowes Dickinson argued for a league in *The Choice Before Us*. A compendium of the most outstanding proleague literature was published in the summer of 1917 under the title *The Project of a League of Nations*.[24] Liberal newspapers and journals opened their pages to debate on the league idea and, in most cases, gave the idea strong editorial support.

A second line of increased proleague activity took the form of further conferences and meetings. Some of the meetings were designed for the general public and included a speech by a prominent proleaguer. Other conferences were arranged to appeal directly to specific groups. On 17 July 1917 a conference of ministers representing the Church of England, the Roman Catholic Church, and the free churches convened in the Central Hall to discuss the league question in the light of Christianity. The Bishop of Oxford, who chaired the meeting, strongly argued the central theme of the conference—that the league of nations project was a necessary extension of the ethical implications of organized Christianity. A committee to facilitate promotion of the league idea through the churches was set up.[25] The support of the churches, both established and free, was vitally important in building respect and influence for the league cause.

Another conference was organized to appeal to the legal profession. Among the leaders were Lords Parmoor, Shaw of Dunfermline, Buckmaster, Pollock, and Phillimore—each of whom played a significant role in the development of the league idea. Discussion largely centered on the difficult international legal issues involved in the creation of a league, but there was substantial agreement on both the necessity and feasibility of some type of peace organization. The discussions of the conference were published as a League of Nations Society pamphlet.[26]

On 20 July 1917 the society convened the first of its annual meetings with forty-seven leaders in attendance.[27] The principal item of business concerned revisions to the original "Objects of the Society." Two principal changes were agreed upon. The first strengthened the resolve to use force to guarantee peaceful procedures, while the second provided for periodic conferences among league members to consider general international business and to codify rules of international law. Clearly, there was a trend away from the original scheme, which saw the league operating only in times of crisis. The society also decided to open a permanent office in Buckingham Gardens.

The League of Nations Society hoped, of course, that the government would go beyond simple endorsement of the league idea and undertake serious study and planning for eventual action. After the Central Hall meeting, W. H. Dickinson circulated prominent public figures to gather signatures for a letter urging government action. On 8 August Lord Bryce delivered a petition to Downing Street, signed by seventeen men of eminence, requesting that the government set up an Anglo-American commission of experts to examine thoroughly the whole league question, with the goal of developing a practical plan.[28]

Through 1917 the increased activities of the society resulted in a significantly expanded membership and much greater public interest in the league ideal. The annual report for 1917 records that between March 1917 and March 1918 membership in the society grew from 400 to 2000, with over 170 meetings organized to further the society's program. The report concluded that, in the previous twelve months, the idea of a league of nations had attained a general recognition among most thoughtful men and women in the Allied countries. Governmental leaders also had endorsed the idea that a year ago had been regarded by many as "the Utopian catch-phrase of a few theorists."[29]

The records also show that, just as the league idea had been generated in liberal and radical circles, the leadership and supporters of the movement came mainly from the Liberal party ranks.[30] The publications of the society were designed to appeal to the professional and humanitarian sections of the middle class. Liberal newspapers provided a public forum for debate on the league program, particularly those papers closest to the Asquith wing of the party.[31] By late 1917 British liberalism, within the official party and without, had made the major contribution to the leadership, organization, and support of a league of nations movement, which, month by month, was growing in its political impact.

The league of nations movement continued to draw major inspiration from President Wilson through 1917, particularly after America entered the war against Germany in April. By this time Wilson clearly stood as the champion of liberal internationalism and a league of nations. On 22 January, after his unsuccessful attempt at mediation, Wilson had enunciated before the Senate his conception of a "peace without victory," a peace negotiated between equals, based on principles of democratic justice. To sustain and guarantee such a peace, Wilson maintained, the world must not return to the balance of power, organized rivalries, or entangling alliances. Rather, the power of the international community must be organized into a "League for Peace," embodying a force "so much greater than the force of any nation now engaged or any alliance hitherto formed or projected that no nation, no probable combination of nations could face or withstand it."[32]

The German submarine campaign ruined Wilson's hopes for a negotiated peace without victory, but in bringing the United States into the war as an "Associated Power," the president portrayed American war aims in the language of liberal internationalism.

America was fighting not for selfish ends, desire for conquest, or indemnities, but for "the rights of mankind," to make the world "safe for democracy," and for "a universal dominion of right by such a concert of free peoples as shall bring peace and safety to all nations and make the world itself at last free."[33]

Wilson's speeches were designed to speak for "liberals and friends of humanity in every nation." British liberalism responded warmly and eagerly to Wilson's program, especially since the major themes of Wilson's New Diplomacy had their roots in the British liberal-radical tradition.[34] Wilson's infusion of liberal internationalist ideology into the politics of the war also had an important effect on the developing political program of the British and Allied Left in 1917. As British labor responded to the third year of bloody warfare, its espousal of the New Diplomacy added further impetus to the league of nations movement.[35]

For the first two years of the war, the mainstream of British labor had cooperated loyally and enthusiastically in the war effort. Labor had participated in Asquith's coalition government, and Henderson was given a seat in Lloyd George's War Cabinet. Only the Independent Labour party and the Union of Democratic Control dissented from the government's justification for the war, but their program found little sympathy in majority labor circles. However, a series of factors through 1917 combined to end the political quiescence of British labor. Wilson's liberal pronouncements struck sympathy in British labor circles and contrasted with the lack of similarly inspiring war-aims declarations in Britain. Events in Russia following the March revolution, the debate on war aims, and the Bolshevik call for peace without annexation or indemnities excited the interest and sympathy of British socialists. After visiting Russia, Henderson advised his government colleagues that the time had come for a public reformulation of Allied war aims to keep Russia in the war. In addition, domestic factors contributed decisively to the political radicalization of British labor in 1917, as the growing pressures, privations, and casualties of the war had their greatest impact on the working classes.[36]

One of the earliest indications of changing attitudes on the part of British labor was the response to Wilson's 22 January 1917 "Peace Without Victory" speech. The Independent Labour party and UDC welcomed Wilson's views. Snowden, on behalf of both organizations, expressed "special gratification with the fact that the head of the greatest neutral Power in the world has come to the support of the same ideas and proposals which they have long advocated."[37] More important, the Labour party, at its annual conference in January 1917, having explicitly repudiated the ILP–UDC line a year earlier, unanimously passed a resolution calling for formation of "an International League to enforce the Maintenance of Peace on the plan advocated by the President of the United States and approved by the British Foreign Secretary; each affiliated nation to cooperate to restrain by any means that may be necessary any Government or Nation which acts in violation of the Laws and Judgements of the International Court."[38]

Through the spring of 1917, as both the hardships of the war and its ideological dimensions grew, the war-aims debate increasingly agitated the British labor leadership. Labor organs of public opinion devoted much more attention to the problem of postwar international organization, generally expressing growing sympathy with the league idea.[39] As the Independent Labour party mounted a parliamentary campaign in the early summer of 1917 to have the government tell the whole truth about its war aims and secret commitments, the position of the Labour party gradually grew closer to that of the Independent Labour party.[40] The shift to a more radical position was illustrated at the special 10 August 1917 Labour conference. Under Henderson's tutelage, the conference voted three to one in favor of sending delegates to an international meeting of Allied, neutral, and enemy socialists in Stockholm to discuss war aims—a decision which quickly led to Henderson's exit from the War Cabinet.[41]

The conference, in a draft statement on war aims, also gave strong endorsement to the league idea. The type of league proposed somewhat reflected the thinking of the Independent Labour party and the UDC. Membership would include all present belligerents and, ultimately, all sovereign states. Its machinery would consist of an international court for the settlement of justiciable disputes and effective machinery for mediation of nonjusticiable disputes. The conference advocated an international legislature, with powers to codify and extend international law. Members would pledge to submit all disputes to peaceful means of settlement and unite against any state violating its commitments. Finally, the draft statement endorsed a league of nations that would exercise important colonial and economic functions. Following the antiimperialist thought of the British Left, the conference recommended that the colonies of all European powers in tropical Africa, as well as those areas of the former Turkish Empire incapable of settling their own destiny, be transferred to the proposed supernational authority or league of nations for "administration by an impartial Commission under that authority, with its own trained staff." Such an administration would guarantee the "open door" and equal trade opportunities to all nations, protect the native populations from exploitation, help develop the area, and maintain its permanent neutralization. After the war, the proposed league could play an important role in economic reconstruction and allocation of scarce resources. The draft statement, therefore, not only placed British labor solidly behind the league idea, but also illustrated labor's commitment to a league with important economic and colonial functions.[42]

Through the late summer of 1917, with the casualty figures mounting from the futile British offensive in Flanders, with the Italian army routed at Caporetto in October, the government faced growing pressures to justify continuation of the bloodshed. The November revolution in Russia not only presented appalling strategic implications for the Allies in the wake of Russia's withdrawal from the war, but Lenin's Peace Decree and Trotsky's publication of the secret treaties threw damaging and embarrassing light on the real nature of Allied war aims.

Given the strategic and political dangers confronting the Allied governments as the winter of 1917 set in, Lansdowne once again sounded the theme of negotiated peace, publicly this time. In a famous letter to the *Daily Telegraph* of 29 November, the former foreign secretary stressed the danger to European civilization involved in continuing the war and questioned the wisdom of striving for a victory that might well leave victors, as well as vanquished, in a state of exhaustion. If the Germans were assured that it was not the intention to destroy their nation or their economy, a negotiated peace might be worked out with the more moderate forces in that country. Lansdowne added his support to the project for a league of nations to force nations to resolve future disputes by arbitration.[43] Lansdowne was bitterly attacked and his suggestions repudiated by the Conservative party, but his letter added to the heavy pressure on the government to justify its war policies in terms that would confront growing public suspicion and alienation.

In December the Labour party made it plain to the government that continued support for the war and further drafts of British manpower for the army were dependent on a clear statement of justifiable British war aims.[44] The peace program favored by labor was spelled out in a "Memorandum on War Aims," endorsed at a special conference of the Labour party and the Trades Union Congress held on 28 December. In this document British labor put itself squarely behind the principles that Wilson had laid down at the beginning of the year and that the Independent Labour party and UDC had championed since early in the war. The memorandum argued that the fundamental motivation behind labor's continued support for the war was "that the world may henceforth be made safe for democracy." The principal war aim was the provision of effectual means whereby "there should be henceforth on earth no more war." These means included the complete democratization of all countries, the abandonment of every form of imperialism, the termination of secret diplomacy, the institution of strict parliamentary control over foreign policy, the international limitation of armaments, and the abolition of conscription and the private manufacture of munitions. Labor demanded that as part of the treaty of peace itself, there should be established "a Super-National Authority, or League of Nations, which should not only be adhered to by all the present belligerents, but which every other independent sovereign State in the world should be pressed to join." The league would immediately set up an international high court to settle disputes of a justiciable nature and appropriate machinery to provide mediation in nonjusticiable disputes. An international legislature would be formed, including an allocated share of representatives from every civilized state, to undertake the gradual development of international law. All states would agree to settle disputes through the procedures provided and, whenever necessary, "by the use of any and every means at their disposal to enforce adherence to the terms of the agreement and pledge."[45] The memorandum, therefore, reaffirmed British labor's commitment to the establishment of a league of nations with extremely broad international power and authority. Clearly the government would have to respond if it hoped to maintain the morale and loyalty of the laboring section of British society.

Early in December Philip Kerr advised Lloyd George that a great speech on peace aims should be made to rally the industrial masses and neutral opinion. Victory over Germany was necessary, but "the old war arguments" were now unsuitable. What was needed was "a statesman who will play the part of Joshua and go forward and explore the promised land of peace" and outline the steps necessary to reach it. Kerr suggested that the prime minister put the creation of a "League of Allied Nations" at the center of a declaration on peace aims. The league could be built up from the Supreme War Council which had recently been established and combine all nations at war with Germany into a permanent international organization.[46] The prime minister and the government, however, chose to continue the hard line for the time being, striking out at those, like Lansdowne, who advocated a negotiated peace, and castigating those who thought that the war could be ended simply by establishing a league of nations to enforce peace. Such would be a fine policy after victory, Lloyd George argued, but to believe that the present German government could be trusted in a league of nations was "a farce in the setting of a tragedy."[47]

After the negotiations at Brest-Litovsk where the Central Powers skillfully exploited the rhetoric of New Diplomacy, and after the special Labour conference of 28 December, the War Cabinet agreed on 31 December that a public statement of war aims, couched in moderate and reasonable terms, was necessary to counter enemy propaganda and that such a statement should be issued unilaterally.[48] The drafting of an appropriate "counteroffensive" was entrusted to Cecil, Smuts, and Philip Kerr. Working through the opening days of the new year, all three had produced draft statements, which were ready for cabinet consideration by the afternoon of 3 January. Each recognized the necessity for an ideological counteroffensive to restore Allied morale in light of the damage done by Bolshevik open diplomacy. With regard to most questions concerning the nature of war and peace aims, the three drafts manifested an essential harmony. There was agreement that the war was not being fought to crush Germany as a great power, nor to impose an alien constitution upon her government—although a democratized Germany was portrayed as contributing greatly both to the ease and durability of the peacemaking. The three drafts basically agreed on the nature of the general territorial settlement desirable for Europe, the applicability of the principle of self-determination, the destiny of captured German colonies, and the ultimate settlement to be drawn for the Middle East.

Each paper, moreover, argued that a necessary part of any peace settlement was the provision of some means whereby future international disputes could be resolved peacefully and war prevented. Here, however, there were important differences in approach among the papers. Smuts called for provisions in the peace treaty that would bind governments to "the abolition of Military conscription and limitation of Armaments and the means and scale of future warfare, to the compulsory submission of future international disputes to arbitration, and to the institution of a regular Conference or League of Nations which shall control the execution of these general provisions and devise adequate machinery for the purpose." Kerr, on the other hand, while agreeing that war must be prevented if civilization were to survive, asserted that "no international machinery or treaties" could "in themselves" bring about lasting peace. The chief securities to be relied upon were the spread of constitutional government among all nations and the growth of an international public determination "that liberty shall be respected and justice enforced in the relations of state with state." Rather than projecting a universal postwar league of nations joined together in solemn covenants, Kerr returned to his previous suggestion of building up from the present "great association of free peoples." From the basis of such an "alliance," Kerr argued that other arrangements could follow for arms limitation, economic cooperation, arbitration of disputes, and the constitution of a "regular conference or League of Nations to watch over the larger affairs of mankind."[49]

Cecil's paper, as could be expected, placed major emphasis on the problem of curtailing future war. In its final section, the paper spoke eloquently of the burdens and horror of modern warfare and argued that the creation of an international organization to resolve disputes peacefully should be stated as a principal war aim, along with the reestablishment of the sanctity of treaties and a territorial settlement based on self-determination.[50]

A synthesis of the Cecil and Smuts drafts was approved by the War Cabinet, and Lloyd George arranged to deliver the speech before the Trades Union Congress since Parliament was not meeting.[51] The prime minister made it clear that he viewed the speech "rather as a war move than as a peace move."[52]

On 5 January, then, Lloyd George went before a labor audience at Caxton Hall and attempted to remove the "misgivings and doubts" concerning war aims which had grown in the past months. Although the prime minister's statement fell far short of the idealism of Labour's 28 December "Memorandum on War Aims," it did pay tribute to the ideological pressure which the war had generated at home and abroad. Trying to clarify both the principles for which the nation was fighting and their "definite and concrete application to the war map of the world," Lloyd George again denied that the desire to destroy Germany, Austria-Hungary, or Turkey formed any part of Allied war aims. Nor was the war being fought to alter or destroy Germany's imperial constitution. While a liberalization of German government would facilitate "a democratic peace," this would be "a question for the German people to decide." For Britain, this was first of all a war of self-defense—"in defence of the violated public law of Europe and in vindication of the most solemn treaty obligations on which the public system of Europe rested." On the other hand, the prime minister presented a damaging critique of the war aims of the enemy. In spite of the "lip service to the formula of no annexation and no indemnity or the right of self-determination," Lloyd George argued, Czernin's 25 December pronouncement was so deceptive and vague that it could include "almost any scheme of conquest and annexation."

Sketching the war aims of the British government, Lloyd George outlined the general features of the settlement ultimately desired. The desiderata with regard to Belgium, Alsace-Lorraine, and other occupied territories followed past pronouncements. If Russia concluded a separate peace, she would be left alone to face the catastrophe such action would surely bring. Keeping the line open for a separate peace with Austria-Hungary, the prime minister denied any wish to see the breakup of the empire, yet called for "genuine self-government on true democratic principles" for "Austro-Hungarian nationalities." Italy and Rumania, Lloyd George felt, should achieve satisfaction of legitimate desires for union with those of their own race and tongue. Outside Europe, non-Turkish portions of the Ottoman Empire would be "entitled to a recognition of their separate national conditions." The prime minister did not specify the exact form of such recognition but expressed willingness to discuss with the Allies the secret "arrangements" that had engendered so much debate, in light of the "new circumstances." The fate of the German colonies would be determined by the peace conference, with the wishes and interests of the natives the prime consideration and the principle of self-determination as applicable as in Europe. Lloyd George made no claim for indemnities—all that was demanded was "reparation for injuries done in violation of international law."

The prime minister's principal tribute to the New Diplomacy came in the final section of his address. Lloyd George followed Cecil's memorandum almost verbatim in asserting that as long as national disputes continued, as long as men were dominated by passion and ambition, and as long as armed conflict was the only means of settling disputes, all nations would be forced to live under continual threat of war. The "crushing weight of modern armaments" and the evils of conscription would remain as blots on western civilization. The prime minister continued, "For these and other similar reasons, we are confident that a great attempt must be made to establish by some international organization an alternative to war as a means of settling international disputes." The address concluded with the three conditions considered essential to a just and lasting peace: "First, the sanctity of treaties must be established; secondly, a territorial settlement must be secured based on the right of self-determination or the consent of the governed; and, lastly, we must seek by the creation of some international organization to limit the burden of armaments and diminish the probability of war."[53]

Lloyd George's address, with its castigation of enemy war aims, assertion of Allied moderation, and allusions to the rhetoric and program of the New Diplomacy, did much to rehabilitate governmental policies in the eyes of British labor and liberalism. But Wilson, in his famous Fourteen Points of 8 January, launched the real liberal ideological manifesto of the war. Since early fall, the president had grown increasingly concerned about the content of Allied war aims, especially in light of events in Russia and the mounting domestic pressures by the Left in Allied countries for clarification. Wilson argued in his 4 December statement to Congress declaring war on Austria that the liberal cause must be brought back "under the patronage of its real friends."[54]

Consequently, when the president faced Congress again on 8 January 1918, he was determined to recapture the ideological offensive for the Allied side. While Lloyd George had admitted, on 5 January, that "the days of the Treaty of Vienna are long past," Wilson rang out the principal tenets of New Diplomacy in fourteen hard-hitting points. That the days of conquest, aggrandizement, and secret covenants were "gone by" was now clear to anyone whose thoughts did not "still linger in an age that is dead and gone." While outlining a just and moderate settlement for Europe, based on the principle of national self-determination, and calling for a "free, open-minded, and absolutely impartial adjustment of all colonial claims," the president called for a new international order built on foundations that would guarantee a lasting peace. The principal elements of this new order were open diplomacy, freedom of the seas, freedom and nondiscrimination in trade, arms limitations, self-determination, and an end to colonialism. To crown the new order, Wilson's fourteenth point insisted that "a general association of nations must be formed under specific covenants for the purpose of affording mutual guarantees of political independence and territorial integrity to great and small states alike."[55]

The liberal manifestos of Wilson and Lloyd George served to rally the tired and dispirited ranks of the Allied coalition at a point when morale was dangerously low. Acting against the menacing ideological challenge of bolshevism, the American and British leaders had pointed to a new order of liberal internationalism that would justify continuing the war until victory was at hand. War conditions of 1917 had resulted in the political radicalization of British labor and the activation of middle-class liberalism in the league of nations movement. Though liberalism and labor differed increasingly on many issues, they at least shared a common attraction for Wilson as the prophet of a new international order. By the end of 1917, although the League of Nations Society had limited influence in its own right, the league of nations movement drew major new strength from Wilson's proclamation of the New Diplomacy and its support from the British and Allied Left. By 1918 the league of nations idea stood at the center of the ideological response of British and American liberalism to the tragedy of modern war and the fear of revolution.

4 Cecil's War: Searching for a Policy, 1918

Through 1918 the ideological alliance of Wilson and the Allied Left continued as the president's speeches elaborated the principles of the New Diplomacy. At the same time, activities of the League of Nations Society contributed to the growing numbers and influence of the league of nations movement.[1] Branch organizations of the society spread from London to other British cities, and the league idea was kept before the public in numerous meetings and several larger conferences, while books and pamphlets continued to pour off the presses.[2] In June Grey contributed greatly to the prestige and power of the league movement with the publication of a widely circulated pamphlet.[3] Grey argued at length that the survival of civilization depended on the substitution of international law for militarism and advocated the creation of a league of nations along the lines suggested by the League of Nations Society.

Later in 1918 the society published a detailed outline of the machinery and institutions that would be necessary if the principle of a league were to be translated into reality.[4] While the society knew that this task would be the responsibility of governments, it, nevertheless, was concerned that the proper detailed preparations be undertaken.

Cecil fully shared this concern, and through 1918 he conducted an unremitting campaign to persuade the government to study the league question thoroughly, reach an agreed policy, and take the necessary practical steps for eventual implementation. In fact, Cecil was behind the Bryce petition of August 1917, which called for the establishment of an Anglo-American committee of experts to look into the league idea.[5] Afterward, Cecil wrote to House on 3 September suggesting that examination of the league idea by some of the "best brains" in Britain and America would be of great value.[6] The tremendous importance that Cecil attached to working with President Wilson and the crucial significance he placed on such cooperation for future British policy are evident in a memorandum he circulated to the War Cabinet on 18 September. Cecil's memorandum urged replacing Spring-Rice as ambassador with Grey, who would get along much better with Wilson, "a Gladstone Liberal." Cecil relayed information from William Wiseman that House and the president hoped to cooperate closely with the British in the peacemaking, perhaps even in collusion against other powers.[7] Cecil did not know how much of Wiseman's information was true but thought it possibly accurate "when one remembers that, though the American people are very largely foreign, both in origin and in modes of thought their rulers are almost exclusively Anglo-Saxon, and share our political ideals." Cecil sketched a grand vision of a future Atlantic partnership led by Britain:

> The United States are entering upon an entirely fresh chapter of their history. For the first time they are taking a part in international European affairs; they will soon begin to realise what vast power they have; and, unless they are very different from any other nation that has ever existed they will wish to make use of that power. If they make use of it rightly, it may be of incalculable benefit to the human race; and by rightly I mean in accordance with our ideas of right and justice. There is undoubtably a difference between the British and the Continental point of view in international matters. I will not attempt to describe the difference, but I know that you will agree in thinking that, where it exists, we are right, and the Continental nations are, speaking generally, wrong. If America accepts our point of view in these matters, it will mean the dominance of that point of view in all international affairs.[8]

Cecil's hopes for a future Anglo-American partnership in world politics, overdrawn though they were, were shared by an important section of British policymakers. However, when the War Cabinet on 19 October considered the more limited proposals for cooperation with America suggested in the Bryce petition, it decided to adjourn the matter until discussions could be held with Colonel House, who was expected in England shortly.[9] When House arrived in Britain, Cecil's hopes for joint Anglo-American consideration of the league project soon foundered on opposition from Wilson. In conversations with British officials, House revealed the president's belief that the creation of a joint committee would be a mistake. Wilson refused to be committed in any way "to a cut and dried plan for the establishment of a League of Nations" and was presently discouraging the efforts of those in America who were active in designing detailed schemes.[10]

Faced with this setback, Cecil subsequently pressed Balfour to create an exclusively British expert committee to consider the league of nations schemes currently circulating and to recommend some practical policy. Otherwise, Cecil feared that at an eventual peace conference the government would be faced with "a lot of windy talk, ill thought out, and leading to nothing." Balfour doubted that speculation on the league idea would be very illuminating, but he admitted the value of analysis by experts and granted Cecil permission to proceed.[11] Accordingly, a committee consisting of historians A. F. Pollard, Julian Corbett, and J. H. Rose and Foreign Office representatives Sir Eyre Crowe, Sir William Tyrrell, and C. J. B. Hurst assembled under the chairmanship of Sir Walter G. F. Phillimore.[12] Established 3 January 1918, its purpose was "to enquire particularly from a judicial and historical point of view into the various schemes for establishing by means of a League of Nations, or other device, some alternative to war as a means of settling international disputes, to report on their practicability, to suggest amendments, or to elaborate a further scheme if on consideration it should be deemed possible and expedient."[13] The Phillimore committee met nine times before submitting its interim report to Balfour on 20 March 1918. This report was of principal importance in molding governmental thinking in both Britain and America, and influenced strongly much of the covenant's ultimate shape. For these reasons the deliberations of the committee and its report merit careful attention.

At its first meeting the committee rejected two widely contrasting approaches to the problem of international peace and security.[14] On the one hand, the creation of a world federation, or superstate, seemed unrealistic, given the current condition of international society. The committee also turned down a scheme submitted by Hankey that called for a wartime league of Allies based on the Versailles Council.[15] Instead, the committee decided to proceed according to the pattern laid down by the more conventional schemes that had attracted so much public support—a league providing peaceful procedures for the resolution of disputes and applying sanctions to states which violated these procedures.[16] Having decided on this pattern, the committee proceeded smoothly and quickly to fill out the details of a plan they believed would be practical in prevailing circumstances. Surprisingly, in view of the committee's membership, there was little attempt to evaluate the developing plan in light of British and imperial strategic traditions.[17] The only major issue on which the committee divided concerned the power to issue recommendations that an international conference should possess. The Foreign Office representatives argued strongly against granting the conference the power to issue recommendations on the basis of a simple majority vote.[18] Given the absence of major dissension, the committee was able to issue its interim report to the foreign secretary seven weeks after its first meeting.

The Phillimore report consisted of a draft convention prefaced by a lengthy introduction, which explained the principal features of its scheme.[19] The committee made no exaggerated claims on behalf of its plan and, in fact, refused to offer an opinion as to whether a formal league of nations should be established or the traditional diplomatic structure should be retained with a few modifications. The draft was submitted on the assumption that a league of nations might be regarded as "a possible solution." In any event, the proposals could serve "as a basis for an interchange of views." None of the schemes examined by the commmittee was considered completely acceptable or practicable. The committee had, however, embodied "their leading ideas" in its Convention, at the same time endeavoring to avoid their more obvious defects. The proposed league was viewed essentially as an alliance, the primary objective of which would be "that whatever happens peace shall be preserved between members of the Alliance." The secondary objective was the provision of means for settling disputes arising between members of the alliance.

After this cautious introduction, the committee's proposals were presented in four parts in a draft convention. Under the section entitled "Avoidance of War," each of the allied states would agree "collectively and separately" not to go to war with another allied state "(a) without previously submitting the matter in dispute to arbitration or to a Conference of the Allied States; and (b) until there had been an award or report by the Conference."[20] Each member state would further agree not to go to war "(c) with another of the Allied States which complies with the award or with the recommendations (if any) made by the Conference in its report." If any allied state should violate these commitments, "this State will become *ipso facto* at war with all the other Allied States, and the latter agree to take and to support each other in taking jointly and severally all such measures—military, naval, financial, and economic—as will best avail for restraining the breach of covenant." The required sanctions were then spelled out in detail.

These provisions did not build an airtight system against all wars. War was still possible if the conference failed to make a recommendation. However, the committee hoped that such cases would be rare and, given the compulsory moratorium on hostilities, thought that "the time will be so long drawn out that passions will have cooled." The commmittee decided against attempting to enforce the recommendations of the conference against recalcitrant states. On the other hand, the sanction provisions were designed to be as "weighty as possible" to ensure that peaceful procedures were utilized.

The second section of the draft convention detailed the procedures and machinery for "Peaceful Settlement of International Disputes." In judicial or legal disputes, the committee recommended that the parties refer the matter to arbitration. If arbitration proved impossible, the disputants would take the matter before a conference of the Allied states. Such a conference would have a permanent seat in a certain country. The leader of that country would convene the conference, and his representative would preside over its deliberations. The Allied states would be represented at the conference by their diplomatic representatives assigned to the country, or such other representatives as they designated.[21] The conference would ascertain the facts of the dispute and, if possible, make a recommendation. Such a recommendation would not have the force of a decision. The Phillimore committee split on the question of whether to grant any authority to majority recommendations or to follow the advice of the Foreign Office members and insist on strict unanimity for all recommendations. Two alternative articles were therefore included in the draft convention.

The third section of the plan dealt with "Relations between the Allied States and States not Party to this Convention." In the event of a dispute arising between a member of the alliance and a nonmember, the latter would be invited to submit the matter to arbitration or the conference. If this invitation were accepted, the nonmember would be treated as a member, and the normal procedures would be followed. If the invitation were declined, the conference could consider the matter ex parte and make a recommendation in the absence of the nonmember. Should a member of the league be attacked by a nonmember, the Phillimore report merely provided that "any of the Allied States may come to its assistance."[22] The final section of the draft, "Conflict of Treaties," provided that adherence to the league would involve abrogation of all treaty obligations inconsistent with the terms of the convention.

The Phillimore report, then, suggested a postwar international peace-keeping system, which, seemingly, involved only minor departures from conventional diplomatic practice.[23] The system was designed primarily to ensure that peace was maintained between members of the wartime alliance. Beyond an ambassadors conference, the committee saw no need for the creation of new international machinery, and such a conference would act only in times of crisis. The report did not clarify the problem of membership in the system. Membership presumably would be confined to the wartime Allies, yet the report's introduction spoke of including neutrals. No mention was made concerning the ultimate inclusion of enemy powers.

The report, nevertheless, did recommend a wide-ranging system of compulsory economic and military sanctions against any member of the alliance that violated the peaceful procedures agreed upon for the resolution of disputes. These sanctions would be a stumbling block for many British officials who resisted all idea of compulsion. Furthermore, there was some irony in a system that provided for compulsory sanctions against Allies but explicitly rejected the idea of a defensive union against external enemies. Clearly, the proposals of the Phillimore committee fell far short of the type of league that, by early 1918, had captured the public imagination. Moreover, the report itself left many questions unexamined and unanswered.

In late 1917 Philip Kerr suggested that a league of nations might be created during the war on the basis of the Supreme War Council. From the inception of the Supreme War Council, Hankey also had surmised that this institution might be made "the germ of the real League of Nations." Hankey and Kerr developed this conception independently, but in early December they exchanged viewpoints. Hankey then went on to elaborate the project systematically. In January 1918 he submitted a lengthy memorandum to the prime minister, the War Cabinet, and the Phillimore committee. Hankey's thinking on the league question had progressed considerably from his earlier blanket condemnation of all such schemes. He began by outlining the political, economic, and military organizations that now existed to facilitate Allied cooperation in making war—ranging from the Supreme Council at Versailles and the ministerial conference down to the smaller economic and technical commissions. In this comprehensive but somewhat loosely organized wartime structure, Hankey saw "the nucleus of the machinery of a League of Nations" and suggested that the time had come to knit this together more closely "with a view to the formation of a veritable League of Nations." As a first step, Hankey proposed that secretariats of the various inter-Allied organizations sit in one place, perhaps Versailles. Thus, the whole economic offensive of the war could be concentrated under a league of nations. Such an organization might also be used to conduct the eventual peace negotiations with the enemy. After the war, this league could be converted from a valuable wartime instrument to a peace-keeping organization. With such a stranglehold on the world's economic resources, neutrals and former enemies could be compelled to join. Hankey also envisioned a central administrative role in postwar economic reconstruction for such a league. Furthermore, international activities such as postal services, telegraph, wireless, railway, shipping, and aerial communications, and financial, commercial, and technological matters could gradually be brought under league auspices.

Politically, Hankey's scheme differed radically from the mainstream of proleague thought and the recommendations of the Phillimore report. No provision was made for contractual obligations requiring peaceful procedures in resolving international disputes. Nor was any mention made of sanctions. Hankey stressed, rather, the great benefits that would result if a league of nations could ensure frequent international ministerial exchanges. The wartime experience had proven how frequent personal contacts often removed the formalities, suspicions, and strangeness which impede the transaction of business. Similarly, in the postwar period, if the league could make continuous personal contact and cooperation possible in administrative matters, the already established trust and cooperation would greatly contribute to the preservation of peace when major disputes arose. Hankey suggested that each of the "Greater States" be permanently represented by a resident minister at Versailles, who would deal with political matters of secondary importance on behalf of the prime ministers, keep their governments fully informed of all that was going on, and coordinate the nonpolitical aspects of international cooperation. Hankey concluded by warning that whether or not his scheme was considered practicable, Allied governments must coordinate their policies on the league question. Failure to do so would make for major problems at an eventual peace conference.[24]

Hankey's plan for a wartime league was dismissed rather curtly by the Phillimore committee as "not the kind of League generally understood in the expression 'League of Nations.'"[25] Hankey was probably as interested in coordinating the Allied economic offensive against the enemy as he was in laying plans for a permanent peace league. His suggestions, nevertheless, carried great weight in the circles closest to the prime minister, and the memorandum offered a clear alternative to the schemes advocated by most proleague societies as well as to the plan outlined in the Phillimore report. Furthermore, the idea of a league growing out of Allied wartime institutions and aimed at promoting conference diplomacy and functional international cooperation received important public support from several quarters through the remainder of 1918.

Hankey's ideas were shared in large measure by Philip Kerr. Kerr, no longer editor of the *Round Table*, kept in close touch with leaders of the movement, and his approach to the league was propounded by the journal in several articles published through 1918. The *Round Table* cautioned against the millennial hopes that various "paper constitutions" for a league of nations had aroused and proposed basing the league on a regularized system of great power consultation, using the Allied wartime machinery and the Imperial War Cabinet as models. Certainly, in the transitional period from war to peace, the Allied machinery must be utilized in carrying out the urgent tasks of reconstruction. Otherwise there would be "small hope for the future of international organization."[26]

When the House of Lords debated the league idea in March and June 1918, Curzon, speaking for the government, referred to the possibility of a "League of Allied Nations." Curzon promised the proleague lords that the government was "in earnest" with regard to creating a league of nations and outlined an approach that paralleled in part the recommendations of the Phillimore committee. But Curzon's speech dwelt mostly on the difficulties all such schemes faced, and he suggested that if the "larger schemes" for a league of nations failed to materialize, the two leagues already in existence—the British Empire and the league of Allied nations—could still provide "a nucleus from which it may be possible to proceed."[27]

The idea of forming a wartime league of nations served as the principal objective of a new group that came together in July 1918. A split occurred within the ranks of the League of Nations Society, instigated mainly by David Davies, Welsh coal and railway magnate and Liberal politician. Subsequent interparty discussions involving Davies, Gilbert Murray, H. G. Wells, Charles A. McCurdy, and J. A. Spender led to the formation of the League of Free Nations Association.[28] Membership in the new group overlapped with the right wing of the League of Nations Society, but the association's supporters were generally more anti-German and prowar. Less closely identified with radicalism or Asquith liberalism, they were more convinced of their ability to mount a vigorous campaign that would appeal to conservatives as well as liberals and labor.[29] Other leading supporters of the association included Wickham Steed of the *Times*, J. L. Garvin of the *Observer*, Sir Mark Sykes, and Labourite J. H. Thomas. The program of the League of Free Nations Association, published in September, followed the basic plan of most of the proleague groups but differed in its desire to form the league immediately, based on the wartime alliance and excluding the enemy states until they were beaten, repentant, and democratized. The program also provided for the eventual creation of an "international force to guarantee order in the world," a project espoused enthusiastically by Davies.[30] With its good press contacts and with access to the fortune of Davies, the association conducted a vigorous campaign for the duration of the war, its goal being a "league now."

Several members of the association also worked at Crewe House under Lord Northcliffe, director of enemy propaganda. H. G. Wells and Wickham Steed suggested to Northcliffe that the idea of a wartime league of free nations might be effective in propaganda aimed at Germany, particularly if the league were portrayed as a powerful economic coalition with a potential monopoly of world resources for the postwar period. The Germans could be threatened with exclusion from this all-powerful economic consortium if they continued the war. But if the Germans sued for peace and were willing to meet the necessary conditions, they could avoid economic ruin by admission to the league. Northcliffe pressed these tactics on Balfour and the War Cabinet and received the latter's approval after the "fighting league of free nations" was given control over the destiny of Germany's colonies.[31] Subsequent British propaganda exploited the threat of vast economic power controlled by the league of wartime Allies, and Lloyd George himself played on this theme in a speech of 31 July to the National Union of Manufacturers on future economic policy.[32]

The idea of a wartime league of free nations, then, had great elasticity, and it had highly placed supporters in Britain. Eventually, House pressed the idea on Wilson. But Wilson proved the stumbling block to all such schemes. Suggestions that the league might be used to coerce Germany economically during or after the war were bitterly opposed by the president, and the British were duly instructed.[33] Furthermore, Wilson opposed all attempts at the end of the war and at the peace conference to develop the league from existing wartime institutions. In Britain, Cecil also opposed the whole concept of a wartime league and argued against confusing the league project with propaganda for an economic alliance against Germany.[34]

Through the summer of 1918, Cecil became increasingly disturbed at the lack of progress the league question was making in official circles. He had obtained the permission of the War Cabinet to send confidential copies of the Phillimore report to House and Wilson in May.[35] House wrote to Cecil 24 June, outlining his hopes for an international moral standard and sketching a plan for universal compulsory arbitration buttressed by a general territorial guarantee.[36]

House's suggestions made Cecil even more anxious that Anglo-American discussions take place to work out a practical plan. At the same time information on French planning for a league of nations was even more alarming. The French government, like the other Allies, had endorsed the idea of a league of nations, but Clemenceau, who became premier in November 1917, greeted the idea with scarcely veiled cynicism.[37] A commission had been established under Léon Bourgeois. In June 1918 the government received its report and forwarded it to the British government as an aid to future discussion.[38] The Bourgeois commission recommended a "Société des Nations" consisting of the standard international council, tribunal, and secretarial committee. But its detailed proposals for an international army organized under an international general staff and charged with carrying out the decrees of the tribunal and with defending members of the league from outside aggression went far beyond any of the British or American schemes. In effect, the French were proposing a perpetuation of the military alliance against Germany under the guise of a league of nations.[39]

In view of the unsatisfactory state of planning for a league of nations in France, America, and his own government, Cecil wrote a letter to the prime minister, outlining his misgivings and proposing a plan of action. Cecil's letter pointed to great dangers ahead if the government's policy were allowed to continue drifting along indefinite lines. The government would arrive at an eventual peace conference with only "vague aspirations" in mind, without definite government proposals backed by public opinion. Feeling that such poor preparation would be fatal to the league cause, Cecil urged three measures upon the prime minister. First, the Imperial War Cabinet, currently in session, should consider the Phillimore report and express general approval. Second, this approval should serve as a basis for inter-Allied discussion. Finally, the Phillimore report should be published, thereby bringing public discussion on the whole league question into some focus.[40]

With this letter, Cecil embarked upon a determined campaign to elicit from the government a definite policy on the question of postwar international organization.[41] Cecil repeatedly pressed the government to proceed along the lines laid down in his letter. He wrote to House, arguing the wisdom of the Phillimore proposals over the plan outlined in House's letter of 24 June and warning about French designs for a new "Holy Alliance."[42] Again and again Cecil met with frustration. It became evident that members of the government held serious reservations concerning the viability of the Phillimore scheme. The government's misgivings were reinforced by Wilson, who persistently opposed any public debate on the constitution of a future league of nations.[43] From America, both Wiseman and Reading advised the government that the president's attitude made any premature policy announcement on the league question or any public endorsement of the Phillimore proposals extremely unwise.[44]

When the league question was debated again in Parliament on 1 August, W. H. Dickinson castigated the government for its failure to take a position of public leadership on the issue. Balfour rehearsed the government's difficulties but reassured members of his personal sympathy. Cecil intervened in the debate, speaking warmly of the general approach put forward in the Phillimore report (without referring to it explicitly) and urging that the time had come for all men of good will to unite behind a practical scheme.[45] Then on 13 August, when the Imperial War Cabinet once again examined war aims, Cecil argued strongly in favor of publishing the Phillimore report. The discussion led to several heated exchanges. Cecil, admitting that he was "very violently in favour of this scheme," reiterated his arguments for immediate publication of the report to prevent the whole project from perishing in a flood of plausible "faddist schemes." The report need not be published as the views of the government, but a standard was needed to stabilize and settle public discussions on the subject. Reading, back from America, advised the cabinet that Wilson was very anxious that nothing be published that would appear to commit the British government to a definite scheme. The president was currently working on a memorandum of his own and hoped to exchange views with the British in a few weeks. Lloyd George argued that there were two strong objections to publication aside from the president's disinclination. First, in spite of any disclaimers to the contrary, if the scheme were published, "everybody will say this is the scheme of the British

Government." Second, the prime minister argued that the publication of such a peace project could detract seriously from the public will to victory.

Similarly, Australian Prime Minister Hughes, while considering general statements in favor of a league as "quite harmless," objected strongly to the publication of a scheme that dealt with the problem in detail. Hughes felt the Imperial War Cabinet should decide on a definite policy first. Faced with mounting objections, Cecil bitterly replied that he had "pressed for months past to have this question seriously considered" and warned that the government could at any time be faced with "a violent demand from the people" to know what its policy really was. In a heated conclusion he observed that it was "only too evident that some of my colleagues do not want this scheme put forward."[46]

The government's opposition to publication of the Phillimore report was reaffirmed 19 August when Reading circulated a telegram from Wiseman recording an interview with House and Wilson. The interview centered largely on the league question. Wilson opposed any attempt to discuss publicly the constitution of a league of nations and would make no public statement on this matter. Such a statement, Wilson felt, would invite damaging criticism, not only from Senate opponents, but also from utopian idealists. Wilson explicitly opposed publication of the Phillimore scheme, which he felt had "no teeth": "I read it to the last page hoping to find something definite but I could not." The president also opposed any wartime creation of a league of nations since it would "inevitably be regarded as a sort of Holy Alliance aimed at Germany." However, Wilson was ready and anxious to discuss the league question privately with the British government and welcomed any representative the government might delegate for this purpose. Wiseman's telegram concluded by stressing the seriousness of Wilson's attitude on this issue. If the government did not meet Wilson's views, it could "easily embarrass our whole relations with him."[47]

The importance of Wiseman's telegram was not lost on Lloyd George. Writing to Bonar Law 20 August, Lloyd George pointed out that it was now clear that Wilson did not share Cecil's view on the league of nations. He concluded, "We must take care that Cecil does not rush us into a premature pronouncement that would get us into trouble not merely with the French but with the Americans as well."[48] Wiseman's telegram distressed Cecil greatly. Writing to Wiseman 19 August, Cecil argued that the president, by opposing the publication of any definite scheme, did not seem to realize all the difficulties to be overcome if a league of nations were to be established. Giving vent to some of his pent up frustrations, Cecil pointed out that all the European bureaucracies would be against the idea, "including probably the bureaucracy of this country." The idea would also be opposed by all the forces of militarism, Allied as well as German. Cecil warned Wiseman that "all these people are working already, more or less secretly against the idea." Cecil wished, therefore, to publish something definite, "in order to create and form public opinion and make it vigorous."[49]

Cecil's desire to see the government clarify its position on the league question was shared by George Barnes, Henderson's labor replacement in the War Cabinet.[50] Labor's attachment to the league cause and the New Diplomacy increased through 1918.[51] Barnes was chairman of the League to Abolish War, a laborite group with a program calling for postwar disarmament and the establishment of a universal system of compulsory arbitration at The Hague, backed by an international military and naval police.[52] In a speech at Cambridge on 5 August, which surely must have violated all the tenets of collective Cabinet responsibility, Barnes called for a league based on a universal guarantee of political independence and territorial integrity and backed by a strong military sanction. To operate effectively, such a military sanction would need a prearranged plan for mobilization and command, or a virtual international army. Barnes was quite willing to admit that some surrender of sovereignty would be necessary if wars were to be prevented. The league must include Germany and make provision for disarmament and nationalization of all armament industries. Voicing his frustration at the inertia of the British government, Barnes called for increased public agitation: "The man in the street is thinking far ahead of Foreign Offices and governments on these matters, and will at once assert himself if the question begins really to be discussed through the public Press and platform in the form of concrete practical proposals." Barnes concluded his address with an appeal for an inter-Allied Hague conference, attended not only by governments but also by labor, religious, and commercial representatives, to examine and "revise" peace aims and agree on practical steps concerning the initiation of a league of nations.[53]

Barnes brought the league question before the War Cabinet once again at its 2 October meeting. Barnes first warned the cabinet of the dangers inherent in the prevailing lack of focus of official views on the league question. He then stressed the importance of formulating a practicable policy that could serve as a basis for inter-Allied discussion and agreement. Balfour explained that Wilson stood in the way of the course of action that Barnes advocated. However, given the insistence of Cecil and Barnes, the growing public demand for a definite governmental policy, and Wilson's intimation of 18 August that he would welcome private discussions on the question, the cabinet realized the time had come for some action. Both Balfour and Reading expressed strong desire that an Anglo-American accord be reached on this matter prior to discussions with France and other Allies. After some discussion, the War Cabinet decided to empower Reading, upon his return to America, to enter into "private and unofficial" discussions with the president or his deputies, "with a view to the free and frank interchange of views on the subject." Reading would make it clear to the president, however, that such discussions "in no way committed His Majesty's government to any agreement on the subject, or to any definite line of action." To acquaint Reading with "the general trend" of government thinking, Balfour was to arrange an informal meeting at the Foreign Office, where ministers could brief Reading on their attitudes. As a preliminary to such a meeting, Cecil was instructed to prepare and circulate a memorandum on the league question "which would differentiate between those points which were controversial and those which were, in the main, generally acceptable."[54]

With this decision the government took a step in the direction which both Cecil and Barnes had been pointing to for a long time. Had Reading's mission been carried out, the effects would probably have been salutary for both future Anglo-American relations and the creation of the league of nations. By the end of the summer of 1918, each government viewed the other through a veil of mistrust and misunderstanding on the league question, economic policy, and general war aims. Wilson continued to suspect the real nature of British war aims, misread the Phillimore report, resented Northcliffe's use of the league idea in enemy propaganda, and refused to cooperate with Cecil in undertaking the necessary practical planning, despite Cecil's appeals. The president's first draft plan for a league, composed in August on the basis of an earlier draft by House, called for a general guarantee of political independence and territorial integrity, a universal system of compulsory arbitration with enforced decisions, and general disarmament.[55] Wilson's plan could have profited greatly from exchanges with Cecil and British officials, who had thought the whole question through much more systematically.

The British government, for its part, was anxious to work closely with Wilson, and there was powerful support for Cecil's vision of a future Anglo-American entente. But all the British had to go on were Wilson's Olympian declarations—the Fourteen Points, the Four Ends, and the Five Particulars—which asserted that the constitution of a league of nations must form "the most essential part" of the peace settlement itself and that no alliances or selfish economic combinations could exist within such a league of nations.[56] The government had to rely on the intelligence gleaned by Wiseman in its attempt to penetrate to the substance behind Wilson's public manifestos.[57] Most of the mysteries and misunderstandings remained with unfortunate results for Anglo-American cooperation in the peacemaking.

Reading's mission was aborted following the unforeseen and sudden German appeal to Wilson of 5 October for a peace based on the Fourteen Points. The energies of Allied statesmen quickly became absorbed in the tense negotiations leading to an armistice. The British government entered the prearmistice negotiations without having reached agreement on the league question with the Americans or the European Allies and without a considered policy of its own.

5   *War and Peace:*
     Preparing for the Peace Conference

The German appeal for peace presented Allied statesmen
with the question of whether they could fashion an armistice that
would guarantee their hard-won position of military superiority.
Moreover, since the German note explicitly requested a peace based
on Wilson's Fourteen Points, Allied leaders were faced with the
additional task of deciding upon the expediency and wisdom of a
commitment to Wilson's program as a basis for the ultimate peace
settlement. Both the military terms and the political preconditions
granted Germany would have major consequences for the eventual
peacemaking, and the tense prearmistice negotiations presaged in
many ways the issues and strategic choices Britain and her allies
would face in the impending peace conference.

House arrived in Paris 26 October 1918 with the express purpose of committing the Allies to Wilson's program. There followed
several days of acrimonious negotiations with the Allies during
which, despite House's threats of a separate American peace, Britain
and the Allies insisted on reservations that protected their major interests and objectives. The compromise suggested by Lloyd George
—Allied agreement to make peace based on Wilson's Fourteen
Points and subsequent addresses, with reservations on freedom of
the seas and reparations—was accepted only after high-pressured
private negotiations and a written promise by the British prime
minister to permit future discussion of the freedom of the seas in
light of changing conditions.

This compromise, which served as the basis of the prearmistice agreement forwarded by Wilson to Germany on 5 November, was viewed by House as a "great diplomatic victory." The Allies, House believed, were now firmly committed to the Fourteen Points, including the crucial fourteenth point. House advised the president that both Clemenceau and Lloyd George had desired to make the creation of a league of nations "an after consideration, and not part of the Peace Conference."[1] Although the issue had not been pressed, House believed the Allies were committed in this matter also.

British leaders clearly did not view the prearmistice agreement in the same terms as House. At the Imperial War Cabinet of 5 November, after a bitter attack from Hughes, who refused "to be bound to the chariot wheel of the Fourteen Points, particularly those dealing with the League of Nations," Lloyd George attempted to mollify the Australian prime minister with assurances that imperial interests had been fully protected during the Paris deliberations. House had been privately informed that captured colonies would "under no circumstances" be returned to Germany, and those conquered by the dominions would not be surrendered. Furthermore, the prime minister emphasized that the government still possessed the widest freedom of maneuver with regard to the ultimate peace terms. These terms were not limited solely by the Fourteen Points, but by all the president's declarations since January 1918. Having studied these declarations carefully, Lloyd George argued that "he could not find a single point which he wanted that was not amply covered, with the exception of the points regarding the freedom of the seas and indemnities, and of our position in regard to these matters notice had been duly given."[2] A few days later Philip Kerr assured Hughes that acceptance of Wilson's Fourteen Points "really [didn't] prejudice the question of peace to any extent." Wilson's points were "mostly verbiage and [would] have to be interpreted in fact by the light of the situation and the determination of the different parties concerned."[3]

Obviously, House's reading of the prearmistice agreement was overly sanguine. His apparent disinterest in the military and naval terms included in the armistice also demonstrated a somewhat naïve view of Allied intentions.[4] Nevertheless, the role of House during the prearmistice negotiations revealed to Allied statesmen that Wilson was dead earnest in demanding a peace settlement based foursquare upon the new diplomatic order laid down in his Fourteen Points and subsequent speeches. From America, Wiseman advised that the president would approach the upcoming settlement with his mind firmly fixed on the creation of a league of nations. The rest of his program would flow from the league of nations, and, if the league project failed, all else would be considered "useless" and "meaningless."[5]

Cooperation with Wilson in the peacemaking and the establishment of a postwar Anglo-American entente was one major strategic alternative open to the British government at the end of 1918. It was a strategy with enthusiastic supporters in Britain.[6] Cecil envisioned a new "pax Anglo-Americana." Balfour was a convinced atlanticist. Wiseman, too, consistently recommended this path. Borden, the Canadian prime minister, favored "a league of the two great English-speaking Commonwealths."[7] Members of the Round Table group expanded their imperial vision to include the United States in an Anglo-Saxon world mission,[8] while British liberalism and labor looked upon Wilson in almost messianic terms by late 1918.

A strategy of cooperation with America formed the central theme in a survey of the major strategic options open to the British Empire circulated to the Imperial War Cabinet in early December by General Smuts, who had been given responsibility for preparing the British brief for the peace conference. Smuts contended that with the demise of Russia, Austria-Hungary, and Germany, there remained only three first class powers in the arena of world politics. The question was what role Britain would play in this new tripartite game: "Are we going to side with France or America as a matter of large policy?" Manifesting a strong anti-French bias, Smuts argued for abandoning the traditional policy of maintaining the European balance of power by supporting the weaker group in Europe. Instead, he favored cooperation with America and support for Wilson "as far as is consistent with our own interests." In taking this path,

Smuts argued that the empire was "only following the line of our true policy for the future which will no doubt link the two great democratic Commonwealths in a common destiny." Language, interests, ideals, and "all fundamental considerations of policy" pointed to a new era of Anglo-American cooperation. Smuts suggested that the most effective way to promote such cooperation was to support Wilson's policy of a league of nations and "to give form and substance to his rather nebulous ideas." Since to Wilson the league was "the root of the whole matter," if Britain helped him realize this project, then he would perhaps be prepared to "drop some of the other contentious points he has unfortunately raised." The general, then, advised telling Wilson quite frankly at the beginning of the peace negotiations "that we are going to support him fully on the League of Nations, and that, in our opinion, the League will be valuable not only from the point of view of future world peace, but also from the way it will enable us to solve some of the most difficult territorial and economic questions arising out of this war."[9]

Smuts's memorandum outlined one possible strategy for British statesmen to pursue at the peace conference. He failed, however, to deal adequately with issues over which Wilson's program and British traditional strategies and interests were in clear conflict. Could the British afford to abandon their traditional concern for the European balance of power? Could Wilson be persuaded to tolerate Britain's traditional naval and maritime position? Could Anglo-American economic and commercial rivalry be contained? British and Allied leaders were already involved in an ugly clash with the Americans over the organization and control of postwar European relief and reconstruction. Both sides understood full well the economic and political implications involved in the relief program. British advisors hoped that this program could be carried out under collective Allied administration through a general economic board, which would take over the work of the Allied Maritime Transport Council and other Allied wartime economic organs. This venture in internationalism was viewed as a "corollary" to the league project, and there was some hope that the relief and reconstruction machinery could later be subsumed under the league of nations organization.[10] But all of these plans ran into the absolute resistance of Hoover, the American food administrator, who convinced Wilson not to agree "to any program that even looks like inter-Allied control of our resources after peace."[11] Hoover and the Americans were intent on using American food and resource surpluses for political as well as humanitarian purposes, not only with regard to enemy, neutral, and liberated areas, but also as a means of influencing allies. The American responses to British overtures for cooperation in relief were considered "brutally negative," "self-regarding," and "dictatorial," and Lloyd George advised members of the Imperial War Cabinet on 28 November that Wilson's attitude on the relief and naval programs "was not a very good beginning for the League of Nations."[12]

Beyond these immediate problems was the larger crucial question of whether Wilson could carry through with his program in light of the growing power of his domestic opponents if the British decided to put their faith in the president. The November congressional elections had seen Wilson and the Democratic party lose control of the House and Senate. Senator Henry Cabot Lodge, soon to be chairman of the powerful Senate Foreign Relations Committee, was openly hostile to Wilson and secretly warned the Allies that the president's program for a league of nations was "hopelessly impracticable in many respects" and would likely meet with "great, and probably effective opposition."[13] In a Senate speech of 21 December, "intended chiefly for the benefit of the Allies," Lodge insisted that the Senate would have no qualms in resisting or amending a treaty that contained "extraneous provisions" violating American sovereignty.[14] In light of the position taken by Lodge, British leaders understandably had reservations about Wilson's program. Even so warm an advocate of Anglo-American cooperation as Grey felt moved to warn House and Wilson discreetly that caution was necessary if a league of nations treaty were not to be "wrecked by the Senate."[15]

Would a policy of cooperation with France possibly offer a better strategy for Britain? Smuts answered this question with a resounding negative. His memorandum castigated the French as thoroughly unsuitable partners for British world policy. Their diplomatic record until 1870 had been black, according to Smuts, and with Germany defeated, France would aim at remaining "mistress of the continent" and keeping the Germans in "a state of humiliating subjection which must create a hopeless atmosphere for future peace and international cooperation." French diplomacy would follow "arrogant," "militant," and "imperialist" lines. Smuts no doubt had reason to react strongly against French policies. The French approach to the peacemaking had been made clear in drafting the military terms of the armistice and in subsequent memoranda and statements by French leaders.[16] French power was to be increased and German power reduced by means of territorial changes, economic penalties, disarmament requirements, and Allied occupation privileges. The French military hoped to gain the strategic frontier of the Rhine and, at the same time, structure a permanent Anglo-Franco-Belgian alliance against Germany. In addition, a large and powerful Poland would be established to counter Germany in the East and contain bolshevism. French leaders spoke cynically of Wilson's New Diplomacy, relegating his league of nations to the realm of "supplementary guarantees." Clemenceau publicly reaffirmed his faith in alliances and the balance of power.[17]

French intentions were revealed more explicitly during the inter-Allied conference in London, 30 November–3 December.[18] Prior to the conference the French made overtures to the British government for an arrangement on the general principles of peacemaking so that Wilson could be faced with "complete safety" at the conference.[19] The French suggestion was too much for the British, as were the plans submitted by Foch at the inter-Allied meeting.[20] At the same time, the French could not be written off as Smuts desired. Britain's continental strategy, for all its costs, had won the war and prevented German domination of Europe. Westerners would be as loath to see France abandoned after the war as they would have during the fighting. Anglo-French cooperation in the armistice negotiations had resulted in cardinal successes for the countries' joint interests. Belgium had been liberated, the destruction of German military and naval power had been assured, and German liability for major reparations had been established. The Foreign Office considered France an indispensable component in sustaining a necessary postwar balance of power, especially since Russia seemed lost beyond recall in British continental strategies. French policies, then, rather than American slogans, corresponded with traditional British interests in several crucial spheres. Close Anglo-French cooperation in the peacemaking and thereafter would remain a central theme in British policy, particularly in light of the uncertainty surrounding the Wilsonian program. As Sir Eyre Crowe noted, "We must remember that our friend America lives a long way off; France sits at our door."[21]

Smuts's memorandum touched on a third major strategic option —imperial consolidation. One of the reasons for Smuts's hostility to France derived from the secret wartime agreements promising France and Italy a share in the strategically crucial area of the Middle East and in the division of Germany's African colonies. To Smuts the Sykes-Picot agreement and the concessions to Italy represented "a hopeless blunder of policy," which Wilson might be induced to "veto." Smuts didn't point out that Wilson might also want to veto the designs of the South Africans, as well as the Australians and New Zealanders, for annexation of the German colonies they had captured. But to a large degree Smuts shared the vision of Amery and the British imperialists of an empire stretching unhindered from the Middle East to India, down to New Zealand, and from the Cape to Cairo.[22] Smuts, therefore, not only opposed sharing control of the Middle East but also supported the annexation of German East Africa, thereby assuring strategic control of the Indian Ocean.

While Smuts, Amery, Curzon, and the Milnerites contemplated extending British and dominion control over new areas, others questioned whether an imperial strategy of the dimensions suggested could be sustained by the empire and whether such extension might not create more liabilities than assets for British security. Such was the view of Balfour and Cecil and others in the Foreign Office. Imperialism carried major political liabilities, given the aversion not only of Wilson but also of the British Left to the colonialism of the old order. Moreover, imperialism disregarded the awakening political consciousness of India and the Arabs.

The dominions continued to present an enigma in calculations of imperial strategy—an enigma which increased with the growing power of dominion nationalism. The fact that Smuts had served in the War Cabinet and was now playing a leading part in calculating future British strategies illustrated the major changes the war had brought in the role of the dominions. While the southern dominions insisted on the realization of their war aims concerning the German colonies, they and the Canadians also demanded a new national status at the impending peace conference. Would the growing power and ambitions of the dominions add to or detract from British security? Could the Empire speak with a united voice in foreign and defense policy? Generally, the reception of Round Table ideas during the war, particularly in Canada, did little to encourage any hope for imperial federation.[23] The reaction of dominion populations to the carnage of the war had led Borden and Smuts to oppose any future imperial commitments on the European continent.[24] Borden voiced Canada's opposition to any policy of imperial annexations. At the moment of victory, therefore, with the British Empire reaching its apogee of power and territorial sway, political factors compounded defense dilemmas and made an imperial strategy at least as problematic in the peacemaking as it had been prior to and during the war.

While Smuts fused an imperial vision with a desire for Anglo-American cooperation, the league of nations providing the nexus, Cecil continued to propound the league and liberal internationalism as the basis for future British strategy. Of course, like Smuts, Cecil was an enthusiast for transatlantic cooperation. When the Reading mission to coordinate Anglo-American views on the league was aborted by the sudden end of the war, Cecil anxiously pressed his government to reach agreement on the league question. The time had come for detailed planning with or without the Americans. Cecil drafted the paper on the league requested earlier by the cabinet. At Cecil's "urgent request," the cabinet committee originally scheduled to brief Reading met to examine Cecil's paper on 16 October.[25]

Cecil's paper sketched a carefully circumscribed league, which followed the pattern of the still secret Phillimore report: "no very elaborate machinery" would be required; any form of international government was rejected. Essentially, the league would be limited to a treaty binding the signatories never to resort to war until an international conference had been held to inquire into and, if possible, resolve the dispute. This process would interfere only minimally with national sovereignty. If a nation resorted to war prior to such a conference, each of the signatories would use its whole force, economic and military, against such aggression. Cecil saw the principal role of a league of nations as ensuring a delay before hostilities occurred and mobilizing the peaceful force of public opinion during such a delay. Finally, Cecil suggested that the league also play a role in the international socioeconomic field and possibly in the control of "backward races."[26]

Despite the limited nature of the league Cecil propounded, his suggestions were received by his colleagues "respectfully rather than cordially" and "no decisions were come to."[27] Christopher Addison, who attended the meeting as reconstruction minister, recorded that deliberations were of a "somewhat indeterminate character and served only to bring out the inherent difficulties of making any scheme of this kind operative and effective."[28] Cecil nevertheless used this paper as the text for a major public address on the league question, delivered upon his inauguration as chancellor of the University of Birmingham, 12 November 1918. Shortly afterward, Cecil resigned from the government over the disestablishment and disendowment of the Welsh church. No doubt he was also disappointed over the government's failure to assume greater initiative on the league question. He wrote Gilbert Murray that he hoped to do more for the league project outside the government than within it.[29]

As the first winter of peace set in, then, initial discussion and analysis had clarified many of the issues and choices facing British policymakers and their imperial colleagues as the peace conference approached. To the traditional choice between an imperial-naval strategy on one hand and a continental-military strategy on the other were added the further alternatives of atlanticism and internationalism. Each of these major strategies had attractions and liabilities. Some could be combined at least partially, but others were largely exclusive. Choices had to be made. Much work remained to be done by governmental departments and the Imperial War Cabinet to clarify these choices in light of British interests. Meanwhile, a general election absorbed the energies of politicians and provided the domestic determinants of the peacemaking.

In Britain the war drew to a close with the same House of Commons sitting that had been elected in December 1910. Because of the prevailing tides of victory, Lloyd George had little trouble justifying to himself and to his coalition partners the necessity for a new mandate from the people. Accordingly, after a party arrangement between Lloyd George and the Conservatives, an election was called for early December.

Leaders of the league of nations movement were well aware that the issues brought to the fore during the campaign and the results of the election would have an important bearing on the government's approach to the peace settlement. As the end of the war approached, efforts were made to draw the principal segments of the league movement together for a concerted campaign prior to the peacemaking.[30] After preliminary discussions, leaders of the League of Nations Society and the League of Free Nations Association agreed to cooperate in a joint effort on behalf of their cause. The first fruit of this cooperation was an immensely successful mass meeting held in the Central Hall, Westminster, 10 October.[31] Here Viscount Grey, who had agreed to act as president of a union of the two proleague groups, addressed an overflow crowd of league supporters. Grey pointed to President Wilson's Mount Vernon speech of 27 September as the pattern to be followed in the peacemaking. Most important, Grey emphasized, a league of nations must be created during the peace conference. To leave its formation until later would be to court failure. It was necessary, therefore, that the government undertake at once the preparation of practical plans for a league that could serve as a guide during the peace negotiations.

Grey's speech, his first major public address since resignation, was widely reported in the press and later broadly circulated in pamphlet form.[32] The warm reception accorded the speech encouraged leaders of the league movement to press on with the task of uniting the two major proleague groups and developing a joint program. The final details of union were worked out in November when Balfour, Lloyd George, and Asquith agreed to serve as honorary presidents along with Grey. On 18 November the new League of Nations Union published a joint program. With a few additions and changes the program closely followed the earlier plan of the League of Free Nations Association and called for the establishment as soon as possible of a league of free peoples who desired to end war forever. Members of the proposed league would agree—

1. To submit all disputes arising among themselves to methods of peaceful settlement.

2. To suppress jointly, by the use of all the means at their disposal, any attempt by any State to disturb the peace of the world by acts of war.

3. To create a Supreme Court, and to respect and enforce its decisions.

4. To establish a permanent Council, which shall provide for the development of international law, for the settlement of differences not suitable for submission to the Supreme Court, for the supervision and control of armament, and for joint action in matters of common concern.

5. To admit to the League all peoples able and willing to give effective guarantees of their loyal intention to observe its covenants, and thus to bring about such a world organization as will guarantee the freedom of nations; act as Trustee and guardian of uncivilized races and underdeveloped territories; and maintain international order; and thus finally liberate mankind from the curse of war.[33]

From this beginning, the League of Nations Union mounted a wide-reaching campaign to explain their objectives and increase popular support for the league cause. Formation of branch groups was accelerated, and by the end of the year a network of union branches had spread throughout the major centers of population in Britain. The country was divided into a dozen regions, and paid organizers were soon operating in many of these regions.[34] As during the war, pamphlets served as the principal means of propagation. In some forty pamphlets published between October and the opening of the peace conference in January 1919, the objectives of the union were explained, various plans were debated, and the necessity for a league of nations was clearly presented.[35] Specific appeals for support were directed to labor, the church, and women's groups. The churches in particular responded with warm support for the league idea. After a meeting at Lambeth on 29 October, church leaders from all the major denominations gave their blessing to the league of nations movement and urged Christians to respond.[36] On 22 December nearly two thousand churches throughout Britain cooperated in organizing a league of nations Sunday.

The union followed the course of the election closely, bringing pressure to bear where possible. The government was petitioned on behalf of the league cause, direct contact was maintained with Cecil and Smuts, and some fifteen hundred candidates were presented with a questionnaire as to their position on the league question. Over a third of the candidates replied, expressing complete agreement with the union's objectives.[37] The warmest support for the league cause came from the Asquith Liberals and Labour. McKenna, Samuel, Runciman, Simon, and Asquith all reaffirmed liberalism's commitment to the league idea and aligned themselves with the Wilson program.[38] At the same time prominent Liberal candidates like Gilbert Murray, W. H. Dickinson, and David Davies continued as leaders of the union. The Labour party, although increasingly absorbed in domestic issues, continued to support warmly the creation of a "League of Free Peoples."[39] Conservative leaders also endorsed the league program, but Cecil was an exception in his enthusiasm.

Lloyd George had been advised by his chief whip as early as August that the adoption of Wilson's policy of a league of free nations would "attract to the government the vast majority of the electors."[40] In his early election speeches the prime minister called for a peace of moderation and justice and portrayed himself as a firm believer in the league of nations. Speaking to the Liberal party on 12 November, he argued that, given the conditions prevalent in Europe, a league "was more necessary now than ever" and pledged to go to the peace conference "to see that the League of Nations is a reality."[41] In their election manifesto published 22 November, Lloyd George and Bonar Law vowed that it would be "the earnest endeavour of the Coalition Government to promote the formation of a League of Nations" in the peacemaking to end militarism and to further international cooperation.[42] The prime minister also warned his colleagues in the Imperial War Cabinet that any government proved not in earnest about the creation of a league "would be sternly dealt with by the people, and sooner rather than later."[43] As the campaign progressed, however, the major interests of the electorate centered more and more on prosecuting the kaiser, extracting huge indemnities, and expelling all enemy aliens. Sensing this popular trend, the prime minister increasingly based his election appeal on these issues and relegated the league question and other aspects of Wilson's program to the background.[44]

The election results, tallied near the end of December, represented a smashing victory for Lloyd George and the coalition candidates. As in the earlier American congressional elections, the forces of the Right had regained ground and authority taken by the Left in 1917. Asquith Liberals, radicals, and the Independent Labour party were decimated by the election, with Asquith and many Liberal and Labour party leaders losing their seats. Cecil was reelected but the union's Liberal candidates were nearly all defeated.

The election results did not mean, however, that the league of nations idea had been repudiated by the British electorate. The idea had never been at issue in the campaign.[45] It had been endorsed by all the major parties and continued to enjoy support from nearly all sections of the British political spectrum, except for the extremes of the Left and Right. All leading newspapers, aside from the reactionary *Morning Post*, gave their sanction to the league idea and

Northcliffe believed the project would "receive a powerful backing in England from all political parties."[46] The public saw no irony in supporting the league movement while wreaking vengeance on the Germans. By December 1918 the league idea had been applauded by those institutions of greatest influence in Britain—the parties, the press, the unions, and the churches.[47]

With the approach of the peacemaking, many of the complex policy questions involved in the creation of a league of nations were studied in various government departments. The Foreign Office had a primary interest in this issue, even though its authority and role had been severely diminished in the government apparatus created by Lloyd George during the war.[48] The Foreign Office faced a particularly difficult quandary in tackling the league question for, as Wiseman put it, Wilson's call for a New Diplomacy presented the government with "a new conception of foreign policy which no amount of agreement will reconcile with, for instance, traditional British policy."[49] The league question in many ways implied a diplomatic revolution; yet, the Foreign Office had received little guidance from the government as to what general approach to develop. The anxiety of senior members of the Foreign Office is apparent in a remarkable letter signed by Crowe, Tyrrell, Mallet, Paget, and Howard and sent on 22 November to Lord Hardinge, the permanent undersecretary, who passed it on to General Smuts. Here Foreign Office leaders confessed they were "much embarrassed by our inability, in the absence of instructions, to grapple effectively with the question of the League of Nations which encounters us at every turn." The league question closely affected and was likely to dominate "the whole complex of arrangements, territorial, racial, economical," particularly since Wilson might insist that the league have priority in principle and in time over all other questions in the settlement. The government had not yet communicated any decision on the Phillimore report. Given this situation, the letter recommended that "without further delay" someone be put in charge of the Foreign Office league of nations section in order to work on this question.[50]

The Foreign Office received some satisfaction when Cecil was appointed to head the league of nations section after his resignation from the government. Smuts, also, soon provided some major policy guidelines on the league question. Meanwhile, memoranda on the league question were produced by two young members of the Political Intelligence Department, Eustace Percy and Alfred Zimmern. Both were members of the Round Table and shared that organization's general approach to international organization, believing that the drafting of detailed paper constitutions involving explicit and rigorous commitments and obligations for participating members would be ruinous for the league.[51] The principal function of the league, Percy and Zimmern felt, should be to provide a forum for regular international consultations among the leaders of the great powers. Both saw this forum evolving out of the existing Allied conference system at Versailles.

Percy's memorandum was the more conservative, questioning whether any new league beyond the Supreme War Council was possible in the likely event of a general breakdown of economic and political conditions in Central Europe. If conditions did permit the structuring of a league, Percy insisted that Wilson's principles of "equality of trade conditions," freedom of the seas, exclusion of alliances and combinations within the league, and disarmament should not form part of the agreements establishing the league. The bulk of Percy's memorandum examined the problems that the principle of equality of trade conditions involved for Britain and the empire and recommended "the complete separation of the League of Nations from questions of economic policy." As for machinery for resolving disputes, Percy advised following the pattern set out in the Phillimore report.

Zimmern's memorandum was the more substantial and positive. It proposed dividing the establishment of a league into two steps. First, the civilized states of the world would conclude collective treaties and agreements at the peace conference. Second, arrangements would be made for regular conferences to maintain and perhaps extend the understandings arrived at. Regarding the collective treaties, Zimmern argued that the principle of state sov-

ereignty precluded long-term engagements, and therefore the collective commitments should be limited to ten years and subject to
renewal. The treaty establishing the league, however, would be
permanent. Based upon a guarantee of peace, such a treaty would
provide for the settlement of disputes and a regular interstate conference.

Like Percy, Zimmern recommended that the pattern of the
Phillimore report should be followed. The heart of the league, then,
would be the machinery for regular conferences, which "would
seem to grow naturally out of the existing conditions at Versailles."
This interstate conference, consisting of victorious great powers
and Germany and Russia (when stable governments were constituted there) would, "as a fundamental principle of the league," be
a meeting of "Governments with Governments." The conference
could be expanded periodically, perhaps every four or five years, to
include the lesser powers. In addition, a congress of delegates from
parliaments of members could meet every four years to provide a
forum for the expression and education of world public opinion
while preventing the socialist international from usurping this
function. An international secretariat, staffed in rotation by great
powers, would act as a channel of communication between the
interstate conference and all international bodies acting under the
supervision of the league.

Zimmern sketched an extensive array of international activities
of a judicial, administrative, and investigatory nature, that would
not only provide scope for practical internationalism, but also
monitor dangerous issues as they developed and suggest possible
solutions. Zimmern also recommended the establishment of a mandate system for former enemy colonies in tropical Africa and the
Pacific islands, along with areas in western Asia, giving individual
states mandatory responsibility under the auspices of the league.
Like Percy, Zimmern advised the exclusion of Wilson's principle of
equality of trade conditions and disarmament from the agreements
establishing the league and cautioned against saddling the league
with responsibility for the protection of minorities. Zimmern felt
the doctrine of nonintervention in internal affairs should be the rule

for the league, a doctrine that would be useful to counter Bolshevik propaganda and subversion.

One of the most difficult and crucial issues facing Zimmern and Percy and all those who addressed themselves to the league question was the problem of guarantees and sanctions. Wilson had put a guarantee of territorial integrity and political independence at the heart of his league program, and Zimmern advised that it would be dangerous to "burke" this "burning question." Zimmern rehearsed the arguments against guaranteeing a territorial settlement that, despite the best intentions to follow the principle of self-determination, could never be considered universally just or immutable. Instead, he argued that it would be best to meet the demands for such a guarantee by including it in the temporary treaties, "even though its inclusion may be otiose," while excluding it from the permanent treaty establishing the league.

Percy's approach was equally ingenious in suggesting that Britain agree to put its naval, military, and economic force behind a general guarantee of the peace settlement and the principle of political independence and territorial integrity, but that this commitment should take the form of an independent and collective guarantee. Such an approach, in Percy's questionable logic, would involve nothing more novel, "technically speaking," than the treaty guaranteeing Belgium's neutrality. At the same time, however, both Percy and Zimmern had endorsed the Phillimore scheme, which limited the coercive power of the league to instances when a member refused to submit a dispute to examination by conference or attacked before sufficient time had elapsed for the proper study of the dispute.[52]

Erle Richards of the Foreign Office, who was assigned to help Smuts in his study of the league question, argued that it was unwise to involve democracies in any compulsory system of military or economic sanctions to uphold abstract principles. While the principles of territorial integrity and political independence should be accorded the status of international law, their guarantee and enforcement should be left to free and voluntary action by members of the league.[53] Headlam-Morley, assistant director of the Political

Intelligence Department, argued, on the other hand, that Britain had everything to gain and nothing to lose from a territorial guarantee of frontiers in Western Europe. Here, permanent and stable boundaries were possible, and a guarantee of these frontiers, particularly with regard to the Low Countries, was in keeping with Britain's traditional interests. Eastern Europe, however, had not yet reached this stage of development, and no league of nations could avoid future wars until stable conditions had been established there.[54] Clearly, territorial guarantees were to follow stability rather than attempt to create it.

The issue of guarantees and sanctions also attracted attention in the service departments. As expected, those steeped in the traditions of the British army and navy were little inclined to entrust the security of the nation to an international organization. No doubt there occurred much loose talk in military circles hostile to the whole league idea. For Henry Wilson it was "futile nonsense" and "rubbish."[55] Amery termed it "moonshine,"[56] while for Milner it was "flapdoodle" and could damage the chances for a postwar compulsory service army.[57] Churchill cautioned that the league of nations was "no substitute for the British Fleet."[58] All of these sentiments were echoed by the *Morning Post*, which kept up its attack on plans for a peace league, warning that Germany hoped to avoid the consequences of defeat by seeking membership in the proposed league of nations.[59]

On the official level, both the War Office and the admiralty submitted important memoranda on the operation of sanctions under a league of nations. A War Office memorandum expressed strongly critical views regarding any attempt to safeguard the world's peace by means of a league armed only with economic sanctions. Economic sanctions would be effective only if backed up by the spirit and machinery of an armed alliance dedicated to the cause of peace. Anything less would be "a shadow and a sham."[60]

Naval authorities were hostile to any suggestion that Britain's maritime supremacy would be any less necessary after the establishment of a league of nations. With eyes now fixed on the American naval program, Admirals Wemyss and Beresford spoke publicly on the necessity of maintaining Britain's naval position unimpaired.[61] The Admiralty Office circulated a memorandum to the War Cabinet that voiced reservations about the wisdom of undertaking binding covenants to prevent war. Such convenants could involve obligations to take collective military and naval actions "without regard to the wisdom of the step as a purely naval and military proposition." Furthermore, if the British navy were given added collective responsibility under the league, naval estimates might well have to be increased.[62]

When Cecil took over direction of the Foreign Office league of nations section in late November, he selected Zimmern's memorandum as a base to work from and instructed that a summary be prepared of the actual organization involved in its proposals. Cecil's instructions were carried out, and on 14 December he was given a "Brief Conspectus of League of Nations Organization." This draft later went to Paris as the "Cecil Plan." Its recommendations closely followed what Zimmern had suggested. The treaty establishing the league would provide for regular conferences between contracting powers. The conferences would constitute "the pivot of the League," and since they would be composed of statesmen responsible to their own sovereign parliaments, any decisions reached would "have to be unanimous." An annual meeting of the prime ministers and foreign secretaries of the great powers would be supplemented by quadrennial meetings of all member states. Special conferences could be summoned on the demand of a great power, or by any member if there was a danger of war.

The draft envisaged that the great powers would remain in firm control of all league affairs and that the smaller powers would "not exercise any considerable influence." The great powers would appoint a permanent secretariat, a national of another country if possible. The secretariat would provide a channel of communication between the interstate conference and all the international judicial, administrative, and investigatory bodies functioning under treaties guaranteed by the league. Provision would also be made for a periodic congress of delegates from the parliaments of member states, thereby carrying on the work of the interparliamentary union.

It was suggested that a central meeting place for conducting league activities should be established and given privileges of extraterritoriality. Geneva was proposed as the most suitable place. Regarding provisions designed to resolve international disputes, the Foreign Office draft followed the Phillimore scheme closely except that members would also agree to act collectively against not only any member but also any nonmember that refused to abide by the peaceful procedures of the league.[63]

The Cecil plan can be taken as representative of the mainstream of Foreign Office thinking on the league question. The general approach of the Foreign Office was to support the project of a league of nations while attempting to build it up from a practical, realistic base. The league was conceived essentially as a great power conference system, an improved and regularized version of the Concert of Europe extended to include America. The idea of guarantees and sanctions held little appeal in the Foreign Office. The league was not viewed as a new basis for British security. The proposals of the Phillimore report to use sanctions only to compel submission of disputes to international study had been adopted by the Foreign Office with misgivings and in the knowledge that anything less would fail to meet the approach favored by Wilson and the enthusiasm of the public for enforced peace. Nor did the Foreign Office favor a "legalist" approach, basing the league on an extended system of international law and arbitration.[64] If, however, the league evolved realistically, the Foreign Office felt, it could be a valuable addition to the future international system by promoting conference diplomacy and coordinating "functional" activities.[65] As Headlam-Morley put it, it was in Britain's interests "to work vigorously and honestly" in cooperating with America along the lines of Wilson's program. At the same time, British security could not be mortgaged to this program. Headlam-Morley thought it necessary to guard against the possibility that the league might fail: "This means that we cannot at present afford to neglect the guarantees for national security and the maintenance of British interests which would be necessary if international relations were to revert to their former conditions." Despite its current denigration, Headlam-Morley felt the doctrine of balance of power would remain "a fundamental point just as much after the establishment of a League of Nations as it had been before."[66]

While the Foreign Office approached the league question with caution and reservations, Smuts's famous *Practical Suggestion*, published in mid-December, once more lit the fires of enthusiasm on behalf of the league cause. Smuts's pamphlet developed the themes put forward in his memorandum of 3 December and fused the strategies of atlanticism, imperialism, and internationalism into a brilliantly argued program, which focused on the league of nations. In moving and persuasive language, Smuts argued that the league must be made the foundation of the peace, with the peace conference as the first or preliminary meeting of the league. A league of allies or an artificial peace-keeping system would not be enough. Rather the role of the league should be woven into the very fabric of postwar international society.

Smuts recommended charging the league with a grand mission of nurturing, controlling, and protecting those peoples left in the wash by the fall of the Russian, Austrian, and Turkish empires. Among these peoples and nationalities, capable only of varying degrees of self-determination and autonomy, the league could institute a mandate system, delegating administrative responsibility to individual states and patterning itself upon the organization and civilizing mission of the British Commonwealth. In this way the league could act as the "reversionary" of the fallen empires and preclude a new "application of the spoils system." At the same time the league would have a direct charge in maintaining peace and order among the newly independent states of Europe. Altogether these responsibilities would keep the league in the vortex of world politics.

Regarding the league's organization, Smuts envisioned the establishment of a council and a general conference of all members. The council, modeled after the Versailles Council and consisting of prime ministers and foreign ministers or their representatives, would be the dominant organ and perform the "real work of the league." The conference would largely be subject to the initiative and direction of the council. The council would be served by a permanent secretariat and would supervise the many administrative, functional, and investigatory activities Smuts designated for the league. The council would also bear the chief responsibility for peace-keeping and for promoting disarmament and advances in international law. Smuts's council broke new ground in its proposals for minority representation of middle and small powers, drawn in rotation through a panel system. The great powers would remain in control, but not absolute control, as three negative votes would be necessary to veto a council action or resolution.

Smuts insisted that all labors for a league would be in vain unless the "taproot of militarism" were cut. Accordingly, his plan included radical proposals for the abolition of all conscript armies, with authority to fix the size and equipment of permissible militia and volunteer forces given to the league council. Furthermore, armaments industries were to be nationalized and their production subject to inspection and monitoring by officers of the council.

Finally, regarding the league's peace-keeping role, Smuts closely followed the provisions of the Phillimore scheme and the Foreign Office plan of 17 December. No guarantee of political independence or territorial integrity was envisaged. Commitments and obligations were to be kept to a minimum. Nevertheless, Smuts argued that an effective sanction would be necessary to ensure observance of a moratorium if the league were not to be "a pious aspiration or a dead letter." For Smuts sanctions formed "the most important question of all."[67]

Smuts's *Practical Suggestion*, written with full consciousness of the mass aversion to war and phrased in language which balanced idealism with pragmatism, met with a wide-ranging response and elevated the whole league movement to a higher level of influence and respect. Wilson was deeply impressed by Smuts's proposals. Lloyd George considered Smuts's memorandum "one of the ablest State Papers he had read."[68] In the Foreign Office, however, Smuts's proposals brought severe criticism from senior members. Headlam-Morley was "very skeptical" about Smuts's plans for disarmament while Crowe felt these suggestions were "crude and bristled with difficulties." Crowe and Tyrrell, head of the Political Intelligence Department, thought Smuts had dangerously overelaborated the whole league scheme; Tyrrell confessed to being "positively frighten[ed]." Only Esmé Howard supported Smuts's proposals as practical and necessary, given political conditions in Europe and Britain. Cecil agreed on the wisdom of a modest beginning, but considered Smuts's paper "useful as propaganda."[69]

On 17 December Cecil had submitted the Foreign Office memorandum on the league of nations (the "Cecil plan") to the War Cabinet with the "very urgent" request for policy direction.[70] The next day, with Wilson's visit to England impending, the Imperial War Cabinet decided to initiate a systematic discussion of the various questions likely to arise in conversations with the president in order to give the prime minister and the foreign secretary the benefit of the opinions of cabinet members.[71] Subsequent meetings of the Imperial War Cabinet focused attention on the major objectives and strategies to be pursued in the peacemaking, a full-dress debate on the league question taking place 24 December.[72] During this debate, with discussion centering on Smuts's *Practical Suggestion*, it was apparent that there were major areas of disagreement within the Imperial War Cabinet concerning the powers to be given to a league of nations. The crux of the matter was whether or not to grant the league independent executive authority in such crucial areas as armament policy, colonial administration, and, most important, collective resistance to aggression. While no one wished to see the creation of a superstate, there were those, like Cecil and Barnes, who believed in the collective idea and were willing to countenance automatic economic and military sanctions against aggressors, as proposed in the Phillimore report and incorporated in the memoranda of Smuts, Cecil, and the Foreign Office. Cecil, who led disucussion on behalf of the league idea, buttressed his argument with a clear warning that unless the government showed itself to be "very seriously in earnest about the league," he believed "the view would grow that the present government machinery was not to be trusted to deal with serious questions."

On the other hand, Conservatives like Bonar Law, Curzon, Chamberlain, and Balfour, together with realists like Churchill and Hughes, who doubted the viability of any collective system, were unwilling to make the potential sacrifices of national sovereignty that such a system necessarily implied. This powerful group had no desire to see traditional strategies abandoned and the security of the empire entrusted to a new and totally untried system. Chamberlain doubted that the Americans "would put their forces at the disposal of an International Council," and, in any event, Smuts's scheme involved "more than we could effect even in our own Dominions" on the point of calling out imperial troops. Hughes rejected Smuts's scheme as "incompatible with national sovereignty," while Balfour cautioned against allowing the league any jurisdiction over the internal matters of any state: "otherwise it would be impossible to foresee where the responsibilities of the League of Nations would end." To Churchill the proper basis for the erection of a league was "a complete and intimate understanding between France, America, and Britain," but "a League of Nations could be no substitute for national defences." Reading advised against loading the league with responsibilities too great from the outset, particularly the responsibility for disarmament suggested by Smuts.

Despite the opposition within the cabinet to a league with wide-ranging authority, there was nearly universal realization that, given the strength of the league idea in popular opinion and the position taken by the American president, the creation of some new international organization was imperative. The solution that presented itself was a league modeled after the Versailles Council and the Imperial War Cabinet—a league that would facilitate the closest international cooperation and exchange in political as well as economic, humanitarian, and administrative matters, but that left national sovereignty unimpaired. This was clearly the path suggested by the prime minister in his summary of conclusions drawn from cabinet discussions. Lloyd George argued that the cabinet generally supported the idea of a league of nations and the framework outlined by Cecil, but there was hesitation, if not disagreement, on the power to be given the league. He agreed with Cecil about the strong popular support behind the idea and the necessity for disarmament, without which the league would be regarded as a "sham." Regarding the league's framework, the prime minister thought the Imperial War Cabinet and the Versailles Council provided "admirable precedents." Lloyd George clearly repudiated the idea of a league with independent executive powers: "It must not be constituted as a body with executive power. But on the basis of the Imperial War Cabinet and of the Supreme War Council you would get a body whose authority rested with the governments."

Lloyd George apparently had entered cabinet debate fully conscious of public support for the league project, hopeful that it could bring about disarmament, and personally impressed by Smuts's memorandum. It is unlikely, however, that the prime minister had studied deeply the implications of Smuts's proposal, or that he had any fixed personal views on the league question other than a generally favorable predisposition. The criticisms levied against Smuts's scheme were enough to convince Lloyd George that it would be a mistake to attempt too much at the beginning. Nevertheless, the prime minister foresaw that the league might provide a valuable forum for personal diplomacy, and "he thought that if only the leaders of the different nations could meet it would make all the difference in international relations." The prime minister's closest advisor on the league question was Philip Kerr, and it appeared from the conclusions of the cabinet that the conception of the league advanced by Hankey, Kerr, and the Round Table group had triumphed.[73]

Shortly after this debate Wilson arrived in England, and British leaders were given an opportunity to learn more about how he would approach the major problems of the peacemaking. In preparing for discussions between Lloyd George and Wilson, Auchincloss, House's secretary, suggested the league question as the best point of departure. Lloyd George assured Auchincloss that he would not leave the peace conference until an effective league of nations had been created.[74] In private discussions, Wilson, following Auchincloss's advice, concentrated on the league issue but generally proved more accommodating on most matters than British leaders had expected. In public speeches, however, responding to Clemenceau's open reaffirmation of France's attachment to the balance of power, Wilson made it clear that the creation of a league was the *sine qua non* of American cooperation in the peacemaking. If attempts were made to revert to the Old Diplomacy and the balance of power, the American government would "take no interest" in future world politics.[75]

When debate on peacemaking resumed in the Imperial War Cabinet on 30 December, Lloyd George attempted to emphasize the areas where common ground had been found with Wilson. The prime minister pointed first to the priority that Wilson placed on the league question: "that was the only thing which he really cared much about." Wilson, however, had said nothing on this question "which would in the least make it difficult for us to come to some arrangement with him." Though he had no definite scheme in mind, the president's thoughts were close to the proposals advanced by Cecil and Smuts. He was certainly not contemplating "anything in the nature of giving executive powers to the League of Nations." Wilson was anxious, nevertheless, that the league be the first question discussed at the peace conference. Both Lloyd George and Balfour agreed that it would be expedient to grant this wish "on the ground that this would ease other matters, such as the question of the 'Freedom of the Seas,' the disposal of the German colonies, economic issues, etc."

Lloyd George continued by describing the president's generally moderate and vague attitudes on the freedom of the seas, disarmament, Russia, and the Near East. When reference was made to Wilson's firm position on the colonial settlement and indemnities, however, Hughes responded with a tirade against the whole strategy of attempting to cooperate with Wilson. The Allies had won the war and should now proceed to "settle the peace of the world as they liked." Hughes berated Wilson, who had "no claim to speak even for his own country." Hughes felt that to start with the league would mean "giving up the substance for the shadow." Hughes's remarks initiated a heated debate that showed that a powerful section of the British cabinet still had serious reservations about siding with Wilson in an Anglo-American strategy.

Curzon pointed out that Hughes's attitudes were "shared by many members of the Imperial War Cabinet." While agreeing that the fortunes of the world must largely depend on Anglo-American cooperation, Curzon insisted that if Wilson attempted to thwart imperial interests, "it might be necessary, on some issues at any rate, for Mr. Lloyd George to work at the Conference in alliance with M. Clemenceau." Walter Long, colonial secretary, "agreed cordially" with these views. Reading, Borden, and Cecil responded with a strong defense of a strategy based firmly on cooperation with America. Borden made it clear that a strategy of working with "some European nation as against the United States" could not count on Canadian approval or support. Canada's view was that the empire "should keep clear, as far as possible, of European complications and alliances." Cecil argued that while the empire would go into the peace conference in a position of enormous power, the greatest objective was to secure a settled peace. Such a peace could only be accomplished through a good understanding with America, "and that good understanding could not be secured unless we were prepared to adhere to the idea of a League of Nations."[76]

When discussion on the exchange with Wilson was resumed the next day, Lloyd George reaffirmed his belief that it would be possible to reach satisfactory agreements with Wilson in most matters, except perhaps indemnities. The president had by no means taken an extreme position on the league question, and even on the question of the South Pacific islands his position was not irrevocable. The prime minister then pointed to the grand strategy that the nature of Wilson's program and British interests suggested:

> He was not pessimistic about inducing President Wilson to agree ultimately, though possibly under protest, to the things to which we attached importance, providing he could secure his League of Nations, which, politically, was a matter of life and death to him. On the other hand, he entirely agreed with Mr. Hughes that if President Wilson should, in the last resort, prove obsti-

nate, then the sacrifices of France and Great Britain were such
that they were entitled to have a final say, and would say it.[77]

The close of this session of the Imperial War Cabinet marked
the completion of preparations for the peace conference undertaken
in Britain. Given the wartime eclipse of the Committee of Imperial
Defence and the Foreign Office in strategic planning and the absorption of the General Staff in operational functions, the Imperial
War Cabinet served as the forum for both strategic debate and
policy making. Of the major strategies open to Britain in approaching the peace conference, the prime minister had determined on a
policy of cooperation with Wilson, at least in the first instance.
Since this policy looked beyond the peacemaking to a postwar
Anglo-American entente, new strategic ground was being broken.
Lloyd George hoped, nevertheless, that an Atlantic strategy could
be fused with traditional themes in British strategy. As in Smuts's
memorandum of 3 December, there was optimism that the realization of the principal imperial objectives would be compatible with
this strategy. Certainly, no one intended to abandon the traditional
status and role of the navy. And although there was little sympathy
for a postwar continental commitment, the principle of the balance
of power was not ignored. The hope was that, given a just territorial
settlement and the disarmament of Germany, the balance of power
could once again take care of itself. Wilson, the prime minister
thought, would help moderate French territorial ambitions.

Although America had been chosen over France as the principal partner for the peacemaking, a powerful wing of the cabinet
had questioned this approach. An alternative Anglo-French strategy
would have to be maintained in the event Wilson attempted to frustrate vital British interests, or if it looked as though he would fail
to carry his program domestically. The strategy of working with
the United States, nevertheless, reflected the assumption that the
Americans would play the role of a major power in postwar world
politics and that there would be more harmony than conflict in
British and American interests. The choice of America over France
also reflected a new link between strategy and politics in a revolu-

tionary age. The carnage of war, together with the activities of the Union of Democratic Control and the League of Nations Union, had converted the mainstream of British opinion to the merits of the New Diplomacy. With the support that Wilson enjoyed as the prophet of the New Diplomacy in the ranks of British liberalism and labor, strategies based on either imperialism or the balance of power were no longer, by themselves, politically viable.

For the leaders of the British government, then, the league of nations question was viewed primarily in the context of Anglo-American relations and domestic politics. Except for Cecil and Barnes, no political leaders viewed a strategy of internationalism based on the league as, by itself, a credible alternative to traditional strategies in the search for security. However, if the league could be fashioned along British lines, if it would facilitate a strategy of Anglo-American cooperation, and if it would satisfy the domestic proponents of the New Diplomacy, then it was in Britain's interests to participate fully in the attempt to create a new international organization to promote world peace. Better still, if a league of nations could facilitate the alignment of American power with British interests in Europe (and perhaps in the Pacific), there was hope for a new and stable world balance of power. A league of nations that provided a forum for a great power concert including America could be viewed as complementing rather than supplanting traditional British strategies.

Smuts was optimistic that the league could provide the means for reconciling traditional imperial strategies with Anglo-American cooperation in a liberal world mission. Cecil clearly was ahead of the cabinet in his enthusiasm for the league and a strategy of internationalism. The choice of Cecil and Smuts to represent the empire on the league question at the peace conference, therefore, illustrated both the political importance placed on the league project and Lloyd George's hope that this topic could serve as a bridge, as well as hostage if necessary, to Anglo-American cooperation.

6 War No More: Drafting the Covenant

When the leading delegates of the victorious great powers assembled in Paris during the second week of January 1919 for what was termed the preliminary peace conference, the first major issue to be resolved involved agreement on procedures and agenda. The leaders all knew that there was a vital link between procedure and substance, and each delegation maneuvered to establish tactical positions and an agenda that would facilitate the realization of its major objectives. The French government put forward an elaborate agenda for the conference that dealt first with the immediate issues of the war, where France's vital interests were concerned, then turned to the organization of a society of nations, and finally considered the more remote territorial, political, and other general international questions.[1] Wilson opposed this scheme, and, with the American Peace Commission, outlined a procedure that put the league question first on the agenda, followed by reparations, new states, territorial changes, and colonial possessions.[2] At the Council of Ten on 13 January, the British and Americans combined to sidetrack the French scheme. Lloyd George agreed with Wilson's proposal that the league be considered first, but generally argued that the agenda for discussion be prepared "from time to time."[3] On 22 January, then, the Council of Ten passed three resolutions on the league for presentation to a plenary session of the peace conference. These resolutions stipulated that to maintain the approaching world settlement a league of nations should be created "to promote international cooperation, to ensure the fulfillment of accepted international obligations and to provide safeguards against war"; that the league should be created "as an integral part of the general Treaty of Peace, and should be open to every civilized nation which can be relied upon to promote its objects"; and that members of the league should meet periodically in international conference and have a permanent international organization and secretariat. Finally, it was resolved that the peace conference appoint a committee representing the associated governments to work out the details of the constitution and functions of the league.[4] On 25 January the peace conference, meeting in plenary session, duly passed these resolutions and established the League of Nations Commission.[5] The commission was to be made up of two representatives from each of the five great powers and five representatives chosen by the lesser Allies.

Wilson gave a moving oration at this session, arguing that it was necessary for the leaders to represent the peoples of the world rather than the interests of governments or classes. The hopes of the world's peoples, including Americans, centered on the creation of a league of nations, which must be made the "keystone of the whole programme." If the league failed, the people would be disillusioned, no permanent peace would be possible, and there would be no American guarantees of European settlements. The principle of the league had been accepted, however, and Wilson, confident in the demonstrations of mass public support during his European tour, interpreted the passing of the resolutions as a major tactical victory. He and his closest advisors viewed the resolutions as involving the incorporation of the covenant of the league in the peace treaty.[6]

Lloyd George, who followed Wilson with a short speech concentrating on the horrors of war and the devastation of the battlefields (which he but not Wilson had visited), was less certain that the league would be a success. But the people of the British Empire were emphatically behind the proposal, and he fully supported the attempt to settle disputes by means other than "organized savagery." Clearly the prime minister did not interpret the resolutions as a victory for Wilson, or as necessarily involving the inclusion of the covenant in the peace treaty. The procedure of laying down certain principles and then referring the league question to a commission had originated with Cecil, had been endorsed by Lloyd George at the Imperial War Cabinet of 31 December, and had been agreed to in negotiations involving Cecil, the prime minister, House, Miller, and Wilson prior to discussion in the Council of Ten.[7] While reference of the league question to a commission was not intended to sidetrack the league project, it was expected that discussion on the issue would be extensive and subject to delay if tactics so demanded.[8]

Earlier, Lloyd George had advised the Imperial War Cabinet that dealing with the league question early in the peacemaking would facilitate the realization of other objectives. Wilson therefore had his league project underway with British support; the next item on the agenda would be the claims on Germany's colonies. The southern British dominions were determined not to allow Wilson to thwart their desire to annex the former German colonies near their respective territories.[9] Wilson, on the other hand, was equally determined to prevent a simple division of colonial spoils and insisted that all former enemy colonies be handed over to the league, which would act as a "residuary trustee."[10] Responsibility for administration of such areas would be delegated to selected mandatories, under conditions established and controlled by the league. The dominions placed their claims before the Council of Ten on 24 January. A week of bitter confrontation followed, with Hughes and Wilson as the principal antagonists. When the colonial claims of France, Japan, and Italy were aired, the president exploded on 28 January with a threat to discontinue discussions since negotiations had revealed "a negation in detail—one case at a time—of the whole principle of mandatories."[11]

Confronted with this impasse, the dominions, under Lloyd George's urging, fell back on a tactical retreat suggested earlier by Smuts. The device was the distinction between A-, B-, and C-type mandates, the latter to be administered under the laws and institutions of the mandatory power.[12] When Hughes and Massey, the New Zealand prime minister, were given assurances that a C-type mandate would allow them to control immigration, tariffs, and navigation in the territories they desired, they reluctantly agreed to this approach.[13]

The plan for A-, B-, and C-type mandates was presented to the Council of Ten on 30 January. Although Lloyd George emphasized the difficulties experienced by the dominions in accepting this compromise, Wilson showed little gratitude and was willing to accept it only as a "provisional arrangement." No final arrangements could be made until the league of nations had been definitely established, thereby providing the foundation upon which the "superstructure" of a mandate system could be created. It would be premature to parcel out mandatory responsibilities until the practical application of the new scheme could be seen. Clearly, Wilson was bargaining for the league. He suggested that the peace conference concentrate on European questions and the preparation of a preliminary peace in a few weeks' time, thereby establishing the league of nations and eliminating "the haunting element of conjecture." Lloyd George retorted that if all delegates adopted similar tactics of precluding agreements on any question until they had achieved their principal objectives, paralysis and disaster would result. The British prime minister argued that the peace conference had given birth to the league in its resolutions of 25 January, and that business should not be held up until the constitution of the league was complete in all its details. That a new constitution for the whole world could be drafted in nine or ten days he considered "rather sanguine." Lloyd George concluded by admonishing his colleagues to accept the suggested compromise provisionally, subject to reconsideration when the complete scheme for the league had been formulated.[14]

Despite further jousting over Wilson's tactics and an explosive confrontation between Hughes and Wilson in the afternoon session of the Council of Ten, the compromise put forward by Lloyd George was accepted. In the end Wilson accepted the thinly veiled annexation implied in the C-type mandate, but he firmly refused any designation at this stage of ultimate mandatory responsibilities. The agreement remained provisional pending completion of the league project. The dominions, on the other hand, had accepted the mandate principle, but, with their forces occupying the desired territories, they felt little uncertainty as to the future of those territories. Hughes had warned earlier that anyone wanting to dislodge Australia from the captured Pacific islands would have to come and do it. Lloyd George, for his part, had seen Wilson's tenacity and intransigence and resented the experience.[15] The prime minister countered immediately with a maneuver to alter the substance of Anglo-American negotiations on the league question.

During this initial phase of the peacemaking, Cecil had entered into detailed negotiations with the American delegation for purposes of coordinating Anglo-American planning on the league question. Since attempts to discuss the question with Wilson in England had been unsuccessful, Cecil arrived in Paris on 6 January with little idea of what the president's conception of a league really involved.[16] The first exchanges with the Americans proved rather alarming. In conversation with House and Lansing on 8 January, Cecil learned that the Americans favored the creation of a universal system of compulsory arbitration together with a prohibition of all war.[17] Cecil knew the American plan would be totally unacceptable within official British circles and immediately instructed Eyre Crowe to draft a memorandum putting forth the objections of the British Empire to any system of compulsory arbitration.

Crowe's memorandum was forwarded to the Americans the next day. Crowe listed four major points against a system of universal compulsory arbitration: disputes touching on "vital interests" or "national honour" were *ex hypothesi* excluded from processes of arbitration—a vital interest, by definition, could not be compromised; many disputes were by nature political and not amenable to judicial-arbitral treatment; there was a real difficulty in finding competent and impartial arbitral tribunals to rule in spheres where very little in the way of agreed law existed; and the United States Senate's jealously guarded treaty-making powers precluded the creation of such a system. Crowe illustrated his arguments with several historical examples and concluded with an appeal to start the league on "workable lines": "We are undoubtably threatened with a very critical attitude on the part of the American Senate. It may therefore be asked whether it is good policy to aggravate the enormous difficulties inherent in any scheme for a League of Nations by tacking on to it at the very outset, proposals for general compulsory arbitration which, apart from the theoretical contradictions involved, and apart from the defects of the machinery which would have to be set up, has hitherto met with such determined opposition in the American Senate."[18]

Despite this rather inauspicious start, agreement was reached on 8 January that it would be desirable for the British and Americans to "settle between them their policy on the League of Nations before they met their Allies."[19] On 9 January, House briefed Cecil in strictest secrecy on the plan he and Wilson had drawn up during the previous summer. With Lansing no longer present, Cecil found House much more cordial and candid. The colonel was sure that the British and American approaches to the league question were compatible and that the issue of compulsory arbitration would not stand in the way of close cooperation.[20]

On 10 January, regular meetings of the British league of nations section began under Cecil's direction. The immediate task at hand was to draw up a British draft scheme for a league that would serve as a basis for exchanges with the Americans. The American delegation had on 1 January been given a copy of the Cecil plan— the Foreign Office plan of 14 December 1918—but this consisted only of the barest outline of organization and principles.[21] Work was now undertaken to draft a detailed blueprint for international organization. Using a draft prepared largely by Philip Baker as a base, the British section had a plan ready for printing on 16 January.[22] This plan was forwarded to President Wilson on 19 January and, in a slightly revised version, served as a basis for exchange with the Americans.

The British draft convention closely followed the framework that had earlier been sketched by the Cecil plan. Three major organs were envisaged for the league: a general conference, a council, and a secretariat. Plans also included establishment of an international court. The general conference would consist of representatives from those governments, major and minor, attending the peace conference, the European neutrals, Latin American states, and such other countries as the Allies would care to invite. The draft specified the right of the "British Empire to separate representation in respect of the Dominions . . . including India" both in the conference and on the council when matters affecting any particular dominion were under discussion. The enemy states would be excluded until policy on their admission had been decided. The conference would meet "from time to time" and at least once every four years.

The draft convention placed major emphasis on the role of the council. It would consist of the great powers—France, Great Britain, Italy, Japan, and the United States—and would meet as required, but at least once a year. The council would be "responsible for ensuring the successful working of the League of Nations, and for seeing that it secures the harmonious co-operation of all the States members of the League." Special responsibility was accorded the council regarding the development of the new states that would result from the peace conference and for "settling all differences which may arise between them." The draft convention clearly assumed that the control of international affairs would remain within the hands of the great powers.

The procedures outlined for the peaceful settlement of disputes and the related system of sanctions followed in large measure what had been recommended by the Phillimore report and the Cecil plan. One major departure was the recommendation that signatories "undertake to respect the territorial integrity of all States members of the League, and to protect them from foreign aggression and that they agree to prevent any attempts by other States forcibly to alter the territorial settlement existing at the date of, or established by, the present treaties of peace."[23] Here the draft convention aligned itself with the territorial guarantee of Wilson's fourteenth point, although no guarantee of political independence was stipulated. The territorial guarantee also required that states abide by recommendations from the league on necessary boundary changes. Otherwise, the guarantee would cease to apply.

On 20 January, Cecil circulated the draft convention to British and dominion plenipotentiaries intending to have it approved as "the British case on the subject."[24] While awaiting official endorsement, Cecil felt justified in using the convention as a basis for the coordination of views with the Americans. On 19 January Cecil was finally given a chance to see what Wilson had in mind when the president invited him to a meeting and explained his latest draft scheme. The president's plan had incorporated many of the suggestions of the Phillimore and Smuts plans, and Cecil's first impression was that the scheme was "almost entirely Smuts and Phillimore combined, with practically no new ideas in it."[25] The plan projected a league divided into three main organs: a general body of delegates, consisting of ambassadors accredited to whatever country was chosen to host the league's headquarters; an executive council composed, as in Smuts's design, of a bare majority of great powers, with secondary and minor powers selected in annual rotation from two panels; and a permanent secretariat. In all his thinking and utterances on the league question, the president had consistently advocated the necessity for security through a solid collective guarantee of political independence and territorial integrity. Accordingly, Article 3 of the plan provided that "the Contracting Powers unite in guaranteeing to each other political independence and territorial integrity, as against external aggression," at the same time stipulating that agreed boundary adjustments could be effected in the interests of peace. The president closely followed Smuts in the proposals for disarmament and in provisions for peaceful resolution of disputes, dropping the earlier design for a system of universal compulsory arbitration.

Wilson's plan included wide-ranging proposals for a mandate system that served to direct his policy in the struggle over the future of the German colonies. Other provisions required signatories to maintain fair hours and humane conditions for manual laborers within their jurisdiction. All new states seeking admission to the league would be required to provide just and equal treatment for their national or racial minorities and to refrain from religious persecution. After the rights of belligerents on the high seas had been defined by international law, no power or group of powers would have the right to violate these agreements, but the league itself could close the seas, in whole or in part, to enforce international covenants. No treaty would be binding until it had been published. Finally, the president stipulated that signatory powers end discriminatory practices in their financial and economic relationships.[26]

The significant differences between the British and American schemes were outweighed by their common features, and both sides wished to reach agreement on a joint draft. Discussions to this end began on 21 January between Cecil and David Hunter Miller, the American legal expert. Meeting in three lengthy sessions during the next week, Cecil and Miller exchanged views, isolated the major differences of approach, and attempted to bridge these differences.[27] Each delegation, having examined the proposals of the other side, revised its draft by incorporating such changes as were acceptable in order to bring the two sides as near accord as possible. Although Cecil, upon reflection, found Wilson's draft "a very bad document, badly expressed, badly arranged, and very incomplete," he agreed with the tactical wisdom of preserving the form of the president's plan while making desirable changes in substance.[28] On 27 January, in a four hour session, Cecil and Miller reached agreement on a revision of the president's draft, incorporating the British modifications that were acceptable and reserving for discussion those points about which differences still had to be reconciled. In what has come to be known as the Cecil-Miller draft, Cecil was very successful in achieving recognition of desired British modifications.[29] Wilson's design for a council including middle and small powers was abandoned in favor of the exclusively great power council recommended in the British draft convention. On this modification Cecil was frank in declaring his view "that the Great Powers must run the League and that it was just as well to recognize it flatly as not."[30] The extensive responsibilities envisaged by the British draft for the league secretariat and its chancellor were recognized in the Cecil-Miller draft. The new draft also recognized the wisdom of creating a permanent international court. Wilson's complex arbitration proposals were placed in the reserved category in lieu of an explicit scheme for a world court forwarded by Cecil. Provision was made in the new draft for the potentially important nonpolitical functions of a league foreseen in the British draft. Cecil was also successful in gaining the right to separate representation in the league for the dominions. Wilson's supplementary agreements concerning the proposed mandate system, protection of national and racial minorities, freedom of the seas, and provisions for equality of trade conditions were all reserved for later consideration. Cecil hoped that the Americans could be persuaded to change these provisions substantially. Cecil's satisfaction with the outcome of these negotiations was expressed in a letter to Miller, 29 January. Pointing to the textually artificial character of the draft, the result of several amalgamations, Cecil nevertheless expressed his "agreement with the substance of the draft" and thought "it should form the basis of our discussion with our Allies."[31] It remained for Cecil to submit the draft to his government for approval.

Until this point Anglo-American negotiations on the league question had proceeded smoothly, largely because Cecil and his American colleagues shared a common vision. There were, however, critics of the Cecil-Wilson approach to the league within both the American and the British delegations. Henry Cabot Lodge stood as the foremost domestic critic of Wilson's peace program and design for a league of nations, and the senator made his views known in detail, not only to Allied leaders, but also to members of the American peace mission.[32] Since Wilson had refused to include representation from the Republican opposition in the American peace delegation, the most fundamental criticisms of the president's plans were provided by Secretary of State Lansing. In particular, Lansing strongly objected to any positive guarantee of territorial integrity and political independence and to the idea of compulsory international sanctions. Such an idea was, in the view of the secretary of state, inimical to American national interests and sovereignty, contrary to the constitution, in violation of the Monroe Doctrine, and unacceptable to the Senate.[33] Lansing favored an international organization based firmly on international law and settlement of international disputes through judicial processes. If a guarantee was inevitable, he was only willing to recommend a "negative guarantee" or "self-denying covenant," whereby nations merely agreed not to violate each other's territory or political independence. The secretary of state's views on this point were shared within the American delegation by House and Miller.[34] Moreover, Lansing was fundamentally at odds with the president's tactic of holding up the other business of the peace conference while the details of a constitution for the league were agreed upon.[35] Instead, Lansing favored the adoption by the peace conference of a resolution embodying principles setting out the nature and purpose of the league that could be included in the proposed preliminary treaty of peace. Detailed plans for the league, based on these principles, could be agreed upon when a final treaty was negotiated or at a separate congress involving neutrals as well as belligerents.[36] When the establishment of the League of Nations Commission on 25 January somewhat interrupted Lansing's proposals, he nevertheless advised Wilson on 31 January that it would be expedient to have the peace conference pass a resolution embodying the salient features of the league, which could serve as a guide for the League of Nations Commission.[37] By this time, however, Wilson had chosen to pay little or no heed to Lansing's advice; consequently, Lansing's criticisms and proposals had no immediate effect.

On the British side, Cecil's negotiations had departed substantially from the approach favored by Hankey, Kerr, and Lloyd George and spelled out before the Imperial War Cabinet in December 1918. Cecil could not be accused of failing to keep his government informed on the substance of discussions with the Americans. On 20 January Cecil attempted to brief Lloyd George over breakfast on how negotiations were progressing with the Americans. The prime minister did not like the idea of Wilson sitting on the League of Nations Commission, but it soon became apparent to Cecil that Lloyd George "did not want to talk about the League of Nations at all in which he takes no real interest."[38] Subsequently, the British Empire delegation became absorbed in the fight over the German colonies, and Cecil was left without policy guidance in his negotiations with the Americans. Cecil received no response to his request of 20 January that the draft convention be officially endorsed as the

British case on the league question. On 29 January, with the Council of Ten deadlocked on the colonial settlement, Cecil submitted the Cecil-Miller draft to the prime minister with a covering note that asked, "May I assume that I have the authority [of] the Government to continue negotiations with the Allies on the basis generally of the enclosed typewritten draft convention?"[39]

Cecil's note went to Philip Kerr. At the same time Wiseman, who was acting as an important liaison in Anglo-American negotiations, feared that Cecil's views on the league went "a good deal further than the Prime Minister" and held very serious implications for future British diplomatic strategy.[40] House had asked Wiseman to arrange a conference for 31 January where Cecil and Smuts together with Wilson and the colonel would attempt to resolve the remaining difficulties on the league in preparation for the convocation of the League of Nations Commission. Wiseman was anxious that Cecil and Smuts be briefed by the prime minister before the meeting with House and Wilson. He therefore arranged with Philip Kerr that Cecil and Smuts meet with the prime minister on 31 January before the conference with the Americans.

The meeting of 31 January revealed a major rift within the British delegation on the proper approach to the league.[41] Probably still smarting from Wilson's intransigence of the previous day in the Council of Ten, Lloyd George confronted Cecil and Smuts with an attack both on the substance of agreements reached to date with the Americans on the league question and on the procedure of attempting to draft a detailed constitution for inclusion in the peace treaty. Reading from a memorandum prepared by Kerr, the prime minister insisted that the league be based upon a permanent system of voluntary great power consultation, bringing smaller powers into the deliberations when their interests were affected. According to Lloyd George, the league should be modeled upon the procedures and institutions that had served the Supreme War Council and were providing the basis for the peace conference. The essence of Lloyd George's plan consisted of plenipotentiary ministers in continuous consultation. These ministers would spend half of their time at the capital of the league and the other half in their own capitals. They would be men of great authority and would supervise "all international organizations, such as relief, waterways and so forth." At stated intervals and in time of crisis, the deliberations of the league would be strengthened by the prime ministers and presidents of member states. The league would operate through "a joint secretariat constituted on the same lines as the secretariat of the Supreme War Council or of the Peace Conference."

The prime minister then singled out for attack the keystone provisions of all Wilsonian-type designs for a league—the guarantee of territorial integrity and the obligation to participate in collective resistance to aggression. The memorandum asserted that if the league were to be a success, "it will not be because the nations enter into solemn covenants to guarantee one another's territories or to go to war with rebellious powers on certain stated conditions, but because it constitutes the machinery by which the nations of the world can remain in continual consultation with one another and through which they can arrive promptly at great decisions for dealing with all international problems as they arise." The major arguments against the paraphernalia of sanctions were presented briefly and bluntly:

> The probable effect of including in the constitution of the League of Nations obligations to go to war in certain stated conditions will be to make it impossible for any nation to join the League, for no nation will commit itself in such a vital matter except by the free decision of its own Government and of its own Parliament, and no Government and no Parliament can come to such a decision except after an examination of the facts at the time when the decision has to be made. The attempt to impose obligations of this kind at the start will either end in their being nugatory or in the destruction of the league itself. The thing that really matters is that the nations of the world should remain in continuous consultation under a system which enables them to come to prompt and great decisions on world problems as they arise or alter from day to day.

In dealing with the problem of what international obligations should be undertaken by league members, the memorandum paralleled Lansing's approach. Each member should merely be required to guarantee negatively that it would not "initiate military or economic action against its neighbours without first having submitted the matter in dispute to the consideration of the Council of the League and given it reasonable time to negotiate or impose a settlement." Any nation violating this obligation would "become *ipso facto* an outlaw of the League and an immediate meeting of the Council of the League [would] take place in order to determine what action should be taken by the League to deal with the matter."

The memorandum also spelled out a very different procedure for creating the league of nations:

> The conclusion then is that we should take the deliberations of the twenty-five nations that constitute the Peace Conference as a kind of preliminary meeting of the League of Nations; that we should accept the procedure and constitution which has worked today as the procedure and constitution, subject to modifications, of the League of Nations; that as soon as the Peace Conference has completed its labours, it should expand into a Conference of the Nations, including the neutrals which, after the question of the representation and status of the newcomers has been settled, should proceed at once to deal with the post-war problems which will be numerous and pressing exactly as the Peace Conference is dealing with current problems. The opening of this second Conference should be made as formal and dramatic as possible, but the paper obligations to be entered into by the several nations should be reduced to the absolute minimum, for otherwise various legislatures will never accept them. If the existing Conference negotiates a settlement which is just and satisfactory it will have the authority necessary to float its own continuance as the League of Nations; if it does not succeed in doing this, no other League of Nations is likely to do better.[42]

The second part of Kerr's memorandum took the form of a brief draft scheme for the league, which, in light of its sponsorship, merits reprinting in whole.

> 1. There shall be constituted a League of Nations for the purpose of securing agreement among all nations in the conduct of international affairs, and for the prevention of war.
> 2. The League shall consist of all powers who undertake to abide by its rules.

3. The League shall conduct its business by means of an executive Council, consisting of plenipotentiaries of the Great Powers who shall have general charge of the affairs of the League, and of a plenipotentiary of each of the other powers who may attend the Council as a member whenever matters specially affecting their nation are under consideration.

4. The function of the Executive Council shall be to secure agreement among all nations in the conduct of international affairs by means of a constant consultation and deliberation together. It shall also have charge of all international services, administrative, inspectional or research which may be initiated by the League.

5. Each power shall appoint a representative who shall be its permanent plenipotentiary on the Council and other plenipotentiaries to the number laid down on the basis of representation annexed hereto: [not included]

6. The permanent members of the Council shall sit in continuous session, but there shall be full meetings of the Council at intervals of not less than six months, or whenever necessity requires, at which the other plenipotentiaries may attend.

7. There shall be an annual plenary Conference of the whole League.

8. The administrative organisation of the League shall be in the hands of a joint secretariat of the Great Powers and the control of the permanent members of the Council of the League.

9. Every member of the League undertakes to take no action, military or economic, against any other member, without first submitting the matter in dispute to the consideration of the Council of the League for a period of not less than three months. In the event of any power breaking this rule it immediately becomes an outlaw, forfeiting its privileges and immunities under the rules of the League, and there shall be immediately summoned a full Council of the League to consider the action to be taken against it.

10. The first meeting of the League shall consist of the members of the Peace Conference and of all neutrals, and the first business it shall consider shall be draft constitutions.

11. Every nation joining the League shall be required to stop line [?] armies, liquor and slave trades, etc.[43]

The substance of the prime minister's proposals obviously represented an elaboration of the approach to the league question he had suggested in the Imperial War Cabinet—an approach favored by the Conservatives, senior members of the Foreign Office, as well as Kerr and Hankey. This approach was conceived as both realistic and compatible with traditional British interests and strategies. It also attempted to discern what would be acceptable to the United States Senate. In light of subsequent developments, the points made by the memorandum appear perceptive and wise. The procedure suggested for the creation of the league, however, represented a direct violation of Wilson's understanding of the resolutions passed by the plenary session on 25 January. The league was to evolve rather than be created as an integral part of the peace treaty. The establishment of the league would be relegated to the final phase of the peacemaking. This, of course, was the procedure favored by the French government and Lansing.

These developments naturally alarmed Cecil. Whatever substantive merits the prime minister's proposals possessed, the procedural suggestions as well as the timing of his advice represented the worst side of Lloyd George. Later the same evening Cecil and Smuts were scheduled to meet with Wilson to agree on the final details of a joint draft. To have adopted the prime minister's suggestions would have resulted in an explosive reaction from Wilson and, perhaps, a breakdown of trust. Cecil was not the man to strike out in this direction. Instead, in an understandable display of independence, he chose largely to disregard the advice offered by the prime minister. In his diary for 31 January, Cecil explained that the prime minister had entered the meeting with no knowledge of the papers that had been submitted by the league of nations section but had simply read Kerr's memorandum.[44] Cecil agreed that the present plans required a good deal of pruning, but he refused to commit himself to the "Prime Minister's plan," which on reflection seemed to him "a thoroughly bad one—indeed only a device for postponing the League till after the peace." Clearly angered by the tactics implicit in Lloyd George's plan, Cecil suspected the whole thing to be "a French proposal."[45]

In conference with the president and House during the evening of 31 January, Cecil made no mention of the earlier British meeting.

Instead, Cecil proceeded on the basis of agreements already reached with Miller and attempted to settle with the president those points of discord that still remained.[46] Cecil was successful again in wringing concessions from the American side. The president agreed to drop his provision that the body of delegates consist of the ambassadors and ministers of league members. This concession made it possible for the British dominions to be directly represented. Cecil convinced the president that the council of the league should consist exclusively of great powers, the smaller powers being represented only when their interests were affected directly.[47] Wilson also agreed to modify significantly his plans for the abolition of conscription.[48] The British plan for a permanent court was accepted by the president, who thereby nullified his own complicated designs regarding methods of arbitration. Finally, it was agreed that Miller would meet the next day with Hurst, the British legal advisor, to draw up a draft embodying the results of negotiations to date and referring to Cecil and House any points that still remained unsettled.

Meanwhile, several important critiques of the British draft convention arrived from dominion leaders to add further complications for Cecil. The dominions, having won independent representation at the peace conference, were anxious to be granted full membership rights within the league in recognition of their new international status. The dominions had pressed this point on the British, and Cecil had been successful in negotiations with the Americans in having dominion right to independent membership recognized.[49] The dominions, however, continued to press for full rights to nonpermanent membership on the league council, refusing to be satisfied with representation as part of the British Empire. In addition, memoranda by the Canadians and Australians criticized the British draft on several key substantive issues. Both dominions attacked the territorial guarantee, the Canadians arguing that such a guarantee went "far beyond what members of the League should be called upon to undertake" and should be replaced with an obligation merely "to respect" agreed boundaries.[50] The Australian memorandum, written by Hughes, proposed that the British draft eliminate all suggestions that the league possess executive or legislative powers of international government. The league, Hughes felt, could exist in prevailing conditions only as a standing "Council of Nations," each nation retaining full national responsibility. Hughes, therefore, argued strongly against retaining the provisions for compulsory sanctions to meet aggression. Any resort to war under the league must remain a decision to be reached freely and independently by member governments. Hughes also recommended dropping from the draft any implication that a system of arbitration or rulings by an international court could have any jurisdiction over such specific matters as Australia's immigration policies, strategic control of Pacific islands, or the freedom of the seas.[51] Clearly the major points made by the dominions buttressed the views put forward by the prime minister on 31 January.

Hurst and Miller met as scheduled on 1 February and, in a marathon session lasting into the early hours of 2 February, completed the text that would serve as the working draft for the League of Nations Commission. The new Hurst-Miller draft, largely as a result of Hurst's contribution, was expressed in concise legal terminology. In matters of substance, changes from the Cecil-Miller draft largely reflected the agreements reached at the 31 January meeting with the president. The new section on disarmament eliminated demands for the end of conscription and merely made it a duty of the executive council to inquire into the feasibility of such a policy. Definite provision was made for the creation of a permanent court of international justice to deal with disputes suitable for litigation. Wilson's supplementary agreements regarding colonies were dropped, and, following the lines of the resolution drawn up by the Council of Ten on 30 January, Hurst and Miller merely inserted a brief statement of principle concerning the future administration of captured colonial areas. The reserved provisions of the Cecil-Miller draft referring to protection of minorities and freedom of the seas were dropped. An innocuous provision requiring league members to agree upon provisions "intended to secure and maintain freedom of transit and just treatment for the commerce of all States members of the League" replaced Wilson's designs for an end to international economic and fiscal discrimination. A final important change resulted from Hurst's suggestion to drop the provisions for peaceful change that formed a condition of the territorial guarantee. Miller readily assented, and the new article stated unconditionally that "the High Contracting Powers undertake to respect and preserve as against external aggression the territorial integrity and existing political independence of all States members of the League."[52] This article, of course, went directly against what the prime minister and the dominions had advised.

Generally, despite the many changes in terminology and arrangement resulting from the Anglo-American negotiations, Cecil had been very successful in retaining the substance of the British draft convention. The Hurst-Miller draft, however, met with negative reaction from both Lloyd George's entourage and Wilson. The president, upon reading the final draft, thought that too much had been sacrificed in both form and substance to the British and ordered a redrafting of his plan of 20 January to serve as a basis for the impending proceedings of the League of Nations Commission.[53] Only heated protests from Cecil and others deflected the president from this last-minute strategy. House, upon hearing the British objections, warned the president on the dangers of alienating Cecil since he "was the only man connected with the British Government who really had the League of Nations at heart."[54] After a tense meeting with Cecil just before the opening session of the League of Nations Commission, the president reluctantly agreed to allow the Hurst-Miller draft to be used as the basis for the proceedings.[55]

When Hankey learned of the substance of the Anglo-American draft, he concluded that the league project was "not proceeding on sound lines" and warned Lloyd George that "an acutely difficult situation" might be produced.[56] Hankey had a direct personal interest in the league negotiations since for some time he had been contemplating the possibility of becoming the league's first secretary.[57] Hankey would not attempt to run the league on the lines presently contemplated, however, since he believed it would "inevitably break down," and he would "be involved in the smash."[58] Attempting to straighten things out, on 5 February he strongly advised Cecil to organize the league "exactly on the same lines as the Versailles Council." Although Cecil was aware that Hankey spoke "the mind of the Prime Minister's entourage," he argued that there were two objections to this policy. Cecil thought the Versailles Council had been "only a very moderate success." Moreover, the conditions behind a peacetime league of nations and a wartime Allied council were different. The league, "lacking the compelling power of fighting an enemy to keep it together," would need "a much more solid organization" with provision for a much greater variety of functions and a well-organized secretariat. The best Hankey could get was a promise by Cecil to circulate copies of the draft convention and subsequent proceedings, thereby keeping everyone *au fait* with what was being done.[59] Clearly, Cecil had a vision of what the league should be, and criticism from other quarters in the government was not welcomed.

The League of Nations Commission convened for its first session on 3 February. Membership on the commission included two representatives from each of the five principal Allies and one representative from each of five, later nine, smaller powers. Wilson served as chairman; the other major delegates included House, Cecil, and Smuts, with Bourgeois and Larnaude representing France. The deliberations of the League of Nations Commission are a well-known story.[60] What follows is an attempt to recapture the major decisions from the viewpoint of the British delegation.

During the first session of the commission, which dealt mainly with procedural matters, the Americans and British immediately asserted their dominance by having the Hurst-Miller draft adopted as the document upon which to base proceedings.[61] The desire of the French, Italian, and Belgian delegations for initial debate on basic principles was thwarted by Wilson and Cecil, who stressed the necessity of expediting business. The acceptance of the Anglo-American draft and a minimizing of debate on basic principles were absolutely essential if a multinational commission hoped to complete the staggering task of designing the first great international organization in the short period of time that would be available.

Accordingly, on 4 February at its second meeting, the commission began by examining the first articles of the Anglo-American draft.[62] Discussion centered mainly on the critical issue of membership on the executive council. Wilson and Cecil defended the Hurst-Miller design for an executive council composed exclusively of great powers. In stating their case, both stressed the importance of making the league acceptable to the great powers. Inclusion of smaller powers on the council would seriously threaten this acceptance. Wilson argued that the greatest burdens, economic and military, fell on the great powers and that this responsibility entitled them to preponderance. Cecil denied that the principle of the equality of nations, though meritorious, could be allowed to operate in this instance, especially when all action would be subject to unanimity. These arguments were attacked vigorously by all the small power representatives on the commission. Hymans, the Belgian foreign minister, led the attack , arguing that a council excluding smaller powers would be unacceptable and would lack the confidence of the majority of league members. When Orlando, Italian prime minister, and Bourgeois both supported the case of the smaller powers, Cecil and Wilson reluctantly agreed to a redrafting of the article that would admit the smaller powers to minority representation on the executive council.

With the principle of minority representation established, the third meeting of the commission attempted to fix a number.[63] The British, Americans, French, and Italians united behind an amendment granting the small powers a representation of two on the council. This proved unacceptable to the smaller powers; Vesnitch from Serbia argued for four, and Hymans pleaded for parity. Cecil strongly resisted the demand, threatening that if parity were granted, "there would be a real risk of one or two Great Powers holding out." When this statement brought the accusation from Hymans that a new Holy Alliance was being proposed, Cecil declared that since there was "a great and fundamental difference of opinion" on this subject, the fixing of the exact number of majority representation should be deferred. Privately, Cecil railed against the tendency of all the "foreigners" to harp perpetually on principle and rights of abstract justice in contrast to the British and the Americans, who were pragmatic and saw that an exclusively great power council would be "a much more workable instrument of administration."[64] Not until its ninth meeting, 13 February, did the commission decide upon four as the smaller power representation on the council. This decision marked a major defeat for Cecil, who anticipated much opposition from his government.

The fourth meeting of the commission, 6 February, examined the critical provisions relating to guarantees of territorial integrity and political independence.[65] Cecil, aware of opposition within the British government to binding contractual obligations, attempted to modify the unconditional guarantee put forward by the Hurst-Miller draft. Cecil expressed concern at the extent of the obligation, "which means war if it means anything," and warned that things were being put in the covenant "which cannot be carried out literally and in all respects." Smuts observed that the article went "further than anything else in the document." In line with the views of his government and the dominions, Cecil proposed an amendment that would have removed the positive obligation to "preserve as against external aggression" and simply left the passive requirement to respect "the territorial integrity and existing political independence of all States members of the League." In proposing this line, the British delegation ran into the united opposition of the rest of the commission. Wilson argued that the words added little to the implied obligation of the whole covenant. Faithful to his earliest approach to the question, the president reiterated his belief that these obligations were necessary to show that the league meant business and would operate as more than simply a forum for discussion; they were "the key to the whole Covenant." This emphasis on the security function of the league was supported strongly by France, Italy, and the small power members of the commission. Wilson successfully proposed an amendment to the article defining its implementation: "In case of any such aggression the Executive Council shall advise the plan and the means by which this obligation shall be fulfilled." The president probably felt this addition merely clarified the operation of the guarantee, but Cecil realized that the amendment considerably "softened" the article.[66] By interposing the direction of a council that could act only with unanimity between the guarantee and its operation, the effectiveness of the guarantee was seriously conditioned if not completely nullified. Nevertheless, the radical obligation to preserve the territory and independence of all league members still stood. Retention of this provision meant a second major defeat for the British delegation within the commission.[67]

The commission next turned to the question of disarmament.[68] The French were successful in having the references to possible abolition of compulsory military service deleted. In their place Wilson inserted an amendment that made it the responsibility of the executive council to determine "for the consideration and action of the several Governments what military equipment and armament is fair and reasonable in proportion to the scale of forces laid down in the programme of disarmament; and these limits, when adopted, shall not be exceeded without the permission of the Body of Delegates." The deletion of the reference to conscription was a setback to British designs, especially as espoused by the prime minister, while the added amendment met with alarmed resistance from British military and naval circles. Finally, on Wilson's initiative an amendment was inserted directing the council to inquire into the possibility of ending private manufacture of armaments.

This session of the commission also began examination of the Hurst-Miller articles dealing with the peaceful resolution of disputes.[69] Since there was virtual agreement, the draft articles were passed with only minor revisions. The principle was set forth that any war or threat of war, whether immediately affecting the league members or not, was a matter of concern to the whole league, and members reserved the right to take any necessary action. Disputes not settled through ordinary diplomatic channels would be referred either to arbitration or to inquiry by the executive council. Resort to force was forbidden until three months after an arbitral award or recommendation by the council, and in no case could a power attack a league member that complied with such an award or recommendation. Plans were also made for the creation of a permanent court of international justice to adjudicate upon disputes that parties recognized as suitable for submission.

The discussion of provisions for the peaceful resolution of disputes continued at the fifth meeting of the commission, 7 February.[70] The Belgian delegation, in suggested amendments to Article 13 of the Hurst-Miller draft, raised important questions of principle concerning the role of the council in arbitrating disputes. As the article stood, after a unanimous report by the council (excluding parties to the dispute), members of the league simply agreed not to go to war with any party that complied with the council's recommendations. Failing unanimity, the council would merely issue a majority report with no legal effect. The Belgian proposals would have made compliance with a unanimous report obligatory—thus inaugurating a system of compulsory arbitration—and would have given legal effect to a majority report by obliging league members to refrain from war with a complying party. The principle of compulsory arbitration, although supported by the French, Greek, and Serbian delegations, was resisted strongly by Cecil and Wilson. With such opposition, the Belgian amendments were not accepted. The article, however, was referred to a subcommittee, which did recommend that, in the event a party refused to comply with a unanimous council recommendation, "the Council shall consider what steps can best be taken to give effect to their recommendation." This addition was accepted at the commission's seventh meeting.[71]

The fifth meeting of the commission also examined the fundamental question of sanctions. Although Cecil was aware of the strong opposition within the British government to these binding commitments, no challenge to the principle of sanctions was put forward. To do so would have involved a fundamental critique of the approach to the league question embodied in the Hurst-Miller draft and would have run into the headlong opposition of Wilson and the rest of the commission. Instead, debate centered on Belgian proposals to extend the operation of sanctions, particularly to include violations of the territorial and political independence guarantee. Within a collective system for security, the Belgian proposals were eminently logical. However, in light of the opposition within both the British and American governments to the principle of sanctions, it seemed inadvisable to be strictly logical on this issue, and the Belgian proposals were turned down.

Subsequent meetings of the commission on 8 and 10 February dealt with the operation of the mandate system, protection of international labor, regulation of trade and transit, and the publication of all future treaties.[72] These matters raised few difficulties since, in the case of mandates, it was largely a matter of accepting the previous decisions of the Council of Ten. In other matters, moreover, the commission contented itself with elaborating principles that were for the most part as ineffectual as they were benign. A suggestion by Cecil and Orlando that the council of the league be empowered to rule on the legality of future treaties was sidetracked by Wilson, who argued that if all treaties were registered and published by the league, public opinion would be powerful enough to prevent the signing of treaties that were inconsistent with the covenant.

At the meeting of 11 February, Cecil returned to the difficult problem of territorial guarantee, attempting to qualify it further by adding provisions for peaceful change.[73] The most Cecil was able to have accepted was an article granting the league's body of delegates the right to advise members to reconsider treaties that had become inapplicable and to review international conditions that, if left unremedied, might endanger the peace of the world.

It was at this point that the French delegation presented the most important and far-reaching challenge to the Anglo-American approach to the league. At the beginning of the commission's deliberations, the French representatives, agreeing to proceed on the basis of the Hurst-Miller draft, had tabled their own draft constitution for a league. This was the plan drawn up by the Bourgeois committee in June 1918. The French delegation now proposed a series of amendments that would have changed the fundamental approach of the Hurst-Miller plan by incorporating the major objectives of the French design. The first would have given the executive council power to request sanctions against any state that, having submitted a dispute to peaceful settlement, refused to accept the award of an international tribunal or a unanimous decision rendered by the league's council or the body of delegates. This amendment, in effect, revived the Belgian proposals for a system of compulsory arbitration. The second amendment would have directed the executive council to establish "an international control of troops and armaments" and to "fix the conditions under which the permanent existence and organization of an international force may be assured." The French hoped to realize their designs for the creation of an international army under an international general staff. The international control of armies and armaments was intended to ensure that the disarmament of enemies and the armament of friends remained effective. Associated with this amendment was a proposed qualification directing the council, in formulating disarmament plans, to pay due regard to the relative strength of the different states and the risks to which they were exposed by their geographical situation and the nature of their frontiers. The third French amendment was designed to ensure that only a thoroughly reformed and disarmed Germany would ever be admitted to league membership. It stipulated that no nation would be admitted to the league "unless it has representative institutions which permit of its being considered as itself responsible for the acts of its own Government; unless it is in a position to give effective guarantees of its sincere intention to abide by its agreement; and unless it conforms to those principles which the League shall formulate regarding naval and military forces and armaments."

These French proposals sparked heated debate in the commission. Underlying Bourgeois's defense of each proposal was the insistence by the French government and people that the league, if it were to be worthwhile, must provide iron-fast guarantees for national security. As Bourgeois argued, if no sanctions were placed behind the league's unanimous decisions, what would protect a state acting in good faith from a state acting in bad faith? Without such protection, the league would be an organization "effective in appearance, but in reality a trap for nations of good faith." In defending the proposed control of armaments and creation of an international force, Bourgeois quoted the president's own words:

"A force must be created, a force so superior to that of all nations or to that of all alliances, that no nation or combination of nations can challenge or resist it." The failure to protect honest nations against every sudden attack would indicate "a real failure in the organization of law." Bourgeois concluded his defense with the threat that unless these types of guarantee were forthcoming, the proposed covenant would meet with vigorous opposition from the senators and deputies who composed the French parliamentary committee on arbitration.

Wilson and Cecil united in opposing these French designs. Wilson stressed the constitutional and political impossibility of America's adopting such proposals and argued that the construction of an international army could be viewed as an internationalized version of militarism. Cecil, after "resisting vigorously"[74] the French scheme, suggested as a compromise the establishment of a permanent commission "to advise the League on naval and military questions."[75] This compromise failed to satisfy the French, and the debate in the commission reached an impasse, with Wilson appealing for mutual good faith in pledges and Bourgeois insisting on explicit guarantees in the covenant. The issue was therefore referred to a drafting committee for further consideration.

When the drafting committee met the next day to deal with pending amendments and clarify the language of the text passed to date, Larnaude once again pressed the French demand for an international army.[76] After the 11 February meeting of the commission, Cecil had privately warned the French delegation that the league of nations "was their only means of getting the assistance of America and England, and if they destroyed it they would be left without an ally in the world."[77] Now, before the drafting committee, Cecil repeated this remarkable warning in more threatening language. The offers for support through the covenant made by Britain and America were in effect a "present" to France. Both America, and to a lesser extent Britain, could afford to stand apart from continental affairs. If France adopted the attitude "that because more was not offered they would not take the gift that was at hand," the alternative to the league would be an alliance between Britain and America.[78]

This threat, which Cecil made without any official authorization, temporarily diverted the French from their declared purpose. The committee did, however, amend the provisions governing admission of new members to take into account the proposed French requirements regarding self-government, observation of international obligations, and disarmament undertakings.

Two more British proposals of importance, designed to extend the humanitarian, technological, and economic functions of the league, were placed before the drafting committee.[79] The first proposal provided that league members agree to carry out, through the league, any other functions assigned to it by the treaties of peace and promote the common study and regulation by the league of "important economic, sanitary or other similar problems." The second proposal, which received the committee's endorsement, provided that league members agree to place all existing international bureaus under control of the league (with the consent of the parties participating in these bureaus) as well as all such bureaus established in the future. Finally, the committee directed the legal experts Hurst and Miller to incorporate the results of deliberations in a document of precise legal terminology.

On 13 February, the commission met in its final two sessions before publishing the 14 February draft convenant.[80] Although business was directed to a vote on each article as revised by the drafting committee and the legal experts, issues of substance still predominated. In the morning session, the French were persuaded to withdraw a distinctly anti-German addition to the preamble specifying the "common feeling of reprobation towards those who began the war." A second French proposal, linking the league to the work of The Hague, was voted down.

Smuts then proposed that an extraordinary session of the body of delegates meet at least every four years with representatives from national parliaments and other groups representative of public opinion. This proposal was, in effect, a revival of plans in earlier British drafts for a representative assembly as part of the league and represented an attempt by Smuts to meet some of the desires of his more radical friends. Cecil and Wilson, however, advised waiting until later to see how public opinion expressed itself on this issue. Smuts's proposal, nevertheless, gave rise to an important debate on the nature and number of representatives each state would have in the body of delegates. It was agreed that while each state would be free to choose whatever delegates it wished, these delegates must be the responsible voice for their respective governments. An amendment was therefore passed, specifying that each league member would have one vote and not more than three representatives in the body of delegates.

In the afternoon the commission's business was taken up largely by a renewed French effort to see provisions for armament control and an international general staff written into the covenant. The French delegation presented its case with dogged persistence, which sorely tried the patience of Cecil, who chaired this session while Wilson attended the Council of Ten. After lengthy and acrimonious debate, Cecil had both French proposals voted down. Extensive debate also occurred on a proposed article preventing religious discrimination by league members. After the Japanese delegation had suggested linking the prohibition of racial discrimination with religious discrimination, the commission advised dropping this potentially explosive issue. The remaining articles of the draft were then passed with only minor revisions.

While the commission was putting the finishing touches on its draft covenant, Wilson was contemplating the next procedural step to be taken on the league question. On 12 February he informed Miller that he did not intend to submit the draft covenant to a plenary session of the peace conference. Rather, Wilson wished to appoint a subcommission to discuss the matter with neutral powers.[81] When Cecil learned of the president's intentions, he advised that the covenant be laid before a plenary session but that no decision be asked for at this stage.[82] Wilson then recommended this procedure to the Council of Ten, 13 February, requesting notice for a plenary session for the next day. Clemenceau favored having the commission's report discussed by the Council of Ten first, but Balfour, no doubt briefed by Cecil, thought it best if Wilson could explain the draft covenant to the conference before he left for his trip back to America. At the same time Balfour made it clear that the president would make his submission "as Chairman of the League of Nations Commission and not as a member of the Conference of the Great Powers." Members of the Council of Ten, therefore, "would not be committed to the scheme in any way." Clemenceau raised no objections to this procedure, and a plenary session was scheduled for the next day.[83]

Accordingly, on 14 February Wilson placed before the peace conference and the world the commission's draft design for international organization. With a full sense of the historical moment, the president read the document article by article, pausing briefly here and there to explain the intent of particular passages. Later, he spoke warmly of the spirit that had marked the deliberations of the commission, of the simplicity of their plan, and of the hope offered for future generations. Several aspects of the plan were singled out for particular elaboration. Wilson acknowledged the widespread popular desire to see the creation of a truly representative assembly and not simply a body of governmental officials. While it had proven impossible to create a directly representative assembly, the method of selecting national representatives in the body of delegates had been left open. Wilson emphasized that this method would allow a variety of representation. According to Wilson the jurisdiction of the body of delegates in dealing with disputes was broad and would give full play to the cleansing and compelling influence of publicity. Although the league would depend primarily and chiefly upon "the moral force of the public opinion of the world," armed force would remain in the background—"and if the moral force of the world will not suffice, the physical force of the world shall." The president spoke further of the definite guarantee against aggression and the role the league would play in promoting international cooperation, particularly with regard to labor protection and the humane development of the colonial areas of the world. "A living thing is born" —with these words Wilson appealed to a war-sick world to join in a "Covenant of fraternity and friendship."

Cecil joined in the president's appeal, pointing to the new principles of international relations being established and emphasizing the hope that international cooperation would replace international competition. At the same time, with an eye on governmental attitudes, Cecil took care to minimize the executive powers of the league. The aim had been "to devise some really effective means of preserving the peace of the world consistently with the least possible interference with national sovereignty." Accordingly, the commission had worked on two assumptions: the league should not in any way interfere with the internal affairs of a state; and, except in clearly specified cases, all action taken by the league would require unanimity.[84]

The presentation of the 14 February draft covenant to the plenary session marked the high point of the peace conference for both Cecil and Wilson. Throughout the war they above all other governmental figures had insisted upon the creation of an international organization for peace and security as the principal objective of the Allied coalition. Now, at the peace conference, they had given their idea form and structure. The draft covenant represented a distinct triumph for the conception of international organization espoused by Wilson and Cecil. There were significant differences between their approaches, but such differences were not of a fundamental nature and were readily amenable to compromise. The deliberations of the League of Nations Commission witnessed the fusion of Wilson's insistence upon collective guarantees of peace with Cecil's desire for a system of multilateral consultation, designed to promote peaceful resolution of disputes and further international cooperation. Both resisted the security-minded military designs of the French government, and each ignored the more conservative approach favored by powerful quarters within their respective governments. Together, Wilson and Cecil believed the draft covenant promised a new order of liberal internationalism based on reforms of the prewar diplomatic system necessary to prevent future war and revolution. It remained to be seen how the draft covenant would be received by the public and by those governments who held the prime responsibility for its acceptance, modification, or rejection.

7 *The Peacemakers at War: Revising the Covenant*

Publication of the covenant sparked off a wide-ranging debate among supporters and critics of the league project. Wilson left for America directly after the plenary session of 14 February, intent upon confronting his American critics and defending the covenant as drafted. During the month the president was away, the European allies attempted to speed up the work of the peace conference and prepare for the realization of their own major objectives. At the same time a project was launched in Paris that would have fundamentally altered the president's approach to the creation of the league. Wilson returned to the peace conference fearing that much of his handiwork had been threatened and insisting that the covenant and the league be fully integrated with the peace treaty. As the peace conference entered its crisis period in late March, the league project was thrown into the fray, with the peacemaking strategies of the major Allies in open conflict.

In Britain publication of the draft covenant brought official and public debate on international organization into focus. The major critiques came from the left and right wings of the political spectrum. The *Morning Post*, through the early months of 1919, hammered away on the theme that British security was founded on the empire, the navy, and a balance of power based on the Allied coalition.[1] The draft covenant was so much verbiage concocted by pacifists and pro-Germans, who didn't realize that "the fate of nations is decided by strength."[2] Colonel Repington, the *Post*'s military correspondent, believed a fundamental error had been made in attempting to "cram as much as possible" into the covenant and that the Anglo-Saxons would find themselves being "talked to death by the Latin races in this new Parliament."[3]

British labor, on the other hand, found the draft covenant wanting when contrasted with the program of radical international reform propagated by the Union of Democratic Control and written into labor war-aims manifestos. Labor newspapers and leaders of the UDC denounced the draft plan as a new "Holy Alliance," dominated by the governments of the great powers, feeble in the provisions for disarmament, mistaken in its exclusion of former enemies, and hypocritical in its endorsement of the division of colonial spoils.[4] After examining the draft, the Labour party Advisory Committee on International Questions recommended on 4 March four major revisions in its report to the party executive. The committee advised the extension of league membership on equal terms to all civilized states, the establishment of a deliberative democratic assembly within the league to represent peoples rather than governments, the universal abolition of conscription, and the inclusion within the mandate system of all colonial possessions.[5]

A special joint conference of the Labour party and the Trades Union Congress organized 3 April reaffirmed labor's critique of the draft covenant.[6] Discontent focused on the limited role assigned to the body of delegates, which, it was argued, should be made representative of peoples and fashioned into the major organ of the league. Labor in effect was calling for a virtual international parliament, with the executive council responsible to a popular body of delegates.

If the Left and Right were critical of the covenant, the Liberals continued to provide the principal support for the league project. Asquith, in his first speech after defeat in the election, presented the league as "the supreme question" of the hour,[7] and Donald Maclean rallied the Liberal remnant in Parliament behind the cause.[8] When the covenant was published, Liberal leaders hailed it as the major accomplishment of the peace conference, while liberal newspapers continued to offer wide and sympathetic coverage to negotiations on the league at Paris and the efforts of the League of Nations Union at home.[9]

The League of Nations Union kept up its campaign for the league, submitting advice to the government[10] and joining with the Allied Societies for a League of Nations in lobbying at the peace conference.[11] When the draft covenant was published, the research committee of the League of Nations Union welcomed "the whole document as a long step—perhaps the longest possible for the time being—in the right direction." Its observations generally were confined to explaining and commending the articles of the draft scheme. Only two substantial "comments rather than criticisms" were put forward. The committee hoped that some provision could be made for a larger representative assembly to complement the work of the body of delegates. A second suggestion was to ban absolutely all wars rather than leave a loophole for a final resort to force after all the procedures of the covenant had been followed.[12] Cecil knew that he could count on the union to support the draft covenant and took steps to ensure that press and union propaganda "should no longer be generally for [a] League of Nations but specifically on [the] Covenant."[13] A second conference of Allied Societies for a League of Nations was held in London, 11–13 March. Again, the draft covenant was welcomed warmly and suggestions for changes were made in a friendly spirit. Most changes were patterned after the previous British suggestions, but the French delegations insisted on provisions for speedy and efficient execution of covenant obligations.[14]

British governmental leaders and officials, in line with Balfour's position in the Council of Ten, viewed the draft covenant as provisional and subject to major modification. Back in London, the prime minister defended the league idea before Parliament on 12 February and argued that American Republican opposition would not thwart the project. He warned, however, that there were differences of opinion on the league "with regard to its functions, and the extent to which it ought to have the power of committing the great nations to war." Lloyd George asserted that the British government would have something to say about these issues, and he agreed "that a nation ought not to be committed to war by any means without having the responsibility considered by itself."[15] Hankey thought the draft covenant "infinitely better" than the earlier drafts, but he still did not like it and emphasized that the government remained "quite uncommitted."[16] Lunching with Cecil on 13 February, Hankey observed that without being a cabinet minister, Cecil "appeared to have 'bounced' the League of Nations Commission very successfully."[17] Cecil mistook this observation for a compliment.

Naval and military leaders focused their criticism on the disarmament provisions of the draft covenant. A joint admiralty, army, and air council memorandum of 7 February had protested "in the strongest possible manner" against the approach to disarmament found in Article 8 as drafted, arguing that "the whole question of the limitation of Armaments should be viewed independently of the general Covenant of the League of Nations."[18] When these criticisms had no effect on the covenant as published 14 February, the admiralty board decided to take its case directly to the War Cabinet.[19] A memorandum of 3 March by Walter Long pointed out the admiralty's objections and proposed three principal amendments. The first would have eliminated any obligation on the part of league members to take definite action on advice of the executive council regarding arms limitation, thereby reducing such advice to the level of recommendation. The second proposed deleting the obligation not to exceed agreed limitation of armaments without the permission of the executive council. The third attempted to state explicitly the implied requirement that, except where otherwise expressly provided, all executive council decisions would require unanimous agreement.[20] The admiralty proposals were considered at the 13 March meeting of the British Empire delegation.[21] Cecil argued that council decisions would definitely require unanimity and agreed that certain features of Article 8 needed redrafting.

Churchill, secretary of state for war, added the voice of the army to that of the admiralty in advising caution on the league. Replying to Liberal and Labour critics in the Commons on 3 March, Churchill explained that the army estimates could not be reduced simply because a league of nations was being created. The league was "on trial" and would have to face "cruel and terrible facts" before confidence could be placed in the security it promised.[22]

Two important commentaries on the draft covenant came from the dominions. On 13 March Borden circulated to the British Empire delegation a comprehensive list of amendments proposed by the Canadian government together with related explanations. Most of Borden's amendments concerned matters of form and were aimed at simplifying and clarifying the language of the covenant. On matters of substance, like the admiralty, Borden argued that draft Article 8 was confusing and ambiguous and needed redrafting to clarify the powers of the council in arranging arms limitation. Borden also suggested that there were loopholes in the draft covenant that might be exploited by a determined aggressor and that could be removed by redrafting or adding further safeguards. The crucial portion of the Canadian memorandum related to the guarantee of territorial integrity and political independence included in Article 10. Following the line of an earlier memorandum by Doherty,[23] Borden advised that this article "should be struck out or materially amended." As it stood, signatories to the covenant would be called upon to declare: "(a) that all existing territorial delimitations are just and expedient, (b) that they will continue indefinitely to be just and expedient, (c) that the signatories will be responsible therefor." Borden argued that even if it were possible to resolve all present territorial issues involving league members, it would still be impossible "to forecast the future." The article failed to provide for the possibility and likelihood of future national aspirations that could not "be permanently repressed." Furthermore, the article seemed inconsistent with the articles dealing with peaceful resolution of disputes, which could include territorial disputes. In Borden's view, the weak provision in the draft for peaceful change failed to bridge this difficulty. Generally, as North Americans, Canadian leaders saw few virtues in Wilson's desire for a collective system of international security, nor did they wish to see the league replace the British Empire as an agent of external control of Canadian policies, considering the assertion of new national status by the dominions.[24]

While Borden differed from the president on the critical issue of Article 10, he could still be counted among those who strongly supported the league idea. The same could not be said of the fiery Australian prime minister, who spared nothing in his attacks on Wilson and on the league project in particular. On 18 February the *Morning Post* reprinted a press release by Hughes comparing the league "founded on words" with "that great *de facto* League of Nations which, cemented by blood, sacrifice, and heroic endurance through the long dark night of trial, has at length led us to final victory."[25] Hughes pleaded for haste in drawing up the real terms of peace and deprecated the time wasted on nonessential issues. On 21 March, Hughes circulated to the British Empire delegation his considered views on the 14 February draft covenant. His memorandum pointed out that there were two rival approaches to the league question: one conceived the league as an international government or superstate; the other saw the league in terms of a more limited system of international consultation. In Hughes's view, while the draft covenant rightly based itself for the most part on the consultative idea, it was still full of ambiguous expressions and provisions that suggested the governmental idea. For instance, the executive council was a misnomer since it had no executive power of its own, nor could the body of delegates be considered analogous to a legislature. It must be made clear, Hughes felt, that all decisions taken by the league could only have the power of recommendations, particularly regarding Article 8 and the role assigned to the league in dealing with the question of arms limitation.

Two further aspects of the draft were singled out for criticism. Hughes argued that, in spite of the strong arguments in favor of some system of international sanctions, the provisions for automatic war embodied in Article 16 were "a mistake." The weight of the league behind the bare covenant would be sanction enough without a definite pledge. The league should be left free to decide on appropriate action as each case arose. Hughes advised, therefore, that Article 16 be recast "with a view to limiting it to an affirmation of the *right* to make war against a Covenant-breaking State." Hughes also objected to the power granted to the league council to define by act or charter the nature of the control to be exercised by a mandatory state if not previously agreed upon by the high contracting powers. The memorandum concluded with a terse warning: "The draft as it now stands, halting between the two inconsistent principles of international cooperation and supra-national government, now leaning to one direction and now in the other—is open to widely different interpretations, and stands in serious danger of combining the disadvantages of both with the advantages of neither."[26]

Clearly there was major opposition, not only from the dominions, but also within the British government, to several central features of the draft covenant. When Cecil returned briefly to London, Lloyd George suggested that he go as ambassador to Washington.[27] Cecil declined, no doubt anxious to see the league project through to completion in Paris. In light of British and foreign criticisms of the draft covenant, Cecil reflected in his diary on 10 March that the League of Nations Commission, "more by good luck than good guidance," had taken the only possible line that could succeed: "A little more and we should have upset the Americans, and a little less and we should have disgusted our left wing supporters, and probably the smaller Powers also." Cecil's formula is revealing in its exclusion of his own government, but his concern for American reactions was well merited.

While the draft covenant was being examined critically by British and dominion officials, no less important a debate was well underway in America. Wilson returned to find powerfully organized Senate opposition to his program, which focused its attack on the draft covenant. The opposition divided into three principal groups: the "irreconcilables" or "bitter-enders," who opposed any departure from isolation; the "strong reservationists," who wished to place clear limits on American international commitments, protect American interests, and guard the diplomatic prerogatives of the Senate; and the "mild reservationists," who welcomed the creation of a league but wished to safeguard traditional American policies and practices.[28] Henry Cabot Lodge, chairman-designate of the Senate's new Foreign Relations Committee and a bitter personal and political enemy of Wilson, led the diverse Republican opposition brilliantly, Lodge's objectives being the protection of American national sovereignty and the political destruction of Wilson.

As a means of confronting Wilson and bringing Senate influence directly to bear on the peacemaking, Senators Brandegee and Knox organized the famous round robin, which Lodge read on the Senate floor, 3 March. By this device, thirty-nine senators and senators-elect, more than one-third of the Senate, joined in declaring that the constitution of the league "as now proposed" was unacceptable to the United States, and urged that the settlement with Germany be completed before further consideration was given to the league question.[29] Since a two-thirds vote was necessary for Senate consent to ratification of a treaty, the round robin constituted a serious threat.

Wilson responded to his opponents with a mixture of conciliation and defiance. At House's suggestion he entertained members of the congressional foreign relations committees in the White House and attempted to explain the covenant in terms that answered their major concerns. This gesture did little to moderate the opposition. Confronted with the round robin, Wilson threw down a defiant challenge in his departing speech at the Metropolitan Opera House on 4 March. When the treaty came back, "gentlemen on this side will find the Covenant not only in it, but so many threads of the treaty tied to the Covenant that you cannot dissect the Covenant from the treaty without destroying the whole vital structure."[30]

Some of the president's supporters, nevertheless, advised making certain revisions in the draft covenant in order to meet the more legitimate and substantial of the various criticisms put forward. On 4 March Senator Hitchcock, acting Democratic Senate leader and retiring chairman of the Foreign Relations Committee, suggested six amendments he believed would bring most of the Republicans into line. These included preservation of exclusive control over domestic subjects, explicit recognition of the Monroe Doctrine, provisions for withdrawal from the league, clarification of ambiguous points in Article 15, insertion of the words "by the several governments" after "adopted" in Article 8, and assurance that a nation could accept or reject mandatory responsibilities.[31] After Wilson had returned to Europe, Taft, the leading Republican supporter of the league, sent the following telegram to the president:

> If you bring back the treaty with the League of Nations in it, make more specific reservation of the Monroe Doctrine, fix a term for duration of the League, and the limit of armament, require express unanimity of action in the Executive Council and Body of Delegates, and add to Article 15 a provision that where the Executive Council of the Body of Delegates finds the difference to grow out of an exclusively domestic policy, it shall recommend no settlement, the ground will be completely cut out from under the opponents of the League in the Senate. Addition to Article 15 will answer objection as to Japanese immigration, as well as tariffs under Article 21. . . .
>
> Monroe Doctrine reservation alone would probably carry the treaty, but others would make it certain.[32]

Although Wilson was loath to acknowledge the necessity for any substantial revision, political wisdom dictated that full account be taken of the advice tendered by Hitchcock and Taft.

Republican opposition to the covenant as drafted and the explicit warnings on how the treaty would be received by the Senate if the covenant were included in its present form increased the reservations and misgivings of Allied leaders on the league project. At the same time, Wilson's domestic difficulties opened tempting tactical advantages to European leaders, who were anxious to bargain hard for the realization of their principal objectives. While Wilson was absent from Paris, the league question once more became entangled as a result of tactical maneuvering and the confusion surrounding efforts to draft preliminary peace terms and speed up the peacemaking.

Wilson had fully endorsed the 12 February decision of the Council of Ten to proceed with the drafting of final military, naval, and air terms of a preliminary peace to be imposed on Germany.[33] Then, on Balfour's initiative and with House's support, the Council of Ten on 24 February expanded the scope of the project for an early preliminary peace to include terms relating to the territorial and economic settlement to be imposed on the former enemies, together with arrangements for trying war criminals.[34] Expert commissions were instructed to submit their reports by 8 March. While these decisions were being made, French leaders pressed their plans for the territorial dismemberment of Germany, particularly the establishment of a separate Rhenish republic under French control. The French hoped these objectives could be included in the preliminary peace and counted on House to be a more accommodating negotiator than Wilson.

As planning for a comprehensive preliminary peace gathered momentum in Wilson's absence, rumors also began circulating in Paris that the covenant was to be separated from the treaty.[35] This tactic seems to have been initiated by the French in an effort to concentrate the energies of the peace conference on their principal territorial and economic objectives and, at the same time, to increase bargaining leverage with Wilson when he returned. Certainly the Senate's round robin was interpreted by French leaders as a critical setback to Wilson's league program.[36]

Likewise, a British group, led by Wickham Steed, editor of the Paris edition of the *Daily Mail* and editor-designate of the *Times*, picked up the theme of an accelerated preliminary peace without the covenant, a tactic which apparently tempted Lloyd George as well. Steed, like Hankey and the circle around Lloyd George, disliked the fundamental approach to the league set out by the draft covenant. He preferred, instead, a much more modest beginning, setting an embryonic league based upon wartime inter-Allied institutions underway immediately and letting it develop naturally rather than trying to provide for everything in a detailed constitution.[37] If an embryonic league were established, the peace conference could concentrate on imposing terms of peace on Germany, referring questions not ripe for immediate settlement to the executive council of the league, which would begin its work "pending the final revision of the Covenant."[38] This course was advocated by the Northcliffe lobby in both the Paris *Daily Mail* and the *Times*.[39]

House was in close communication with Steed and, according to Steed, shared his thinking on peacemaking procedure and plans for the league.[40] House's tendency to be all things to all men probably led Steed to read too much into their exchanges, but on 28 February the colonel cabled Wilson that Cecil and Balfour had agreed to a plan to get the league functioning at once. The members of the League of Nations Commission would form a provisional executive council, which could study and make recommendations on matters referred to it by the Council of Ten or the plenary conference. House also recommended that Hankey be appointed secretary general, thereby making Lloyd George and his confreres, "who are not strong believers in the League," more enthusiastic.[41] Wilson replied to this proposal on 3 March, cautioning House that critics of the league could seize upon formation of the provisional executive council as an attempt to commit America to the league before action by the Senate. However, if the plan could be carried out with the clear understanding that the machinery was purely provisional and designed merely to facilitate the peacemaking, then Wilson thought the danger of criticism would perhaps disappear.[42] House made no progress on this project as he informed the president on 4 March.[43] In light of the round robin of 3 March, however, the colonel apparently contemplated separating the covenant from the peace treaty as a means of conciliating the Senate opposition.[44] House found Miller totally opposed to this course, and the matter was dropped.

Rumors continued to circulate in Paris, nevertheless, that the covenant was to be separated from the preliminary treaty. These rumors reached Wilson upon his arrival back in Europe,[45] and, after he had had an initial taste of the atmosphere prevailing in Paris, the president reacted with a forceful press release issued through Ray Stannard Baker on 15 March. Wilson's press release referred to the 25 January plenary conference resolution that the league should be created as an integral part of the peace treaty and insisted that there was "no basis whatever for the reports that a change in this decision was contemplated."[46] When Pichon, the French foreign minister, told press representatives the next day that there was indeed an intention to fashion a preliminary peace without the covenant,[47] Wilson drove home the points of his press release in private conversations with British and French leaders. On 18 March

Cecil came to the support of the president, informing British press representatives that the British delegation was committed to the incorporation of the covenant in the peace treaty.[48] Cecil claimed to speak with the blessing of his government, but two days later a press interview by Lloyd George disavowed Cecil's statement, casting further uncertainty on the relationship of the covenant to the peace treaty.[49] Lloyd George, mindful of the Republican opposition's warning and the tactical advantages to be gained over the president, was apparently as eager as French leaders to stall on Wilson's league program.

The confusion over the possibility of a preliminary treaty continued for some time after Wilson's arrival back at the peace conference. At a meeting of the Council of Ten on 17 March, the muddle over the legal status of proposed preliminary military, naval, and air terms became obvious, and Wilson requested postponement of any decision on this matter until he could get legal advice.[50] Wilson apparently thought that peace preliminaries would not necessarily involve submission of a treaty to the Senate and that the covenant might perhaps be included in preliminary terms dealing with military, naval, and air matters.[51] His legal advisors quickly disabused him of this notion, and the mystifying project for accelerated preliminary peace terms was allowed to lapse.[52] The confusing story of the preliminary peace project, with the simultaneous rumors about the covenant's separation from the treaty, not only increased the suspicions Wilson harbored about the integrity of his European colleagues, but also contributed directly to his estrangement with House. After Wilson returned to France and learned of the proposals House had entertained on the Rhineland issue and his unsteadiness on the league project, the relationship between the president and the colonel altered fundamentally, the former bonds of trust now being severed by Wilson.

Cecil had closely followed American reactions to the draft covenant and was, if anything, more anxious to meet the suggestions of the moderate critics in the Senate than he was to heed the advice put forward by British and dominion leaders.[53] He was eager, therefore, to begin the process of revising the covenant to meet legitimate American criticisms. On 16 March, however, when Cecil had his first chance to meet with Wilson again, he found the president "in a very truculent mood, fiercely refusing to make any concessions to Republican senators."[54] House, nevertheless, later advised Cecil that he was sure the president would make considerable concessions. Cecil agreed to draft proposals and meet Wilson again on 18 March.

On the morning of 18 March, Cecil advised House and Miller of the most important proposals he intended to make. These included an amendment to Article 3 empowering the council to expand by coopting other states with the approval of a majority of the assembly. This amendment was designed to facilitate eventual acquisition of council seats for Germany and Russia and, thereby, counter certain leftist criticisms. Next, Cecil spoke of the views of the admiralty about Article 8 and advised making it clear that the limitations must be adopted "by the Governments." With reluctance, Cecil revealed the admiralty's insistence on removing the necessity for council permission to alter adopted limitations of armaments. The strong Canadian views on Article 10 were read, and Cecil, again with reluctance, suggested removing the positive obligation to "preserve" as against external aggression the territorial integrity and political independence of members. He also suggested that Article 10 should include a reference to Article 24 (revision of treaties), thereby making the guarantee conditional. Cecil advised clarifying Article 15 to provide for an instance in which none of the parties to the dispute agreed to a unanimous report by the council. Finally, Cecil raised the sensitive issue of the Monroe Doctrine, requesting House's views on a statement he intended to make before newsmen. The statement would imply that if the Monroe Doctrine permanently separated the American hemisphere from the rest of the world, it was pernicious and opposed to the covenant; if it meant only that nothing was to be done in the American hemisphere without United States consent, then it was in accord with the covenant. Neither House nor Miller raised objections.[55]

That same evening Cecil dined with the president and Colonel

House. Cecil's proposals were carefully examined one by one. First, Cecil achieved agreement on a rewording of the preamble to the covenant, whereby Germany, in signing the treaty, would be bound by the obligations of the covenant, though not a member of the league. The president readily agreed to the proposed British amendment to Article 3 providing for future expansion of the council. Cecil successfully advised an insertion in Article 4, specifying that all decisions taken by the council or body of delegates would require unanimous agreement of all states represented at the meeting unless otherwise expressly provided in the covenant. Consensus was not so easily reached on other matters. When Cecil put forward the admiralty's views concerning Article 8, aside from agreeing that adoption of limitations would be "by the several governments," the president refused to countenance the admiralty's desire to allow changes in agreed limitations simply upon "notice to" the executive council. Regarding Article 10, Cecil no longer attempted to delete the obligation to "preserve," but merely advised making the guarantee "subject to the provisions of Article 24." Article 10, of course, lay at the heart of the president's program for a collective system of security, and he refused to accept this attempt to weaken its operation, citing the inevitable French opposition.

At the Americans' turn to suggest revisions, Wilson had obviously thought twice about adopting an unbending line on the draft covenant. Referring directly to Senate opposition, the president advised deleting the provisions of Article 15 requiring the council, when faced with a refusal to comply with one of its unanimous recommendations, to propose the measures necessary to give effect to such a recommendation. This change was agreed to, thereby removing the suggestion of compulsory arbitration implied by the original wording. Wilson suggested an amendment that would allow withdrawal from the league upon two years' notice. Furthermore, after mentioning the problems of Irish Home Rule and Japanese immigration, the president suggested explicit exclusion of domestic affairs from the jurisdiction of the league. No decision was reached on either of these suggestions. A proposal by Cecil, however, was put forward to quiet American fears about having to accept mandatory responsibilities. It was agreed to spell out explicitly in the mandate article that no state could be compelled to be a mandatory. Finally, the meeting began discussion of possible reservation of the Monroe Doctrine in the covenant. The president attempted to place a limited construction on the meaning of the doctrine, but Cecil strongly opposed specifying the doctrine in the covenant; the meeting could reach no agreement.[56] This exchange marked the beginning of an issue that very quickly assumed major proportions.

After interested neutral states were given an opportunity to submit suggestions on the draft covenant in two meetings arranged by Cecil and House,[57] the League of Nations Commission reconvened on 22 March. In meetings held on 22, 24, and 26 March, the major substantive changes to the draft covenant agreed upon in the previous Anglo-American negotiations were endorsed by the commission.[58] Many difficulties of terminology and procedure were passed on to a drafting committee. Wilson was successful in these meetings in having matters of domestic jurisdiction excluded from the authority of the league and in providing for withdrawal from the league upon two years' notice.

The French representatives raised the most serious difficulties during these negotiations, returning to their previous insistence upon an international general staff and a disarmament verification commission. The French further suggested the extension of the sanctions of Article 16 to cover violations of Articles 8, 13, and 15, as well as Article 12. Cecil and Wilson continued to oppose the French attempt to turn the league into an armed alliance, but on Cecil's suggestion Article 16 was extended to include resort to war in violation of Article 15.

By 26 March, the reconvened League of Nations Commission had made important modifications in the covenant, most of which were designed to blunt the opposition of the United States Senate. Wilson had been successful in having nearly all of the changes suggested by Hitchcock and Taft accepted by the League of Nations Commission. He had also given notice to the issue of recognition of the Monroe Doctrine, and much behind-the-scenes activity was

underway on this point. Many issues had been referred to the drafting committee, but none seemed insurmountable. The French continued to raise awkward issues, but both Clemenceau and his chief
assistant on foreign affairs, Tardieu, freely admitted to Cecil that
Bourgeois's insistence on an international general staff and a disarmament inspection commission was a bargaining tactic directly
related to the progress of negotiations on Germany's western boundaries.[59] At this point, however, the work of the League of Nations
Commission became deeply entangled in the politics of the peace
conference, and for a while the whole league project seemed to be
seriously endangered.

In the last week of March the peace conference entered its
crisis stage, with the British and the Americans resolutely opposed
to the French designs for the Rhineland and the Saar, with the
Allies and the Americans widely split on the reparations question,
with the Italians anxiously waiting for an opportunity to press their
Adriatic claims, and with the British and Americans preparing for a
major confrontation over naval isuses. To the frustrating delays in
fashioning the German peace treaty were added growing apprehen-
sions that revolution might upset all the efforts at peacemaking.
Policies on Russia remained in a state of confusion. Hunger and
social disintegration went hand in hand with revolutionary ferment
in Germany. On 23 March a Communist regime under Béla Kun
gained power in Hungary, immediately appealing to Bolshevik
Russia for aid and an alliance.[60]

The pressures of peacemaking weighed with particular force
on Lloyd George, who faced not only mounting labor unrest at
home but also growing demands from the right wing of his parliamentary coalition and the Northcliffe lobby to impose a harsh
peace on Germany. There was a general sense in Lloyd George's
circle that by late March the peace conference was taking on the
form of "a race between peace and anarchy."[61]

Faced with French determination to separate the Rhineland
from Germany, Lloyd George had responded by convincing Wilson,
immediately upon the latter's return to Paris, 14 March, to offer

an Anglo-American guarantee to France as an alternative basis for French security. This guarantee, as Harold Nelson has argued, "constituted a signal success for Lloyd George's diplomacy," with its goal of the commitment of American power to uphold the continental peace settlement in the vital western sector.[62] Lloyd George's move was also basic to the grand strategy of cooperation with America set down in the December 1918 meetings of the Imperial War Cabinet. Now this strategy encountered not only the strong French insistence on "physical guarantees" to supplement the Anglo-American offer but also major differences with the Americans on the question of reparations and a looming confrontation on naval policies.

The latter issue centered on the threatening new naval bill before the United States Congress. This bill was designed explicitly by the American administration as a club with which to coerce Allied governments into compliance with the American peace program should heavy-handed methods be called for.[63] Attempts by British and American naval officials to come to some agreement had resulted in a heated deadlock by the last week of March. Both sides resorted to their biggest guns, the Americans forswearing any modification in their naval program until the peace was signed and the league in operation, the British threatening to ruin the whole league project.

Faced with concurrent crises in Anglo-French and Anglo-American relations and the growing specter of bolshevism in Eastern and Central Europe, Lloyd George withdrew to the quiet of Fontainebleau on 22 March to put in what he termed "the hardest forty-eight hours' thinking I have ever done."[64] At Fontainebleau, the prime minister undertook the first major review of British peacemaking strategies and tactics since the previous December. With him as his principal advisors were Hankey, Kerr, and Henry Wilson. Montague also attended, but there was no Foreign Office representation.[65] The major strategic themes that emerged from the discussions of 22–23 March and were embodied in the Fontainebleau memorandum of 25 March included the warning that a vindictive peace might drive Germany into the arms of Russia, with the result that "all Eastern Europe will be swept into the orbit of the Bolshevik revolution and within a year we may witness the spectacle of nearly three hundred million people organized into a vast red army under German instructors and German generals equipped with German cannon and German machine guns and prepared for a renewal of the attack on Western Europe."[66] To prevent such an occurrence the prime minister advocated a peace based on liberal principles of justice, which could be accepted and implemented by a German government, and which avoided provocations for future wars. The major portions of the memorandum were aimed at France, with advice to accept the Anglo-American guarantee offer in lieu of a policy of territorial dismemberment of Germany.

A second theme of the Fontainebleau discussions centered on Anglo-American relations. With the Anglo-American guarantee to France already promised, British leaders adopted a hard bargaining line on the American naval program. One of the earliest working papers at Fontainebleau, a memorandum by Kerr and Hankey entitled "British Empire Interests," listed as the first requirement "strict limitation of German naval strength. An agreement with the United States of America as to naval shipbuilding."[67] The paper went on to specify the tactic to be used in realizing this requirement: "Signature of League of Nations Covenant by British Empire to be conditional on such an agreement." This tactic was then incorporated into subsequent drafts of the Fontainebleau memorandum.[68] The memorandum, as delivered to Clemenceau and Wilson on 26 March, stressed the importance of creating a league of nations as an effective guardian of international right and an alternative to bolshevism. But the memorandum predicated the success of any such league—and even its creation—on prior inter-Allied agreement on naval and military limitations: "The first condition of success for the League of Nations is, therefore, a firm understanding between the British Empire and the United States of America and France and Italy that there will be no competitive building up of fleets or armies between them. Unless this is arrived at before the Covenant is signed, the League of Nations will be a sham and a mockery. It will be regarded, and rightly regarded, as a proof that its principal promoters and patrons repose no confidence in its efficacy."[69] Part II of "Outline of Peace Terms," annexed to the Fontainebleau memorandum, directed an even more ominous warning to Wilson. The covenant was to be "signed as a separate Treaty by those Powers that are admitted," and acceptance was to be subject to a series of conditions, with the first "an agreement between the principal members of the League of Nations in regard to armaments which will put an end to competition between them."[70]

The adoption of this tactic illustrated the general level of conviction on the league project shared by Lloyd George's immediate entourage. In fact the records of the Fontainebleau conference contain important revelations about how the prime minister and some of his closest advisors viewed the league in private. Sir Henry Wilson, for one, advised placing no confidence whatever in the league project. Wilson argued bluntly "that to build on the League of Nations was to build on shifting sands." While the claim was that the league would internationalize the world, Sir Henry argued that "in truth [it] was a machinery set up to interfere with everyone's business, and this by 3rd or 4th rate men and by 10th rate Powers."[71] Wilson represented an extreme antileague position and was probably alone in the sarcasm he expressed at Fontainebleau. Others recognized the importance of creating the league but showed little inclination to put much trust in its immediate contribution to British security. A working paper, dictated by Lloyd George himself, argued that a league of nations would undoubtedly help accommodate postwar difficulties but cautioned that it would take "generations for an organization of that kind to acquire the necessary authority to dictate the action of independent nations charged with angry emotions and moved by interests as well as patriotism." The paper predicted the league might well "split up into two great parties, as all great assemblies have a tendency to divide, into warring parties, first of all warring in words, and you have only to add one letter to make 'words' 'swords.' "[72] The working paper by Kerr and Hankey included in its outline of peace terms a tenth point: "League of Nations to be set up to deal with international quarrels, especially in the opening stages, and generally to keep small States in order."[73] Clearly, Wilson's contention that the whole peace settlement and future world security should be based squarely upon a league of nations found no supporters at Fontainebleau. In fact, Smuts's suggestion of December 1918 that the league project should serve as a bridge in formulating an Anglo-American world strategy now was supplanted by Lloyd George's tactic, also spelled out in December, that the league could be used as a hostage in managing Wilson.

The Fontainebleau memorandum, then, contained a strategy for peace based on liberalism and designed to contain French reaction as well as Russian bolshevism. The memorandum also included a strategy for security based on traditional British naval hegemony and the protection of the empire. Certainly a naval-imperial strategy held priority for Hankey over atlanticism, the league of nations, or a continental commitment. In appealing for impartiality and justice, in using the liberal principles of self-determination and disarmament against France and America respectively, and in threatening to ruin the league project to protect Britain's naval position, the Fontainebleau memorandum was worthy of Lloyd George's tactical wizardry. The memorandum had a counterproductive effect on both Clemenceau and Wilson.

Even before he had received a copy of the Fontainebleau memorandum, Wilson determined once and for all to scotch the rumors still circulating that the covenant was to be separated from the treaty. The president chose to bring this matter directly before the Council of Four, which had just been established in an attempt to deal at the highest level with the divisions and delays in the peace conference. Accordingly, on 25 March at Wilson's insistence, the first decision taken by the Council of Four reaffirmed that the covenant would be included in the peace treaty.[74]

This decision, however, did not divert Lloyd George from his tactic of using the league to exact naval concessions from the Americans. The next day he revealed to Cecil the new tactics to be employed. Cecil had come to seek advice on an appropriate formula for protecting the Monroe Doctrine in the covenant. It was apparent that a covenant reservation protecting the doctrine was essential for Wilson to undermine Senate opposition. To Cecil's alarm, the prime minister opposed the inclusion of any reference to the doctrine in the covenant. When pressed, he admitted that "his real reason for resisting it was that he wanted to have something to bargain with, and he was anxious to induce the Americans to give up their plan of building ships against the British."[75] Cecil argued in vain against this line of action. He was instructed to inform Wilson that the matter must be taken up directly with the prime minister. The president was so informed that same day, and on 27 March Cecil told House that until a naval agreement had been reached, Lloyd George would neither agree to the inclusion of the covenant in the treaty nor sign the treaty itself.[76]

A deadlock of nearly two weeks resulted during which not only Anglo-American relations were severely strained but the peace conference itself came perilously near disintegration. Concurrent with the Anglo-American "naval battle of Paris," the peace conference entered a critical state on the Rhineland and Saar issues. Cecil resented the prime minister's tactics and repeatedly threatened resignation. On 4 April he wrote to Lloyd George objecting to the heavy-handed tactics of the admiralty and demanding information on government policy concerning the league and the Monroe Doctrine: "Does it mean that your policy is no longer favourable to the League? If so, please let me know."[77] In a letter to his cousin Balfour on 5 April, Cecil left no doubt as to the depth of his estrangement from the prime minister. Lloyd George's tactics, if they became public knowledge, would put the league project "on the rocks." The letter continued with an indictment of the prime minister's whole peacemaking strategy: "His whole attitude is really inconsistent with any belief in the importance of the League, and if that is really his feeling in the matter I doubt very much whether the League can be made a success as long as this government remains in office. It can only work with the hearty cooperation of the British and Americans." Cecil concluded with a bitter warning of resignation:

> My own position is becoming, as you will see, an exceedingly difficult one. I accepted the invitation of the government to come out here in charge of the League of Nations section, in the

express belief that it was going to be made a genuine part of the British policy, and pushed with all the strength of the government behind it. If that was no longer to be the case, I ought to be told quite definitely that the policy of the government has changed. I certainly am not prepared to try and carry out a policy which, in my judgment, is wrong in itself, and exceedingly hazardous to a cause in which I passionately believe, and to which I am pledged by every obligation of honour.[78]

Despite Cecil's threats, the deadlock continued until 6 April, when Wilson, sick of Allied obstruction tactics, called for the *George Washington* and prepared to return to America. Wilson's threat to leave had the desired effect on the French. It also seems to have moved Lloyd George to seek some way through the Anglo-American impasse. House conferred with the prime minister on 7 April, and the next morning Lloyd George instructed Cecil to discuss outstanding issues with the colonel.[79] In the next few days, thanks largely to the industry of Cecil, an understanding was reached.[80] In a letter of 9 April to Cecil, House promised that if the peace included the league of nations, the United States would be ready to "abandon or modify our new naval program."[81] House also intimated that the American government would be "ready and willing" to consult the British government on a yearly basis concerning naval programs. While this compromise failed to satisfy Lloyd George, who desired the Americans also to halt construction of American ships not already begun under the 1917 program, the agreement reached the next day ran substantially along the lines of this letter from House. The 10 April memorandum embodying the agreement expressed also the possibility that construction of ships not yet begun could be delayed until after the peace signing.[82] The memorandum stressed the aversion felt by the president to any program of naval competition and pointed to the desirability of joint Anglo-American naval negotiations directly after the signing of the treaty. The "naval battle of Paris" thus ended in a stand-off rather than a victory for either side. But the deadlock had been breached and, since Lloyd George no longer refused to countenance a reservation on the Monroe Doctrine, progress was once again possible in the work of the League of Nations Commission.

The League of Nations Commission reconvened 10 April to study the changes suggested by its drafting committee (which had continued its work during the impasse on the Monroe Doctrine) and to resolve the remaining issues of substance.[83] Geneva was finally adopted as the seat of the league. The principal item of business, however, concerned provision for a Monroe Doctrine reservation. Cecil gave strong support to the president as if to atone for the recent sins of his government. The French, however, put up lengthy and tenacious resistance to Wilson's proposed reservation of the Monroe Doctrine under Article 10. Perfectly aware of the political plight of the president, the French pointed out the obvious injustice and illogic of specifying a diplomatic doctrine of one state—a doctrine that lacked clear definition and carried historic isolationist implications. If the doctrine was not inconsistent with the covenant, why should it be specifically reserved? If it must be included, why should it not be defined? It took all of Wilson's patience and skill and a stirring midnight oration to overrule the French objections. Early in the morning of 11 April, the commission approved the reservation, not as part of Article 10 but, to meet French objections partially, as a separate new article.

The commission held its last session the evening of 11 April, readily passing most of the changes put forward by the drafting committee.[84] There were still outstanding issues, however, that gave rise to acrimonious debate. The Japanese withdrew proposals they had previously submitted for a moratorium on war preparations during periods of crisis after the British reiterated arguments illustrating the futility and hazards involved in this suggestion. Regarding Article 15, when a British amendment was passed which left members of the council free to decide individually how they would respond if a state refused to comply with a unanimous council recommendation, Bourgeois remarked sarcastically that the whole idea of obligation had disappeared. Consequently, Bourgeois argued, it would be necessary "to continue and to conclude separate alliances, inasmuch as the League admitted its inability to offer a formal guarantee of protection to its own members." Discussion of Article 20 brought another French attempt to rephrase the Monroe Doctrine reservation in a way unacceptable to the president. After further argument, Wilson declared the French amendment not adopted. The French reserved the right to bring the matter before the plenary session of the peace conference.

The final form of the covenant's preamble was discussed last. The Japanese had been waiting patiently for some time to present an amendment incorporating the principle of racial or national equality in the covenant.[85] Much behind-the-scenes activity had occurred in an attempt to find a formula that would satisfy the Japanese without incurring the absolute veto of the southern dominions. No arrangement of words could be found to disguise the fundamental impasse on this issue. The Japanese had lobbied on behalf of the principle of racial equality with a quiet but understandable tenacity. Hughes, on the other hand, voiced the implacable opposition of Australia and New Zealand to recognition of any principle that threatened the "white only" policy of immigration— an opposition equally shared by the west coast states of America and the province of British Columbia in Canada. The Japanese now submitted their minimal request—merely "endorsement of the principle of the equality of Nations and the just treatment of their nationals."[86] No one attempted to deny the overwhelming justice of the Japanese proposal. Several delegates, including the French and Italians, spoke in its favor. An embarrassed Cecil stated the opposition of his government to this obviously just, but politically explosive, amendment. When the Japanese insisted on a formal vote, Wilson declared the amendment not adopted since the affirmative vote was not unanimous. By this device the president spared Cecil the ignominy of casting a negative vote.

After this unhappy episode, the commission cleared up a few procedural items and provided for an organization committee to begin work on preparing the league for operation. Given the disappointments, disillusion, and bitterness that had marked the final sessions of the commission, no one felt at all inclined to offer words of inspiration celebrating the conclusion of the commission's efforts. The tides of idealism had ebbed greatly since 14 February.

Cecil had one more important step to take before the covenant could be laid before a plenary session of the peace conference. On 21 April the British Empire delegation met twice to consider the revised covenant. Cecil explained that the criticisms submitted by the dominions had been given careful attention and had resulted in several changes. The new draft took care "to avoid the impression that a super State was being created." These words, however, failed to satisfy dominion leaders, and Cecil was confronted with a barrage of criticism. The Canadians pressed for assurance that the dominions were clearly eligible for election to the council of the league. Cecil assured the dominions that such was the intention and agreed that the covenant should be amended to refer to "member of the league" rather than "state" so as not to prejudice the standing of the dominions in any way.[87] Borden also protested that the Canadian objections to Article 10 had not been met. Cecil related how attempts to amend this article had been unsuccessful and claimed that the article would be qualified by Article 19. This explanation was not enough for the Canadians. Doherty brought forward an argument that would be used frequently by Canadian officials in the next few years: "The proposal constituted in effect a system of mutual insurance, but was it fair to place the same liability upon all? The risks to which different members of the League were subject were by no means equal. In Canada, for instance, the risk of invasion was remote, while in France or in some Balkan States it might be great. Accordingly the element of consideration in the contract was violated by unfairness." Doherty continued by arguing that the covenant involved greater liabilities for Canada than those that had formerly existed under the empire. Borden still thought Article 10 should be omitted. Its inclusion "would mean in effect that Canada should not join the League."

Cecil replied to the Canadians by insisting that a fundamental principle of the covenant was that all nations had an interest in the preservation of peace. The argument of differing liabilities did not recognize that it was impossible to foretell how a conflagration, once lighted, would spread. The remainder of Cecil's reply was devoted to putting a minimalist construction on the meaning of Article 10. Members were pledged to preserve territorial arrangements only against "external aggression." It was impractical that members should go to war on issues remote from their own interest. Hence, the council would determine the means whereby this obligation was to be fulfilled. The council could only act on unanimous decisions and must include all parties interested in the question under consideration. Cecil then pointed out that if Canada were ever asked to contribute militarily to a league operation, "a Canadian representative must be invited to attend the Council, and if he disagreed there was an end to the matter." Cecil did not attempt to explain how any security could be derived from the article, given this interpretation of its operation.

Both the admiralty and the Australians objected to certain provisions in the revised Article 8. Cecil defended the article, explaining that the government would not be bound by anything to which it had not agreed. The admiralty's contention that governments should be free to exceed agreed limitations merely upon "notification" of the council, instead of by "concurrence," would result in the article's complete futility, according to Cecil.

Cecil then addressed himself to changes that had been introduced to meet American objections. Article 16 had been amended slightly to meet certain American constitutional requirements concerning declaration of war. No longer could any league member be committed to ipso facto war in defense of the covenant; war could only be declared unilaterally, according to the constitutional arrangements prevailing in each member state. Cecil explained the commission's feeling that the extreme measures contemplated in the article should only be brought into force in the extreme instance of a definite "resort to war" in violation of covenants. The reference to the Monroe Doctrine had been necessary in order to ensure the assent of the United States Senate to the covenant. Wilson had denied that the doctrine excluded the League from intervention in the American hemisphere for peaceful purposes or that the converse side of the doctrine was isolationism.[88]

Cecil's defense of the revised covenant left the dominion prime ministers with many lingering misgivings and the feeling that little had been done to meet their earlier criticisms. Later both Hughes and Borden insisted that the British Empire delegation have time to reconsider the final covenant before its submission to the peace conference.[89] As it turned out, no time was found for such a discussion.

Clearly, there was little enthusiasm within the British Empire delegation for the type of league fashioned by Wilson and Cecil. Hankey had already decided not to risk his career on the league of nations. He had wrestled long with the offer of becoming the league's first secretary general, tempted by the prospect of exercising his administrative talents on a world stage. He had gone so far as to draft an organizational plan for the secretariat, based explicitly on his experience as secretary to British and Allied institutions and designed to facilitate a major, if covert, political role for the secretary.[90] Hankey was convinced, however, that the league would succeed only if it received the strong support of British political leaders. The soundings he took on this point were all discouraging. Esher advised him at an early date that if he went to Switzerland, he "would be a wasted force for England." The league, should it survive, could be entrusted to less accomplished hands. Hankey's talents were needed at home developing a "new England" and a new imperial Commonwealth.[91] Curzon, soon to replace Balfour as foreign secretary, doubted very much whether the league would turn out to be the great instrument of world pacification that its creators desired. The league, Curzon predicted, would experience "many and great disappointments" and might well fail. Curzon advised Hankey to remain as "the most valued and influential servant of your own country," rather than wasting his talents on such an "impersonal and soulless international bureau" as the league secretariat.[92]

Balfour similarly advised Hankey to remain in Britain. Cecil Hurst warned that Miller, his American counterpart, did not believe the covenant would pass the United States Senate.[93] The determining advice, however, came from the prime minister. Hankey had earlier advised Lloyd George that he wished to have nothing to do with the league unless the government planned to give the new institution full support and to develop it into an organ of great importance in world politics.[94] On 18 April there was an opportunity to discuss the matter at length with Lloyd George after they had returned together from London to Paris. The options placed before Hankey were continued service to the British cabinet—the world's most powerful body—or service in an international institution, which, however promising, was totally unproven.[95] Hankey was convinced, and he immediately wrote to Cecil withdrawing his name from consideration as a possible secretary general.[96] That evening Hankey confided to his diary that his visit to London had persuaded him that "the British Empire is worth a thousand Leagues of Nations."[97] The position of secretary general was subsequently offered to Eric Drummond—a less influential figure than Hankey, but one more dedicated to the spirit of the league.

The final draft of the covenant was presented before a plenary session of the peace conference by President Wilson on 28 April. Wilson spoke briefly, explaining the principal changes made in the 14 February draft covenant. The president nominated Sir Eric Drummond as the league's first secretary general. Belgium, Brazil, Greece, and Spain were designated the first nonpermanent members of the council. A committee was authorized to prepare plans for organizing the league, establishing its headquarters, and arranging for the first assembly meeting. The Japanese delegation expressed deep regret over the failure to incorporate the principle of racial equality in the covenant. The French made yet another lengthy defense of their proposals concerning arms inspection and an international military staff. Pichon's suggestion that the principality of Monaco be added to the list of states invited to join the league was too much even for Clemenceau, who cut him off tersely. The covenant was then adopted unanimously, but without celebration, by the conference.[98]

The covenant laid before the 28 April plenary session of the peace conference formed the first section of the treaty presented to the Germans at Versailles on 7 May. The covenant was also incorporated into subsequent peace treaties with the other enemy powers. Cecil and Wilson had won the battle for the covenant at the peace conference, but Wilson had been forced to pay a heavy price in concessions to the Allies in order to keep the league project intact. The struggle for the covenant had been won over the opposition of the French, who put no trust in an unarmed league, and over attempts by the British government and the dominions to base the league on very different foundations. In their victory, however, both Cecil and Wilson had alienated important sections of their countries' political elites. For Wilson, the crucial battle for the covenant and the treaty in the Senate lay ahead. Cecil, more than anyone else, deserved credit for the successful outcome of the second phase of the work of the League of Nations Commission. By the end of the struggle, he, too, was estranged from Lloyd George and his circle, who, Cecil felt, cared little for the league. Yet, both Cecil and Wilson knew that if the covenant were to result in the creation of a functioning international organization, the support of the British and American governments was absolutely vital. In the crucial months immediately ahead, when the foundations of the league were being constructed, the fortunes of the whole project depended largely on the outcome of the struggle in the United States Senate and equally on the support of the British government.

8 War No More for Ten Years: Retreat from the Covenant

In a statement to the press after having reluctantly signed the Treaty of Versailles, Smuts voiced the hope of many who shared his concern at the harshness of the settlement that the League of Nations could provide the path of escape out of the ruin brought about by the war. He continued: "But the League is as yet only a form. It still requires the quickening life, which can only come from the active interest and the vitalizing contact of the people themselves. The new creative spirit, which is once more moving among the peoples in their anguish, must fill the institution with life, and with pacific ideals born of this war, and so convert it into a real instrument of progress."[1] The period from May to December 1919 witnessed the first phase of the attempt to translate the formal league into an organism possessing the life and spirit spoken of by Smuts. These initial months perhaps marked the most critical interlude of all in the league's genesis.

During this time the league's organizing committee, meeting in London under the impetus of House and Cecil, set the preparatory machinery of the league in motion and established the secretariat. At the same time Eric Drummond, the secretary general, recruited an international staff, which laid plans for the first meetings of the council and the assembly and attempted to chart the ground rules for the new international organization in world politics. Proleague associations continued their fight to bring public support to the league cause. Concurrently, the great powers were determining their attitudes and policies on what role the league should play in the post-war international system. The most dramatic debate on the league occurred, of course, in America. But no less significant a debate occurred in Britain as the government began formulating strategies and policies to protect the interests and security of the empire in the postwar world. When the Americans defaulted on the peace treaty in late 1919, the future of the league—indeed its very existence—became dependent on the policies of the British government and the support of the British people.

The final draft of the covenant, published on 26 April, received a mixed reception from British officials. In attempting to institute an international security system of enforced peace based on territorial guarantees, obligatory procedures for resolution of disputes, and sanctions to punish aggressors, the covenant was a long way from the type of league favored by the prime minister, his closest advisors, the Conservatives and dominion leaders. Aside from George Barnes, who was absorbed in the creation of the International Labour Organization and who, in any event, carried little weight in government circles, no British minister offered public support to the final version of the covenant. In private, there were serious misgivings about the type of league projected by the covenant. Writing to his wife early in May, Hankey argued that the prime minister and his entourage were already alienated from the league: "The more we look at the famous Covenant the less we like it!" Plans were already being made to continue using the Supreme Council as the principal forum for postwar diplomacy rather than the league: "The real League of Nations will be the Council of Three (or Four)."[2] Sensing where the real power would lie, Hankey was anxious to continue as secretary to the Allied councils and glad he had turned down the position of secretary general to the league.

Lloyd George made clear his criticisms of the final shape of the league to Cecil over breakfast on 3 May. Cecil found the prime minister "inclined to curse the covenant of the League on various grounds, particularly because there were four small Powers on the Council."[3] At the meeting of the British Empire delegation held on

5 May, Lloyd George returned to this criticism. It was "unthinkable that the present system of membership of the Council could last." The five great powers on the council, representing roughly seven hundred million people, shared authority with four small powers, representing fifty million people at most. To the prime minister, it was "unreasonable to suppose that any Great Power could tolerate a position in which these four representatives might possibly take action which would involve that Power in war."[4]

Eric Drummond, faced with major and completely novel challenges in filling out the structure of the league, received little support from the British government. When, in mid-May, Chancellor of the Exchequor Austen Chamberlain was presented with a request for a £100,000 credit by the organizing committee, the response was an offer of merely £5,000. Chamberlain resented this unexpected demand, particularly since the French and Americans, pleading constitutional difficulties, were contributing nothing. Only after a lengthy dispute between the Foreign Office and the Treasury Board, and strong representations by Balfour and Curzon, was a £24,000 advance found for Drummond in July. Chamberlain complained bitterly to Balfour about Wilson's leaving "his offspring on our doorstep."[5]

Cecil resented the parsimony of the Treasury Board and found himself becoming more and more suspicious of and estranged from the government through the spring and early summer of 1919. In the debate within the British Empire delegation over revision of the peace treaty after its initial presentation to Germany, Cecil joined with Smuts and others who argued strongly in favor of moderating many of the harsher features.[6] Writing to the prime minister on 27 May, Cecil insisted that the treaty was "overwhelming." The territorial and economic provisions violated both the spirit and the terms of the professed Allied war aims as put forward in the Caxton Hall address and President Wilson's Fourteen Points. Most critical, Cecil emphasized the general fear that "the present Treaty may be an unsound basis on which to erect the League."[7]

When German protests and counterproposals had been received, those within the British Empire delegation who favored softening the harshness of the treaty suggested that one positive step was to promise the Germans an early invitation to join the league. Smuts argued that the British Empire delegation should press to have Germany admitted to the league "as soon as the Treaty was signed." Lloyd George, though favoring major concessions in other areas, acquiesced in the French opposition to immediate admission of the Germans to the league, where, it was felt, they would exploit Allied differences. The prime minister advised a waiting period of no longer than twelve months to allow time for Allied disputes to settle down; then the Germans would be invited to join the league.[8] Cecil subsequently submitted a memorandum to the prime minister advising admission of Germany to the league within "a few months" if the new government had given genuine proof of its "pacific tendency." This step would be highly popular among European neutrals, would be a severe blow to bolshevism everywhere, would prevent a German counterleague, and would establish the league once and for all as part of the European system.[9]

In the final terms granted Germany, few significant concessions were made. Regarding the league, the Allies merely denied any "intention of indefinitely excluding Germany or any other power from the League." If proof of Germany's intention to fulfill her treaty obligations was forthcoming, then there was no reason why she could not be invited to join the League "in the early future."[10] This concession, along with others on territorial and financial matters, failed to satisfy those, like Cecil and Smuts, who deplored the harshness of the settlement. Cecil left Paris on 9 June, disappointed that Lloyd George had failed to overcome French resistance to an early invitation for German admission to the league and glad to be getting away from the frustrations of the conference.[11] With Wilson and Smuts, Cecil saw the League of Nations as one bright spot in a very dark situation. But would the government make full use of the league to put the world back on the right track?

Both Smuts and Cecil, like Wilson, looked to public opinion to support and sustain the league of nations project. Smuts directed his appeal to "the peoples in their anguish" to bring spirit and life to the league, privately telling C. P. Scott that the diplomats were "all against" the league and would probably try to sabotage it.[12] Cecil plunged into the activities of the League of Nations Union. In June the union organized a campaign to increase membership and build financial support. The campaign was launched 13 June with a large rally in the Royal Albert Hall. With Viscount Grey presiding, an audience of 10,000 heard speeches by Grey, Cecil, Clynes, representing labor, and national religious leaders welcoming the covenant of the league and commending the work of the union.[13]

In July a reconstruction committee chaired by Cecil submitted plans to the union for redefining its objectives and operations in light of new conditions. The underlying theme of Cecil's report, accepted by the union, was that efforts must concentrate on building a powerful lobby in Britain to ensure that the government carried through with the construction of the league and placed the league at the center of British foreign policy. Cecil's report specified the necessary tactics:

> 1. Formation in all parts of the Empire of groups of persons who will promote and popularize the principles of the League.
> 2. Vigorous propaganda to arouse and maintain national interest in the work of the League, and to secure public support for the League in carrying into effect the principles of its constitution.
> 3. Bringing influence to bear upon Members of Parliament and governments throughout the Empire, and rallying all political and national organizations to the support of the League.
> 4. Organizing research and discussion upon matters of international concern, and influencing education in schools and universities so as to increase public relations and promote a just appreciation of the principles and spirit of the League.[14]

The union found a sympathetic audience among a postwar public dedicated to the slogan, "Never Again." Though dogged by recurring financial problems,[15] it sustained a wide-reaching program of proleague activities and established a network of branch organizations, all the time building up its membership. Hundreds of meetings were organized and countless pamphlets distributed.[16] The liberal press opened its pages to publicize the work of the union and editorialized regularly on behalf of the league.[17] With the union's leadership largely dominated by Asquith Liberals, Cecil, as chairman of the executive committee, was anxious to attract prominent Conservatives and solicit the backing of labor.[18] Several Conservatives were brought into the executive, but more important, labor, disappointed that the covenant had not projected a more radical "peoples' League," rallied to the support of the union by the fall of 1919.[19] On 6 November at a Trades Union Congress in Glasgow, Henderson, Clynes, Thomas, Snowdon, and other Labour leaders endorsed a resolution calling for national propaganda in favor of the league. The league was portrayed as complementing the work of the Socialist International while initiating "the greatest experiment tried upon the face of the earth." The union was commended to all who wished to see an end of war.[20]

The League of Nations Union had launched a great fall campaign on 13 October with a mass rally in Mansion Hall.[21] The lord mayor read messages from the king and prime minister, and Asquith gave the major address, followed briefly by Cecil, Clynes, and Venizelos, the Greek prime minister. On 11 November the union organized seventy League of Nations Day rallies in cities and towns throughout the country. At the London rally, Balfour and national religious leaders addressed a full house at the Queen's Hall. By late 1919, with its meetings well attended and its membership 14,665 as of December and rapidly increasing, the union functioned as Britain's most influential pressure group on foreign affairs.[22] The league of nations project continued to attract solid support through the mainstream of British politics, with hostility only from the extreme Right and Left. With a good press and powerful backing from the churches, the league enjoyed a public support that the government could not afford to disappoint.

While the government was aware of the public support for the league, it was nevertheless anxious to place its own interpretation on how the league should operate. In June, with the Treaty of Versailles due to be presented before Parliament, the government had published a white paper on the covenant that clearly revealed the conservative definition British leaders wished to place on the league's role in world politics. British leaders did not want the covenant viewed as the constitution of a superstate, rather as a solemn agreement between sovereign states that consented to limit their complete freedom of action on certain points in their own interests and in the interest of the world at large. The League of Nations Commission, recognizing that one generation could not hope to bind its successors by written words, had assumed throughout its work that, in the last resort, the league would depend on free consent. Thus, the ultimate and most effective sanction "must be the public opinion of the civilized world." The league could not compel cooperative behavior: "If the nations of the future are in the main selfish, grasping and warlike, no instrument or machinery will restrain them."

In describing the operation and intent of Article 16, the government commentary argued that each league member would remain its own judge about what contribution it would make to a common military action. Any standing international staff or strategic planning to implement military sanctions was ruled out: "It would plainly be impossible for British officers to take part in concerting plans, however hypothetical, against their own country, with any semblance of reality." Recognizing the meager security against sudden aggression afforded by the league under these conditions, the commentary advocated that members make their own arrangements for immediate self-defense, "relying on such understandings as they have come to with their neighbours previously for this purpose." The commentary stressed that the covenant did not preclude defensive alliances so long as their terms were published, but rather welcomed them insofar as they tended to preserve peace.[23]

Presenting the Treaty of Versailles to the House of Commons on 3 July, Lloyd George chose his words carefully in dealing with the League of Nations. The league was portrayed as "the greatest guarantee of all" in the settlement. However, "this great and hopeful experiment" was only rendered possible if other conditions were met. In words perhaps intended mainly for the Americans, the prime minister warned that unless nations were willing to disarm and to enforce respect for treaties, the League of Nations would be just like similar conventions in the past, "something that would be blown away by the first gust of war or any fierce dispute between the nations." Nevertheless, had the league been in existence during 1914, Lloyd George argued that war could have been averted. Given the savagery of mankind, perhaps not all wars could be prevented, but if the league prevented just one war, then it would have justified itself. In any event, the prime minister believed the "experiment" deserved a fair trial and cautioned his colleagues not to "sneer" at it. The league might not "stop everything," but it would at least make war more difficult. Lloyd George, therefore, viewed it "with hope and with confidence."[24]

Debate at this time on the peace treaty and the future course of British foreign and defense policies increasingly revealed serious divisions of opinion—divisions that often centered on the expected role of the League of Nations. On the one hand, there were Donald Maclean, representing the independent Liberals; Clynes, representing labor; and Cecil, who, together with the forces of the League of Nations Union, believed the league heralded a radical change in the international system and in the requirements of British security. The traditional themes in pursuing British security—naval hegemony, armaments, alliances, the balance of power—would have to be subordinated to a strategy designed to achieve peace and security for all through the League of Nations. Moreover, defense expenditure could be reduced drastically. For Cecil, if "the jungle theory of international relations" were to continue, he could "see no hope for the world."[25] British officials such as Arthur Salter and Frank Walters, launching new careers as international civil servants, based their hopes and their planning in the league secretariat on the fundamental assumption that the league marked the beginning of a new era in international relations.[26]

The government, on the other hand, while quite willing to countenance the league as a "noble experiment" and a valuable forum for international cooperation and consultation, firmly opposed any abandonment of traditional safeguards in favor of the potential security promised by the league. Once again, the issue of security emerged as central to the league question, with a clear division between those who believed in a new collective approach to security and skeptics who put their trust in traditional safeguards. The attitude of government leaders and officials became clearer through July and August in discussions on postwar strategy and defense estimates. In mid-July, when the prime minister and his entourage retreated to Criccieth for a conference on future economic policy, Hankey produced a wide-ranging study paper dealing with economic issues in the context of strategic planning. Hankey admitted the necessity of reducing defense expenditure to the lowest point "consistent with national safety." But he derided those "idealists [who] would have us believe that the establishment of the League of Nations was sufficient guarantee of the peace of the world." The paper revealed strong doubts about the cohesion of the league and its ability to function effectively, given the diversity of its membership and the inevitable conflicts of interest. Would the league survive a succession of failures or even one serious failure? Hankey contended, "While our policy must be to try and make the League of Nations a success, and it must become the focus of our foreign policy, it is an experiment on the success of which we cannot yet afford to base our national security."[27]

Outlining the conditions that future British strategy must be designed to meet, Hankey argued that Germany and Russia were exhausted and would remain so for years. The principal danger to European peace was eventual exploitation by Germany of Russian resources, but such exploitation was far distant and could be prevented with a proper policy. The United States, with an impregnable geographic position and massive commercial, military, and naval potential, was identified as the principal threat to British security. However, given the Anglo-American community of ideals, this threat, too, was a "remote contingency."[28] With these considerations in mind and considering the requirements for maintenance of law and order throughout the empire, Hankey recommended a two-power standard as a possible basis for naval planning. This standard would in theory exclude the United States, but Hankey emphasized that the British fleet should never be allowed to sink below the level of the American navy. The paper made a cursory examination of other future military and aerial requirements and concluded by suggesting that the Committee of Imperial Defence be reactivated to draw up a policy on which navy, army, and air force estimates could be worked out.

In discussions on defense estimates, which followed in August, little reference was made to the League of Nations. An admiralty memorandum referred to the possible role the league might play in arranging general naval reductions "if it makes an auspicious start," but the major hope for reducing naval estimates centered on the possibility of dissuading the Americans from completing their 1916 program and, thereby, rivaling the British fleet.[29] Milner, as colonial secretary, spoke publicly of the "somewhat stoney soil" in which the league would have to strike root, pointing to the development of the British Commonwealth as the major hope for the future. If, in reaching out after a dubious *pax mundi*, Britain let slip from her grasp a well-tested *pax Britannica*, she would be substituting "the shadow" for "the substance."[30]

On 15 August the cabinet ruled that in framing their estimates the service departments should proceed on the assumption that "the British Empire will not be engaged in any great war during the next ten years, and that no Expeditionary Force is required for this purpose."[31] No reference to the League of Nations was made in the strategic decisions laid down by the cabinet. Given the failure to acknowledge that the league made any difference in strategic calculations, Cecil concluded to House that the government was "not particularly favourable to any such League of Nations as the rest of us have in mind," but wanted "one that will give some advantage to the British Empire."[32] On 13 August, however, the government had announced that Lord Grey would undertake a special mission to the United States, pending the appointment of a permanent ambassador. In Grey's instructions, three major issues in Anglo-American relations were singled out: naval rivalry, the Irish problem, and the League of Nations.[33]

Through the summer of 1919 British leaders had been following the development of the debate in America over the peace treaty and the League of Nations with growing concern. The friction of Anglo-American bargaining during the peace conference, together with naval competition and a revival of tensions over Ireland, had severely tested enthusiasm for atlanticism within British governing circles. Nevertheless, in spite of the rough methods sometimes used in handling Wilson at Paris, a central feature of British peacemaking strategy remained cooperation with the Americans and perpetuation of this cooperation in postwar world politics. Kerr had responded to Hankey's distrust of the Americans and skepticism on the league with an extensive defense of continued efforts to fuse an Anglo-American strategy with a far-reaching joint liberal imperial mission. Kerr charged this Anglo-American strategy with keeping peace by referring disputes to the League of Nations, "which we will mainly control," and with cooperating in a movement "for the education and betterment of the backward races of the world." If the "stagnant pools of humanity" in Africa and Asia were not "cleaned up," according to Kerr, they would soon "infect" the rest of the world. American resources, wedded to the ideals of British liberal imperialism, would be vital to such a mission.[34] Kerr argued that only the league could provide the forum for postwar Anglo-American and Allied cooperation for peace and progress. Otherwise, diplomacy would sink back into "the ancient and hopeless" channels of the European foreign offices and embassies.[35]

British leaders continued to view the League of Nations primarily in the context of on-going Anglo-American cooperation. A league without the United States offered few attractions and, indeed, contained potentially dangerous liabilities. Even so warm an advocate of the league as Lord Bryce thought that "without the United States, the whole thing will fail."[36] Yet, as the summer of 1919 passed into autumn, American ratification of the peace treaty and participation in the League of Nations became less and less certain. In the absence of a permanent ambassador, Wiseman and R. C. Lindsay, the British chargé d'affaires, provided the main intelligence on American politics when Wilson returned from Paris in early July to defend his handiwork. From an analysis of the forces of opposition arrayed against the president, Wiseman contended that although the Republicans were attacking the treaty and the league and attempting to gain political capital against the president, they were divided among themselves and not likely to succeed. A group led by Senators Lodge and Knox hated Wilson and would attempt to attach reservations to the treaty; an extremist faction of irreconcilables, led by Borah and Johnson, opposed the league and any American participation in foreign affairs; the majority of the party, however, was still uncommitted and waiting to see how Wilson would be received. Wiseman concluded that there was "no serious opposition in America to the League of Nations" and that the president could "force the Senate to ratify the Treaty without amendment or reservation."[37]

After an interview with Wilson on 18 July, Wiseman advised the British government that the president was taking the opposition seriously but was unwilling to countenance any amendments or reservations. Wilson firmly believed he had the support of the people and was contemplating a tour to raise support for the treaty. In confidence, however, he admitted that "some reservation defining or interpreting [the] language of one or more clauses of the Covenant" might be necessary in order to secure a really satisfactory majority. But such a measure would be a last resort. The president also suggested that the course of ratification by the Allies was being watched closely by the Senate since Lodge was spreading the story that he had received letters from a member of the British government that indicated the proposed Republican amendments would be welcomed at Westminster.[38]

Lindsay took the Senate's opposition more seriously and thought the president was erring in not seeking the cooperation of the "mild reservationists." He believed, however, that interpretive resolutions would suffice in the end.[39] Wiseman's early optimism proved unfounded and failed to convey the intense personal and partisan hatred that the treaty debate was now generating in America. As Lodge used his control of the Senate Foreign Relations Committee to submit the treaty to exhaustive criticism and to build up opposition to the league, Wilson embarked in early September on a desperate mission to take the issue of the treaty and the league directly to the people.[40] After three weeks of constant traveling and speaking, Wilson collapsed in Pueblo, Colorado, and suffered an incapacitating and near-fatal stroke in Washington on 2 October.

The president's collapse did nothing to abate the intense hatred of his enemies in the Senate. The collapse did mean that the forces of the administration were without leadership from the White House in the bitter struggle that was reaching a climax. On 6 November Lodge introduced into the Senate a series of fourteen reservations to the treaty behind which he had united the various factions of the Republican party.[41] The most important of these reservations effectively exempted the United States government from any obligations under Articles 8, 10, and 16 of the covenant, granted to Congress the right of unimpeded withdrawal from the league any time it so desired, declared the primacy of the Monroe Doctrine, and empowered the United States government to define unilaterally what constituted a question within its exclusive domestic jurisdiction. A final reservation, aimed at the British Empire, exempted the United States from any league decision in which any government together with its dominions or colonies cast more than one vote. The preamble to the reservations gave them clear constitutional and international legal consequence by presenting them as a condition of ratification and requiring that they be accepted by three of the four principal Allied signatories before Senate approval of the treaty would be effective.

The Lodge reservations set the stage for the critical phase of the drama in the United States Senate. They also presented major policy dilemmas for the British government. Grey arrived in Washington 27 September, just before the president's collapse. He soon found himself absorbed in the fate of the peace treaty and the problems raised by the Lodge reservations, particularly those relating to the League of Nations. The former foreign secretary had temporarily left retirement in the hope that he could render major service by promoting Anglo-American cooperation in the final stages of the peacemaking. Grey was a strong atlanticist as well as a proleaguer and had agreed to the mission only after assurances had been written into his instructions that the government's policies on the league, the navy, and Ireland would facilitate cordial relations with the Americans. The British hoped that Grey would be able to work closely and sympathetically with Wilson, using House once again as the major channel. House, who had had a major hand in arranging Grey's mission, did all he could to promote a role for himself as a liaison between the British and American governments in seeing the treaty and the league through the current storm. With this role in mind, House followed Grey back to the United States.[42]

Despite Grey's prestige and the apparent advantages he held, his mission was bedeviled almost from its inception. Even before arriving in America, Grey and Curzon, his chief at the Foreign Office, were seriously estranged. Grey's insistence on not only writing his own instructions, but also appeasing the Americans on imperial, naval, and Irish issues, sat ill with Curzon, whose priorities remained focused on India and the Middle East rather than on the Atlantic or the league. Curzon was worried that Grey's support for Wilson on the league issue might lead to trouble with the Republicans.[43] Then, after receiving three memoranda by Grey on Armenia, Syria, and the Anglo-Persian agreement, with the insistence that the latter must be submitted to the League of Nations council as proof of the government's faith in the league, Curzon could contain his annoyance no longer. Writing to Lloyd George, Curzon charged that Grey was "too disposed to dictate a policy to your government than [sic] to carry out their views, and I shall for that reason be glad when he fails."[44]

Upon taking soundings in Washington, Grey learned of the difficulties he faced. In a letter to Lloyd George, Grey explained that Wilson was desperately ill and probably would not be able to resume public business; it was improbable that he would ever see the president; House was without influence; and there would probably be "chaos in American policy" for some time, compounded by a wave of anti-British sentiment.[45] Grey argued that, given the president's collapse, the reason for his special mission had disappeared, and he recommended the early appointment of a permanent ambassador and his own return by the end of the year.

In the meantime, however, Grey was anxious to do whatever

he could to promote good relations with the Americans and facilitate passage of the treaty. He urged Lloyd George to announce a generous new policy for Ireland, as this question was increasingly poisoning all aspects of Anglo-American relations.[46] Grey repeatedly pressed the government to clarify publicly the question of the voting powers of Britain and the dominions under Article 15 of the covenant to counter opponents of the league, who portrayed America as being outvoted six to one in the league by the British Empire.[47] Such clarification would have involved an intimation by the government, perhaps in response to a planted question in Parliament, that no votes of the British Empire would be used in the assembly of the league in a dispute under Article 15 to which any member of the empire was a party.

Grey received little support from Curzon or the government for his suggested tactics. After Curzon initially agreed that Grey's interpretation of voting procedures under Article 15 was correct, he cautioned against any formal declaration on the subject since the dominions had not been consulted.[48] Grey responded that Curzon's advice appeared to him "an incredible statement of impotence," and "very unfair as well as unintelligible to those in the United States who are friendly to us."[49] Grey continued without success to urge upon the government the wisdom of a public announcement.

Grey also pressed for instructions on what approach to take in light of the Lodge reservations. In private and secret discussions with Lansing, Grey gave his personal opinion that the preamble requiring the other powers' consent to the reservations was "most objectionable" and that any reservation violating the written commitment of Lloyd George, Clemenceau, and Wilson regarding the rights of the dominions to nonpermanent membership on the league council would have to be repudiated. He advised, however, an interpretive reservation defining voting procedures in the assembly would not be objectionable as long as it was phrased in general terms and did not imply a subordinate position for self-governing dominions. Reviewing the other reservations with Lansing, Grey suggested alternatives and compromises that would be "less objectionable" and "less damaging" to the league, making it clear always that he spoke as an individual and "a strong supporter of the League of Nations" and could not commit his government concerning matters on which they had not been consulted. Grey suggested to Lansing that the Senate might drop all the reservations if one reservation asserted the right of the Senate to give advice and consent to instructions directing the American representative on the league council. Grey acknowledged, however, that Wilson might consider this proposal more objectionable than all the other reservations put together.[50]

The British government had initiated an urgent policy debate on the question of reservations as soon as the content of the Lodge reservations became clear. On 30 October the prime minister requested the views of the Foreign Office about whether the British Empire should formally ratify the treaty before it was known if the American government would ratify only with reservations concerning the covenant and what these reservations would be. Lloyd George also requested a legal opinion from Hurst, the Foreign Office chief legal advisor, about the effect on the British Empire if it ratified the treaty without reservations while the United States ratified with reservations. The fears of the prime minister were explicit: he did not wish "the British Empire to be bound by all sorts of obligations which the Americans may afterwards say that they do not feel themselves also to be bound by."[51]

On 2 November Hurst produced a memorandum dealing with the legal implications of American reservations proposed by Lodge. Assuming the Senate passed and the president accepted the proposed reservations, Hurst argued that no reservations could affect or modify the rights or obligations of any other signatory to the treaty without its consent. The American reservations could not be deposited, therefore, without the consent of Germany and the Allied powers. Refusal to accept the reservations might lead to an American refusal to ratify the treaty. The United States government was under no legal obligation to ratify, and the test that must be applied in determining British policy should be "whether it is preferable that the USA should stand outside the Treaty altogether, or come in on the terms proposed." Hurst then described the reservations, arguing that those on limitation of armaments, trade with a covenant-breaking state, and withdrawal from the league would profoundly affect the basis on which the League of Nations was established. He concluded that previously, notably in the case of China and Shantung, Allied policy had been to allow no reservations.[52]

The issues dealt with by Hurst set the framework for an intensive debate during the next two days among senior members of the Foreign Office, Kerr, Hankey, and Balfour. In a conversation with Hurst on the evening of 3 November, Kerr revealed in detail the questions that occupied the prime minister's thoughts. The covenant of the league imposed considerable obligations upon its members, particularly upon great powers, and "most of all upon the British Empire with its world-wide interests." The one factor that led the representatives of the great powers at Paris to accept the obligations of the covenant "without exhaustive consideration" was the belief that all the nations, especially all the great powers, would be in the same boat and share the burden imposed by the covenant. Consequently, any modification of the obligations entered into by a great power or a failure to ratify the treaty would profoundly alter the situation. In particular, if by any chance the United States might not join the league or might join on a basis differing substantially from other members, then "the question of the British Empire undertaking these obligations at all ought to be considered very carefully." Would it be safe for the Britsh government to ratify the treaty before the American position was clarified? The conversation brought out the dangers in further delay of ratification. Not only the league but the whole peace treaty stood in danger of being lost by further delays. The British government should have made its agreement to the covenant dependent upon the same condition attached to the Anglo-American guarantee to France, thereby freeing itself if the American government refused to ratify. But Kerr felt it would be humiliating to admit this serious oversight now. After Britain had taken so prominent a part in the creation of the league, it would be difficult to persuade the British public and the world at large that the whole scheme must be abandoned because of the Senate reservations.[53]

In response to the difficulties raised by Kerr, Hurst recommended that the best policy would be to stand by the covenant as drafted, refuse all reservations, and, if necessary, proceed with ratification without America, endeavoring at the same time to render the league as nearly universal as possible by the early inclusion of the former enemy powers and all the neutrals. Hurst, who had established friendly links with Wilson and his entourage at the peace conference, argued that a refusal to countenance American reservations would strengthen the position of the president's party and hopefully contribute to an unconditional ratification. Subsequently, Lord Hardinge, head of the Foreign Office, approved this strategy and suggested that Grey be given freedom to communicate the government's position privately to those with influence in American politics.[54]

The next day Hurst discussed matters at lunch with Hankey, Kerr, Balfour, and Drummond. Hankey and Kerr argued strongly that the League of Nations could not really exist if the United States was not a member. Balfour was inclined to agree with them. Drummond, on the other hand, passed on an opinion of Colonel House that even if the United States did not enter the league initially, the pressure of public opinion would force America to join within a year or so. Kerr then suggested an addition to the strategy advocated by Hurst. Britain should ratify the treaty, but if the American government had not agreed to become a member of the league by the time of ratification, then Britain should accompany her ratification with a notice of intention to withdraw from the league at the end of two years. This strategy would enable the treaty to come into force. At the same time the world would be informed that, in the British view, "the basis of the League of Nations was so changed as to render the scheme unworkable."[55]

On 7 November, Curzon, now foreign secretary, forwarded records of these discussions to the prime minister with an outline of the suggested tactics. Curzon advised that, if the policy of ratification with or without the United States was accepted, Lord Grey should be informed immediately about British intentions. There would be ample time before the ratification date (scheduled at this point for 25 November) to decide whether or not to accompany ratification with a notice of withdrawal from the league.[56] A further memorandum of 10 November by Kerr added yet another feature to the tactics endorsed by Curzon. In light of British opposition to reservations, if the Americans did stay out, and if the British Empire accompanied its ratification with a notice of withdrawal from the league, the government should simultaneously propose a general conference to revise the covenant so that all could enter the league on equal terms. Such a policy, of course, would have meant the abortion of the league project designed by Wilson and Cecil and, perhaps, the eventual substitution of the type of league favored by Kerr, Lloyd George, and the British government as well as the Lodge group in America. In the meantime, however, Kerr argued that Britain and the Allies should stand firm against any reservations, thus putting great pressure on the United States to come into the league on the original terms.[57]

Balfour conveyed the government's concern over reservations and the league in a thinly veiled warning to the United States on 11 November. Speaking to a large League of Nations Union rally in the Queen's Hall, he defended the league project and declared his unwillingness to discuss the future of international relations with any man who did not accept a league of nations in some form or other. A necessary condition for the league's success, Balfour emphasized, was that all the great powers bear an equal share of the burden. If one power were allowed reservations, these would inevitably be copied by other powers, and the future of the league would be "dark indeed." Balfour concluded with words intended for Lodge and his followers: "Therefore I venture to say to any friends of mine in any country who are considering their responsibility at this great moment of the world's history that they ought clearly to understand that, unless they are prepared to bear an equal share in an equal task, they are threatening with ultimate dissolution the whole of that new system which all of us, in common with the great nations, most sincerely desire to see work effectively."[58] The next day Kerr privately informed Grey and House that the British government would not be able to accept "any American reservations whatever."[59] On 14 November, after Anglo-French discussions in

London, *La Presse de Paris* published an officially inspired statement advising that while the Allies would view interpretive reservations as a purely domestic matter for America, they would find it "difficult to accept" any reservations requiring their assent as conditions of American ratification.[60] Privately, Grey and Jusserand, the French ambassador, advised Hitchcock, Democratic leader in the Senate, that the Lodge reservations were unacceptable.[61]

The warnings of Balfour and the Allies had no effect on the course of events in America. The key reservations were passed in the Senate by 15 November, and the crucial votes on the Treaty of Versailles took place 19 November. On Wilson's instructions the Democrats prevented the passing of the treaty with the Lodge reservations. A motion for consideration of the treaty with milder reservations suggested by Hitchcock was also defeated with the Republicans holding firm. Finally, the Lodge forces blocked passage of the treaty free of all reservations. The Senate adjourned with nothing to show but deadlock, neither side commanding the necessary two-thirds majority.

The American deadlock deepened the political quandary of the British government. For Kerr, the experience of pursuing American cooperation in world politics had become profoundly disillusioning. Writing to the prime minister immediately after the Senate vote on 15 November, Kerr argued that the prevailing assumption that America would cooperate in running future world affairs was no longer tenable. Without America, the league and the mandate system would not work. Kerr felt that Britain should reshape her European and Middle Eastern policies accordingly.[62] Cecil, too, despaired at the course of events in America and talk in Britain about the "ultimate dissolution" of the league project. Speaking in Parliament on 17 November, Cecil considered that the Lodge reservations amounted "almost to a repudiation by the United States of the Covenant." Although pessimistic about the final outcome of the American dilemma, Cecil drew a conclusion different from Kerr's: "Whatever happens, the league must go on, for that is the sole hope of permanent peace."[63] Henderson, Thomas, and the Labour party solidly supported Cecil on this point.

But what could the government do? Was there any way to influence directly the outcome of the American struggle? A public government announcement of opposition to any reservations might strengthen the president's hand. Such a step, however, not only involved a major intervention in American domestic politics but also offered little chance of breaking the power of Lodge. Alternatively, to announce publicly a willingness to tolerate reservations offered little chance of breaking Wilson's intransigence.[64] Even if enough Democrats in the Senate broke rank and joined Republicans in passing the treaty with reservations, the president had let it be known the treaty would be pocketed.[65] In any case, Grey warned that the government must be extremely careful in saying anything that might allow either of the American factions to blame Britain for the death of the treaty.[66]

Grey by now was becoming more and more dissatisfied with his position in America. The problem of dominion voting rights in the league dragged on. Curzon and Milner informed Grey that dominion opposition, especially from Australia and South Africa, made any public declaration on the matter "most unwise."[67] For Curzon, to allow a rift on the sensitive issue of voting rights in the league to develop publicly would be "disastrous" for the empire.[68] For Grey, who lined up Canadian support for his position, the "calamity" would be the failure of the Senate to pass the treaty.[69] What was necessary now was to do everything possible to facilitate an acceptable compromise on reservations. Grey insisted on maintaining his interpretation of voting precedures and simply told the government to accept his resignation if they could not support him.[70]

Curzon and Grey also divided on the naval question. Grey advocated a unilateral policy of reduction by Britain in the hope the Americans would follow this example. Curzon argued that it was part of Grey's instructions that, if Britain agreed to reduce, the Americans should be asked and should promise to do the same: "He took out our pledge and now we are to forego theirs."[71]

Grey's position in Washington was further bedeviled by a messy issue of protocol. Lansing, on instructions from the White House, informally and then formally, had requested that the British government recall a member of Grey's staff. Kennedy Crawford Stuart, who was running the social side of the embassy for Grey, apparently had offended the Wilsons politically and socially during Reading's ambassadorship. Crawford Stuart's alleged indiscretions included criticizing Wilson's decision to attend the peace conference, circulating an off-color ditty about the Wilsons, and spreading scandal about a member of the president's entourage. Indeed it seems that Crawford Stuart doubled as a British intelligence agent, and had been responsible for "bugging" the boudoir of a lady friend of Bernard Baruch, when the lady in question had previously been the mistress of Bernstorff, the former German ambassador. A widower suffering from partial blindness, Grey was personally and socially dependent on Crawford Stuart's services. Perhaps not fully aware of the Wilsons' feelings, Grey resisted carrying out the administration's instructions without an inquiry. Consequently, the White House, dominated by Mrs. Wilson during the president's incapacitation, rigidly denied Grey access, even on an informal basis.[72] Finally exasperated, Grey expostulated to Curzon that he hadn't come out of retirement "to put up with this indignity and nonsense."[73] Reviewing the frustrations of his American experience for the prime minister, Grey argued that his situation was "more intolerable to me than any position I have ever been in."[74]

Grey had still received no detailed instructions regarding the Lodge reservations. He informed Curzon on 23 November that House thought the British and French ambassadors were to be consulted privately by the State Department and possibly Senators Hitchcock and Lodge about a compromise on reservations. Grey asked for any observations or instructions Curzon or the prime minister cared to forward.[75] Curzon replied to Grey on 27 November in a lengthy telegram setting forth the government's views on the American impasse.[76] The foreign secretary's directive followed closely what Hurst and Kerr had advised previously and was based largely on a revised Hurst memorandum of 18 November, which had been circulated to the cabinet.[77] Curzon argued strongly that the admission of any American reservations would violate the principle, adopted as the basis for the peace, that "the external political obligations incumbent upon civilized States should in future be shared in common and that this principle should be substituted for the disordered conditions which prevailed hitherto in international relations." To allow particular powers to stand outside the settlement or enter only on a special footing would reintroduce the uneasy conditions that had prevailed in prewar European politics. Consequently, the British government hoped that the United States would accept the treaty as it stood. Indeed, the government doubted very much "whether it will be possible to admit the United States to the League with any reservations having an external effect without automatically breaking down the Covenant."

Curzon particularly objected to the reservation on Article 10. For Britain to be bound by the obligations of this article while the United States remained free "would place a burden upon the resources of the Empire which no government could face." Furthermore, such a situation would destroy any confidence that smaller powers placed in the league for protection. The reservation on Article 16 compounded these difficulties, for, if America stood outside an economic boycott and traded with covenant-breaking states, the whole machinery of the boycott would be brought to grief. The reservation on domestic questions, including the American-Canadian boundary, could never be accepted by the British government. Likewise, the reservation that would allow America to exceed any agreed arms limitation when it felt threatened would destroy all hope for disarmament and render Article 8 of the covenant worthless. Curzon concluded that the government felt

> ... so impressed with the difficulties that would accrue if the United States fail to become a party to the Treaty or endeavoured to become a party on terms in any way approximate to those indicated in the reservations, that we should have to consider the question of giving notice to withdraw from the League at the end of two years. Such notice of withdrawal might be coupled with intimation that if within two years all the States accepted the Covenant or agreed to amend the Covenant in a way to render it universally acceptable, the notice would be withdrawn.

In a separate telegram on the same day, Curzon passed on an ingenious means around the American deadlock, which had been suggested to Frank Polk, acting head of the American Peace Commission, when the latter visited London from Paris on 24 November.[78] The proposal suggested the United States ratify the treaty as it stood, accompanying ratification with a notice of withdrawal from the league in two years unless necessary modifications were made in the covenant.[79] Such a plan would allow Republicans and Democrats to fight the next election on this issue and give the next administration a free hand to withdraw from the league or insist upon amendments. Curzon added that this plan would enable the Americans to avoid the charge of "having wrecked the Treaty and the League," and, in any event, all powers would very likely want to amend the covenant after one or two years.[80] Although the foreign secretary did not specify it, this tactic also made it possible to avoid alienating Wilson in the short run while preparing to work with the Republicans should they head the next administration. Grey was advised to make whatever use of the suggested tactic he thought wise.

Curzon's instructions could hardly have pleased Grey. After a meeting with Elihu Root in New York, Grey advised Curzon on 28 November that the British government must be prepared to accept either an American failure to ratify or ratification with the Lodge reservations virtually unaltered. The most to be hoped for was an alteration of the preamble and the dropping of the first part of the Lenroot reservation, which violated the specific commitments to the dominions concerning their status in the league. He thought it very doubtful that Wilson would accept such a one-sided compromise, but rather, like Curzon, would probably view the reservations as destroying the treaty and the covenant.[81]

By early December, still burdened with the Crawford Stuart affair, frustrated by his failure to see the president or even make contact with the White House, and not in sympathy with his own government's hard line on reservations, Grey concluded that his presence in Washington served no useful purpose. A long private letter that Grey received from Curzon about this time must only have added to Grey's aggravation.[82] In the letter Curzon defended the government's policy on the Anglo-Persian treaty and the voting powers of the empire in the league, welcomed the difficulties over the Anglo-American guarantee treaty to France, which would make the latter more pliable on Near and Middle Eastern questions, and advised that Crawford Stuart was not worth a serious quarrel with the Americans. On 6 December, despite Curzon's advice that he should remain in America, Grey informed the foreign secretary of his intention to leave for England on 2 January, arguing that the greatest service he could render Anglo-American relations was to explain the situation in Washington to a British audience, with a "full understanding of [the] American point of view."[83] Privately, Grey let out that he was shocked by his government's disregard of his recommendations and that he intended to "shake them out of some of their misapprehensions by face to face conversations."[84] Grey thought it important for him to be in London "to persuade the British government" to accept the treaty with the necessary reservations.[85] Moreover, the former foreign secretary was already arranging with the editor of the *Times* to put his views across publicly after his return to Britain.[86]

Grey was not alone in favoring an accommodating approach to the American reservations. Arthur Willert from Washington urged the wisdom of Grey's approach upon his chiefs at the *Times*.[87] Smuts advised Lloyd George that most of the reservations were of "minor importance" and did not affect the real essence of the covenant. According to Smuts, only the limitations on the voting power and the status of the dominions were unacceptable. Otherwise no efforts should be spared to bring the Americans into the league, even if they "were not quite reasonable." The British government should not allow the situation to drift but should take the initiative in securing a workable compromise that would give the league a fair start.[88] Cecil and Drummond now also favored accepting the Americans on their own terms to ensure United States participation in the league.[89]

The most important initiative behind a European attempt to break the deadlock in the United States Senate originated within the American Peace Commission with the support of Clemenceau. Just

before the peace commissioners were ordered to leave Paris and return to America, General Tasker Bliss drew up a memorandum suggesting how the Allies might influence the American situation. Bliss
argued that a principal reason for the current impasse in America
was the belief of the president and his party that the Allies also
opposed acceptance of the proposed reservations. The deadlock
could only be broken by a compromise involving the retention of
some reservations and, perhaps, the modification of some others.
Such a compromise could only come if the Allies indicated to Wilson what reservations, modified or not, they would accept. Furthermore, none of the proposed reservations embodied anything to
which the Allies could not subscribe. Bliss proposed a joint Anglo-
French declaration, accepting the ten or eleven reservations that
related to the covenant on condition that the others, which related
more directly to the peace with Germany, be abandoned. Bliss concluded with a rather deftly worded promise:

> If you will give to the Treaty and to the President the support of
> your declaration that you have no objection to certain of these
> reservations upon the acceptance of which the American people
> are very earnest, and that others of them will be acceptable to
> you by certain indicated modifications, the ratification of the
> Treaty by the United States Senate will be made as certain as
> possible, even though there may be one or two or three of the
> reservations which you entirely reject. . . . If you really wish the
> Peace Treaty to be ratified by the United States, it is possibly
> easily within your power to accomplish it. But there is not time
> to be lost.[90]

Clemenceau communicated Bliss's unsigned memorandum to
the British government on 9 December, as he prepared to attend an
inter-Allied conference in London scheduled for 12–13 December.[91]
With both the treaty and the Anglo-American guarantee endangered
in America, the French government perhaps felt fewer qualms than
the British about supporting reservations and working with Wilson's enemies. In fact Clemenceau had switched from his tactics of
September, when he was expressing a new-found support for the
League of Nations and backing the president's program, and was

now secretly working with Lodge through Jusserand in return for Lodge's promise to support the Franco-American guarantee treaty.[92]

Just before the Allied conference began, Grey telegraphed important information and advice from America. By now Grey, almost certainly, had entered into direct, highly secret, discussions with Lodge, along with Jusserand.[93] Given the pressure of the irreconcilables, Lodge had little desire to modify the reservations beyond perhaps a change in the preamble. In three telegrams sent on 11 December, after discussions with Lansing, Elihu Root, and probably Lodge, Grey conveyed the following information: Lansing thought that any intervention by foreign governments would only do harm; there seemed little hope that either the Republicans or the Democrats would significantly modify their positions; the treaty might be passed minus the league after the Senate's Christmas recess, and then the league would be made into a party issue in the upcoming presidential and congressional elections, with the fight being concentrated on the anti-British issue of the six votes to one; and the Franco-American treaty would be ratified minus the league. It was Grey's opinion that, serious though the Lodge reservations were, it would be better to accept all of them "in the last resort rather than lose [the] whole of [the] Treaty." In practice, the reservations would probably not affect American performance in the league. Grey advised that it was most important that the British Empire and the French government should reach an agreement on reservations and have it recorded eventually in writing with the American government, so that British reluctance to accept reservations could not be made responsible for the league's becoming an issue in the American elections. All of this confirmed Grey in his decision to return home where, he argued, he could be more useful and explain the situation with greater candor.[94]

Bliss's memorandum and the possibility of joint action to influence the American situation were considered in Anglo-French discussions on 13 December. Lloyd George, reiterating Lansing's opinion that Allied intervention in opposition to, or in support of, reservations would only stiffen the Senate or alienate the president, advised that discussion of possible Allied action be deferred until Grey returned.[95] No action was taken, therefore, on Bliss's memorandum.

After the London conference, the government faced renewed parliamentary pressure to clarify its intentions on the treaty and the league. On 18 December Maclean, representing the Liberals, urged Lloyd George, who had often allied himself with difficult causes in the past, "to gird up his loins, and his courage" and proceed with the league, even if the Americans failed to come in.[96] Cecil followed by expressing uneasiness and suspicion about the government's real intentions concerning the league.[97] He admonished Churchill, the secretary for war, for making slighting public remarks on the league. Was the government making the necessary departmental preparations for the commencement of the league's operations? Was the government going to go into the league intending to make it a success, putting all the power of the country behind it? Cecil called for a reassuring statement, backed up by evidence, from the prime minister.

Later in the debate, Lloyd George replied directly to the questions raised concerning the government's league policy. The prime minister berated Cecil for casting suspicion on the sincerity of the government. He spoke briefly of how the government had done everything it could at Paris to further the cause of the league. The government had appointed two "zealots," Cecil and Smuts, to sit on the drafting commission and had supported their recommendations. There had been doubts during the peace conference about the wisdom of starting with a constitution "all written out, tabled, and with all the details." But the government had deferred to the views of its representatives, and the covenant had gone into the treaty. The government, however, could do no more until the treaty was ratified by its allies. On this point the difficulties came from America. The prime minister did not doubt that America would come in, but it would be very difficult if she came in on conditions that left her absolutely free while others had their hands tied behind their backs. The league must meet as a league of "equal nations."

With this foreboding opening, the prime minister nevertheless delivered vital words of reassurance on the league: "Without presuming in the least to say anything about what America is doing or is likely to do, the League of Nations is so vital to the peace of troubled Europe that the government are convinced that this country, at any rate, must go on with it." After speaking eloquently of the horrors of another war, Lloyd George gave the converse side of the government's league policy. The league would be supported, but the government would look elsewhere for the foundation of its security: "Until the League has been founded—until the League has been formally established, until we know that the nations of the world, including America, will work the League—we must make our own country secure. If Britain is insecure, civilization is insecure."[98]

The British government now proceeded to ratify the peace treaty. Ratification was not accompanied by an announcement of intention to withdraw from the league in two years unless America came in unconditionally or unless the covenant were amended to make membership on equal terms possible for all. Such an announcement would have been greeted with a storm of opposition from liberals, labor, and all those who supported the program of the League of Nations Union. Although few cabinet ministers would have shed any tears over the abandonment of the league, abandonment would have meant that certain sections of the peace settlement linked to the league would have had to be renegotiated. Allied leaders had no stomach for tampering with the Treaty of Versailles in late 1919. Still, on the same day as Lloyd George's speech in Parliament, Kerr informed Drummond that he thought the covenant in its present form was "done for."[99]

With Allied ratification the Treaty of Versailles entered into force on 10 January, 1920. The League of Nations Council officially inaugurated the league at a meeting in Paris, 16 January, with speeches by council members to mark the occasion. Curzon's remarks, however, contained little enthusiasm. The foreign secretary expressed the loyalty of the British Empire to "the spirit which underlies the Covenant" and declared the intention of his government to facilitate in every way the development of the league into a practical instrument for promoting international peace and cooperation. At the same time Curzon referred to the "anxious symptoms" surrounding the league's birth and ruled out any possibility of the league's functioning as a superstate or supersovereignty. The league was "an association of sovereign states whose purpose [was] to reconcile divergent interests and to promote international cooperation in questions which affect—or may affect—the world at large."[100] Clearly, the British government had its own reservations about the League of Nations.

Curzon's speech also expressed the hope that America might still join the league. This hope, however, did not last long. Senate factions, after a new series of intensive negotiations to strike a compromise, deadlocked once again in late January. Publication by the *Times* on 31 January of a powerful private appeal by Grey for sympathetic understanding of American constitutional and diplomatic traditions and willingness to accept most of the reservations in the larger interest of facilitating United States participation in the league failed to bring about the desired compromise.[101] A final failure of the treaty in a Senate vote of 19 March indicated that further efforts to break the deadlock would be futile.[102] Wilson was determined to make the league issue into "a great and solemn referendum" in the upcoming elections.

9   *Dilemmas of Security*

The League of Nations, as it emerged from the peace conference, embodied a multifaceted approach to the promotion of international peace, cooperation, and security. The league provided for the first time permanent political institutions to facilitate peaceful resolution of international disputes. It established new agencies and coordinated many already in existence to further international cooperation in nonpolitical or "functional" areas. It set forth a new code of principles, rights, and obligations to regulate the behavior of nations in international relations. Members pledged to seek agreement on arms limitation, to respect each other's territorial integrity and political independence, and to recognize that any war or threat of war was a matter of concern to the whole league. Each member possessed the "friendly right" to bring any threatening circumstance to the attention of the league. Clear procedures were spelled out on how disputes of a legal or political nature were to be dealt with by the league. Resort to war was forbidden until these procedures had been exhausted. Provision was made for the establishment of a permanent court of international justice. A mandates system was instituted with the league assigned indirect authority to monitor the transition away from traditional imperialism. Finally, the league pledged members to resist collectively any aggression against another member's territory or independence or any resort to war in violation of the procedures stipulated for peaceful resolution of disputes.

Most of the themes written into the covenant had a long history in the various phases and streams of the peace movement. But the immediate origins of the league lay in the response of Anglo-American liberalism to the challenge of total war and its social consequences under modern conditions. British liberalism and radicalism and the British Left played a leading role in defining the league idea and in mobilizing support for the New Diplomacy. While Wilson served as the major prophet of liberal internationalism, his ideas were consciously rooted in the history of British liberalism. The hope of Wilson, Cecil, Smuts, and the forces represented in the league of nations movement was that liberal solutions were as applicable to the problems of international relations as they were nationally. The old order, the international anarchy, could be transformed through an international social contract that would define the rights of nations and provide for the necessary political and legal organization of the world. Given peace and stability, prosperity would follow in the wake of a liberal international economy of open trade. The idea of a covenant, moreover, symbolized for the league's religious supporters the spiritual and moral underpinnings of the project. For Wilson, Cecil, and the nonpacifist section of the Christian peace movement, the league cause took on the form of a mission to give international expression to a social gospel of peace. Without the political, legal, and moral reform of the old order, liberals feared that war and revolution would sweep away the institutions and values that lay at the foundation of western civilization. A new order was needed to sustain a liberal, progressive view of the future against the ideologies of both revolution and reaction. The League of Nations stood as the principal expression of this new order and represented the heart of the ideological, political, and moral response of Western liberalism and Protestantism to the world crisis of 1914–18.

By the end of the war, the league of nations movement had captured the support of British public opinion, both secular and religious, and the British government stood committed to the project along with its allies. During the war British political leaders, beginning with Grey, had responded sympathetically to plans for a peace league. The idea also proved extremely useful in building diplomatic rapport with America and, later, in retaining the political support of the British Left when liberal war-aims manifestos were needed. Studies of the league idea by officials, however, demonstrated that there were many difficulties involved. Despite Cecil's best efforts, the government reached the end of the war without any specific policy on the question of international organization and without having been able to exchange official opinions with the Americans.

For Cecil, Barnes, and the League of Nations Union, a strategy of liberal internationalism offered a definite alternative to traditional methods for seeking security. Senior diplomatic and military advisors and nearly all members of the cabinet, however, rejected this suggestion. When the Imperial War Cabinet discussed policy on peacemaking in late 1918, the league idea was examined in the context of traditional strategies and imperial interests, Anglo-American relations, and domestic politics. Since Smuts played the leading role in preparing the government's brief for the peace conference, the league project was given a central place in a complex strategy that attempted to integrate atlanticism, imperialism, and internationalism. But Conservatives and realists in the cabinet made it clear that Smuts's *Practical Suggestion* was quite unacceptable in several respects, particularly when it seemed to violate national sovereignty in such areas as disarmament, mandates, and sanctions. The policy that emerged from the Imperial War Cabinet as defined by Lloyd George was that the league project would be supported as part of a general Anglo-American strategy in the peacemaking, but that traditional strategies and interests, naval and imperial, would not be sacrificed. The league would be a limited league to promote conference diplomacy and international cooperation, but it would not be accorded executive power. Following the approach advocated by Hankey and Kerr, the prime minister pointed explicitly to the Imperial War Cabinet and the Supreme War Council as the precedents to be emulated.

At Paris when it was learned that Anglo-American preliminary negotiations on the league question were proceeding on a basis contrary to British policy, Lloyd George intervened and instructed Cecil at greater length. The league was to begin simply and modestly as a forum for diplomatic consultation under the control of the great powers and as an agency to promote international cooperation. Any attempt to construct an elaborate constitution or include wide-ranging obligations to resort to war in certain stated conditions would end either in futility or the alienation of the great powers.

The prime minister's intervention, however, had little effect and was not repeated. The British government's conception of the league stood no chance in the League of Nations Commission, given Wilson's desire for elaborate covenants and the insistence of France and the smaller powers that the league provide definite guarantees of security. Cecil stood much closer to Wilson than to his own government on this question and, although he attempted to qualify the general territorial and political guarantee of Article 10, which Wilson saw as the heart of the whole scheme, the guarantees remained. Like his friends in the League of Nations Union, Cecil favored a clear security function for the league and always insisted that sanctions must undergird provisions for peaceful resolution of disputes. Although Cecil attempted to put a minimal construction on the covenant in defending his work before the British Empire delegation, his critics remained unconvinced. Lloyd George, however, was willing to tolerate the results coming from the League of Nations Commission as long as Wilson did not frustrate the realization of other, more vital British interests. When a confrontation with the Americans arose on naval issues, Lloyd George, like the other Allied leaders, was willing to exploit Wilson's commitment to the league to exact concessions elsewhere.

Despite the contribution of Phillimore, Smuts, Cecil, and British liberalism to the creation of the League of Nations, the British government found itself in fundamental disagreement with the type of organization that emerged from the Paris Peace Conference. To a large degree this disparity was the government's own fault, given the haphazard lines of policy making and control fostered by Lloyd George and Balfour within the British Empire delegation. The opposition of the government and the leading dominions centered on those features of the covenant that attempted to institute a new system of international security. Sanctions, guarantees, and obligations to resist aggression had always presented the central dilemma, and this dilemma had been resolved in the way favored by Wilson and the internationalists of the league of nations movement.

The British government acquiesced in the final version of the covenant, anticipating that in practice it could be interpreted to suit British interests and that America would be a full partner in sharing the responsibilities of the league. When in late 1919 the latter assumption was negated by Wilson's failure to carry his program through the Senate, the British government reacted with bitterness and alarm. Rather than facilitating a strategy of Anglo-American cooperation in international relations as had been intended, the league (specifically Article 10) proved the rock on which such a strategy was grounded. There were powerful temptations for British leaders to abort the whole league project before it began.

Wilson and Cecil had fought tenaciously for the league at the peace conference, and deserved full credit for the personal and historical achievement associated with creating the world's first great international organization. However, given the present perspective on the history of international organization, much could be said in favor of the more limited approach to the league preferred by the British government. If the plan for a league placed before Cecil by Lloyd George on 31 January 1919 lacked the idealism and inspiration of Wilson's rhetoric, its vision, nevertheless, was firmly fixed on the power realities of international relations and Britain's diplomatic and strategic traditions. In its evolutionary approach, it envisioned realistic reform in the international system and embodied the hope that a lasting peace could be built upon a new world concert and balance of power that included America. Certainly, this approach would have received a sympathetic response from Lodge and the United States Senate. The British government's approach can be interpreted as representing a conservative world policy, in contrast to the radical-liberal internationalism of Wilson and the scorn for international organization shared by bolshevism and fascism.

Whatever criticisms British officials leveled against the covenant and liberal internationalism, Wilson, Cecil, and the League of Nations Union converted the mainstream of British society to their cause. After the war popular support for the league continued to grow, carefully nurtured and directed by the League of Nations Union among a generation committed to the slogan "Never Again," until the league and British foreign policy became almost synonymous in many government pronouncements. As early as 1916 Hankey had predicted that the British people, with their idealism, would be particularly prone to the allurements of a peace league. He also warned that such a league would create illusions of security that would greatly endanger the task of strategic planning. Hankey's words were largely borne out in the interwar period, when, with naval and imperial strategies in disarray, a continental commitment unthinkable, and America in diplomatic isolation, collective security under the league and appeasement became virtual surrogates for foreign policy and defense strategy, until a second world war destroyed the foundations of Britain's world power.

Notes

INTRODUCTION

1. David Lloyd George, *The Truth about the Peace Treaties*, 1:89, 274–82, and chap. 14.
2. Ray Stannard Baker, *Woodrow Wilson and World Settlement*, 1:chap. 14.
3. Frank P. Walters, *A History of the League of Nations*, pp. 19, 73.
4. E. A. Robert, Viscount Cecil, *All the Way*, pp. 155–56.
5. Henry R. Winkler, *The League of Nations Movement in Great Britain, 1914–1919*, p. 254.
6. A. J. P. Taylor, *The Trouble Makers*, pp. 17–18.

CHAPTER 1

1. The debate is analyzed in Michael Howard, *The Continental Commitment*, chaps. 1 and 2.
2. For the new advisory roles of the Foreign Office and the General Staff, see Zara S. Steiner, *The Foreign Office and Foreign Policy, 1898–1914*, and John Gooch, *The Plans of War*. Nicholas d'Ombrain has shown how conflict between the General Staff and the admiralty led to the eclipse of the Committee of Imperial Defence and the monopolization of strategic planning by the General Staff (*War Machinery and High Policy*, pp. 74–111).
3. Great Britain, *Parliamentary Debates* (Commons), 5th ser., 65 (1914):1801–19.
4. For cabinet politics through the crisis, see Cameron Hazlehurst, *Politicians at War*, pp. 25–117.
5. Radical reactions and behavior in the war crisis are analyzed in A. J. Anthony Morris, *Radicalism against War, 1906–1914*, chap. 10.
6. Great Britain, *Parliamentary Debates* (Commons), 5th ser., 65 (1914):2059–60.
7. John Clifford, *The War and the Churches* (London, 1914), in Keith G. Robbins, *The Abolition of War*, p. 32. The Reverend Dr. Clifford was a former president of the National Free Church Council and had led pacifist opposition to the Boer War.
8. *Daily Chronicle*, 7 August 1914.
9. *Nation*, 15 August 1914. Wells's response to the war is analyzed in Norman and Jeanne MacKenzie, *The Time Traveller*, chap. 19.

10. For an analysis of the new radicalism's prewar thought on international relations, see Morris, *Radicalism*, and A. J. P. Taylor, *The Trouble Makers*, chap. 4.

11. For the formation and history of the UDC, see Marvin Swartz, *The Union of Democratic Control in British Politics during the First World War.*

12. Swartz, *Union of Democratic Control*, p. 42.

13. Arno J. Mayer, *Political Origins of the New Diplomacy, 1917–1918*, p. 50.

14. Swartz, *Union of Democratic Control*, pp. 48, 60, 61, 225–27.

15. For analysis of the peace movement, see A. C. F. Beales, *The History of Peace.*

16. G. Lowes Dickinson, *The Autobiography of G. Lowes Dickinson*, p. 6.

17. G. Lowes Dickinson, *A Modern Symposium*, pp. 26–27.

18. Dickinson to C. R. Ashbee, 4 November 1914, Robbins, *The Abolition of War*, p. 49.

19. G. Lowes Dickinson, "The Way Out," pp. 345–46.

20. For Dickinson's role in starting planning for a league of nations, see E. M. Forster, *Goldsworthy Lowes Dickinson*, pp. 157–64; Dickinson, *Autobiography*, pp. 189–92; and W. H. Dickinson, "Note as to the Origin of the League of Nations Union," n.d., W. H. Dickinson Papers, vol. 403. See also Henry R. Winkler, *The League of Nations Movement in Great Britain, 1914–1919*, pp. 16–18.

21. For a detailed examination of the role of the Bryce group, see Martin David Dubin, "Toward the Concept of Collective Security." See also Keith G. Robbins, "Lord Bryce and the First World War," pp. 257–61. Bryce, highly respected as a scholar and Liberal politician, served as British ambassador to Washington, 1907–13.

22. Many of the early draft plans and much of the correspondence can be found in the Bryce Papers and the W. H. Dickinson Papers, vol. 402.

23. James, Viscount Bryce, *Proposals for the Avoidance of War with a Prefatory Note by Viscount Bryce. (As revised up to 24th February 1915)*. Private and Confidential: Not for publication. Bryce Papers; W. H. Dickinson Papers, vol. 402.

24. The *Proposals* were circulated widely in liberal and radical circles during 1915. Various comments and criticisms were compiled in a large chart, "Proposals for the Avoidance of War, Summary of Replies," n.d., W. H. Dickinson Papers, vol. 402.

25. W. H. Dickinson, "Note as to the Origin of the League of Nations Union"; Winkler, *League of Nations Movement*, p. 50. Rea was a junior lord of the Treasury and later a Liberal politician.

26. Williams was a Radical M.P.

27. D. H. Mills, untitled draft history of the League of Nations Union, W. H. Dickinson Papers, vol. 406. Keen was a lawyer and author of *The World in Alliance* (London, 1915); Unwin was a Fabian town planner and architect.

28. Ibid.

29. Ibid.; *League of Nations Society. Explanation of the Objects of the Society* (League of Nations Society Publications, no. 2. Printed for Private Circulation). London, 1916, p. 4. See also Winkler, *League of Nations Movement*, p. 51.

30. Gilbert Murray, "The British People and the League of Nations," P. Munch, ed., *Les Origines et l'Oeuvre de la Société des Nations*, 1:94; W. H. Dickinson, "Note as to the Origin of the League of Nations Union"; Winkler, *League of Nations Movement*, pp. 52–53.

31. Mills, draft history.

32. Robbins, *The Abolition of War*, pp. 107–9.

33. W. H. Dickinson, "Note as to the Origin of the League of Nations Union."

34. Early discussions on the league idea in America and the steps leading to the formation of the League to Enforce Peace are chronicled in John Latané, ed. *Devel-*

opment of the League of Nations Idea, 1:v–x, and 2:703–50; Ruhl J. Bartlett, *The League to Enforce Peace*, pp. 25–47; and Warren F. Kuehl, *Seeking World Order*, chap. 9. For an analysis of the thought of leaders of the League to Enforce Peace, see Sondra R. Herman, *Eleven Against War*, pp. 55–85.

35. Bartlett, *League to Enforce Peace*, pp. 40–42. Leaders of the American league had studied the Bryce *Proposals* and were in correspondence with the British group.

36. For the organization and campaign of the League to Enforce Peace through 1915–16, see Bartlett, *League to Enforce Peace*, pp. 43–83.

37. Leonard Woolf, *Beginning Again*, p. 183. The husband of Virginia, Leonard was one of the saner members of the Bloomsbury circle.

38. For the evolution of the Fabian schemes, see Winkler, *League of Nations Movement*, pp. 7–8.

39. Leonard Woolf, "An International Authority and the Prevention of War," pp. 1–24; and "Articles suggested for adoption by an International Conference at the termination of the present War by the International Agreements Committee of the Fabian Research Department," pp. 1–8.

40. Leonard Woolf, *International Government*. Here Woolf no doubt owed something to Norman Angell's *The Great Illusion* (London, 1911).

41. For Woolf's influence on Cecil and, later, the league of nations section of the Foreign Office, see the obituary notice by Philip Noel-Baker in the *Times*, 21 August 1969.

42. John A. Hobson, *Towards International Government*, and H. N. Brailsford, *The War of Steel and Gold*, Appendix. See also Winkler, *League of Nations Movement*, chap. 2.

43. Wells's schemes are analyzed in Winkler, *League of Nations Movement*, pp. 41–46.

44. Kerr's unsigned articles in the *Round Table* through 1915–16 are analyzed in John E. Kendle, *The Round Table Movement and Imperial Union*, pp. 250–51.

45. For debate on sanctions, see Beales, *The History of Peace*, pp. 222–23, 225, 241, 249–50, 261–62.

46. Joel Larus, *From Collective Security to Preventive Diplomacy*, p. 8.

47. Ibid.

48. Ibid., p. 11. Roosevelt's oft-quoted Nobel address was based almost entirely on an editorial by Hamilton Holt in the 12 March 1910 *Independent*.

49. LNS, *Explanation of the Objects of the Society* (1916), p. 18.

50. For the attack from the Right, particularly the *Morning Post*, see Winkler, *League of Nations Movement*, pp. 119–20.

51. "Mr. Ponsonby's Note on the suggested Amendment to the Proposals for the Avoidance of War," [n.d., c. November 1914], W. H. Dickinson Papers, vol. 402. The earliest draft composed and circulated by Bryce had contained no obligations to use collective force. ("When the War comes to an End," c. November 1914, Bryce Papers).

52. For the skepticism of labor leaders and the UDC on the league of nations panacea, see Taylor, *The Trouble Makers*, pp. 136, 142–44. Hobson was an exception and favored sanctions.

53. Lowell to G. Lowes Dickinson, 7 August 1915, W. H. Dickinson Papers, vol. 402. Dickinson later argued that although the inclusion of sanctions would alienate many pacifists from the league cause, he doubted "whether a League without this power of coersion would receive . . . the support of statesmen like Sir Edward Grey and Mr. Wilson" (*The Friend*, 29 September 1916, Keith G. Robbins, "The Abolition of War," p. 219).

54. "Memorandum on Mr. J. A. Hobson's Notes," 9 January 1915, W. H. Dickinson Papers, vol. 402.

55. Good modern treatments of the concept of collective security can be found in Larus, *Collective Security*; Roland N. Stromberg, "The Idea of Collective Security"; Inis L. Claude, Jr., *Power and International Relations*; Kenneth W. Thompson, "Collective Security Reexamined"; and Marina S. and Lawrence S. Finkelstein, eds., *Collective Security*.

56. The analogy of vigilance committee justice in the American West was first publicized September 1915 in an article by Lowell, "A League to Enforce Peace," *Atlantic Monthly*, pp. 392–93. The British analogy was first given currency in A. J. Jacobs, *Neutrality Versus Justice* (London, 1917). See also A. E. Zimmern, *The League of Nations and the Rule of Law*, pp. 178–79. Later in the war, Cecil, Wilson, and House each used this appealing but misleading analogy.

57. For the opposition of pacifists to a league to enforce peace, see Robbins, *The Abolition of War*, pp. 107–9, 134–36.

CHAPTER 2

1. The Earl of Oxford and Asquith, *Memories and Reflections: 1852–1927,* 2:47.

2. Ibid.

3. *Nation*, 14 March 1914, in A. J. P. Taylor, *The Trouble Makers*, p. 115.

4. Grey to T. Roosevelt, 20 October and 18 December 1914, in Viscount Grey of Fallodon, *Twenty Five Years*, 2:140–43.

5. Grey to Spring-Rice, 22 December 1915, F. O. 800/84. Also in G. M. Trevelyan, *Grey of Fallodon*, pp. 314–15.

6. Grey to Spring-Rice, 2 January 1914, Trevelyan, *Grey*, p. 315.

7. Spring-Rice to Grey, 24 December 1914, F. O. 800/84.

8. The colonel's first peace mission is analyzed in Arthur S. Link, *Wilson*, 3: 223–31; and Patrick Devlin, *Too Proud to Fight*, pp. 263–82.

9. House to Wilson, 9 and 10 February 1915, Charles Seymour, ed., *The Intimate Papers of Colonel House*, 1:352–53, 367–70. See also Keith G. Robbins, *Sir Edward Grey*, pp. 316–19.

10. House to Wilson, 23 February 1915, Seymour, *Intimate Papers*, 1:383.

11. Grey to House, 24 April 1915, ibid, 1:425. In subsequent British discussion of proposals to ensure freedom of the seas, Balfour and Asquith advised caution while Spring-Rice repeatedly warned Grey that America could never be trusted to enforce international obligations. Only Eric Drummond, Grey's private secretary, advised that it would be in Britain's interest to promote collective efforts at preventing future war and eliminating navalism as well as militarism. Discussions can be followed in F. O. 800/50, 58, 94, and 95. See also Devlin, *Too Proud to Fight*, p. 279.

12. House noted in a memorandum to Wilson his belief that "if every belligerent nation had a Sir Edward Grey at the head of its affairs, there would be no war; and if there were war, it would soon be ended upon lines broad enough to satisfy any excepting the prejudiced and selfish" (Seymour, *Intimate Papers*, 1:364). See also House to Wilson, 23 February 1915, ibid., 1:382.

13. Grey to House, 6 June 1915, Seymour, *Intimate Papers*, 1:54.

14. House Papers, 9–8; Seymour, *Intimate Papers*, 1:87. See also Grey to House, 14 July 1915, House Papers, 9–8.

15. Seymour, *Intimate Papers*, 2:89. Grey's reply was communicated by Spring-Rice, 13 October 1915. See also Link, *Wilson*, 4:102–4.

16. House to Grey, 17 October 1915, Seymour, *Intimate Papers*, 2:90–91. The president insisted upon the qualifying "probably." The American note, although dispatched on 19 October, did not reach Grey until about 8 November due to delays in shipping and decoding. Devlin, *Too Proud to Fight*, p. 383.

17. Seymour, *Intimate Papers*, 2:91, 98.

18. Ibid., 2:98, (received 25 November 1915).

19. Wilson to House, 24 December 1915, Arthur S. Link, *Woodrow Wilson and the Progressive Era: 1910–1917*, p. 199.

20. House to Wilson, 7 January 1916, Seymour, *Intimate Papers*, 2:116.

21. House to Wilson, 11 January 1916, ibid., 2:119–20. See also Link, *Wilson*, 4:114–15, and Devlin, *Too Proud to Fight*, pp. 396–403.

22. For the full text of this memorandum, see Seymour, *Intimate Papers*, 2:200–2. See also Robbins, *Grey*, p. 337; Link, *Wilson*, 4:131–41; and Devlin, *Too Proud to Fight*, pp. 431–71.

23. Seymour, *Intimate Papers*, 2:202.

24. "Addendum to the Proceedings of the War Committee on March 21, 1916, Most secret." Cab. 22/13/1. For most of the key documents and an analysis of debate on the House-Grey memorandum, see John Milton Cooper, Jr., "British Response to the House-Grey memorandum."

25. Grey to House, 24 March 1916, Seymour, *Intimate Papers*, 2:273–74.

26. House to Grey, 10 May 1916, ibid., 2:278–79.

27. Grey to House, 12 May 1916, ibid., 2:282–83.

28. Diary of Edward House, 13 May 1916, House Papers.

29. See Seymour, *Intimate Papers*, 2:283–92 for continuing House-Grey correspondence. For further discussion of the House proposals in the War Committee, see Diary of Maurice Hankey, 24 May 1916, Stephen Roskill, *Hankey*, 1:274. Hankey, who was not present at the secret session of the War Committee held on 24 May, learned from McKenna that the Army Council had threatened to resign if ministers insisted on an inquiry into the peace question. McKenna probably exaggerated the support of Asquith, Grey, and Balfour for American mediation.

30. Ray Stannard Baker and William E. Dodd, eds., *The Public Papers of Woodrow Wilson*, 2:184–88.

31. Spring-Rice to Grey, 30 May and 1 June 1916, Cab. 271/148. Also F. O. 371/2794.

32. See the interview with Edward Price Bell published in the Chicago *Daily News*, 13 May 1916, and widely reprinted (F. O. 395/45); and the interview with foreign press representatives in London, 23 October, published in the *Manchester Guardian*, 24 October 1916.

33. See particularly Grey's correspondence with Marburg in John H. Latané, ed., *Development of the League of Nations Idea*, 1:100–1, 103, 149, 163–64.

34. Grey to House, 28 August 1916, House Papers, 9–8. See also Robbins, *Grey*, pp. 340–42.

35. "The Future Relations of the Great Powers," 8 April 1915, Cab. 37/127. See also Robert J. Gowen, "Lord Haldane of Cloan (1856–1928)."

36. "The Future Relations of the Great Powers: Observations on the Lord Chancellor's Note," 21 April 1915, Cab. 37/127.

37. "Irresponsible Reflections on the Part Which the Pacific Nations Might Play in Discouraging Future Wars," printed for use of Cab., January 1916, F. O. 899/3. Initialed by Grey.

38. "Suggested draft in response to Private Telegram sent to Sir E. Grey," 24 May 1916, Cab. 37/148.

39. Hankey to Balfour, 25 May 1916, Balfour Papers, Add. Mss. 49704. Hankey and Balfour had discussed American designs for a peace league on 23 May. As head of the secretariat to the Committee of Imperial Defence and then, during the war, the War Council, the Dardanelles Committee, the War Committee, and, finally, the War Cabinet, Hankey enjoyed an influence and power far beyond a purely secretarial role. Probably more than any other man, Hankey kept the threads of British policy in his head and in his files.

40. Hankey subsequently initiated a historical analysis of peace plans by the naval historian Julian Corbett, working in the historical section of the Committee of Imperial Defence. Corbett concentrated on Wilson's 27 May proposal arguing that it was incompatible with his design for the freedom of the seas. Britain's naval superiority would remain the best guarantee of peace. Cab. 17/161.

41. On 10 April 1916, speaking to a visiting delegation of French politicians, Asquith pointed out that Germany's defeat would "pave the way for an international system which will secure the principle of equal rights for all civilized peoples" (*Times*, 11 April 1916).

42. For the war-aims debate in the fall of 1916, see V. H. Rothwell, *British War Aims and Peace Diplomacy, 1914–1918*, pp. 41–45.

43. [Sir William Robertson], "General Staff Memorandum, Submitted in Accordance with the Prime Minister's Instructions," Cabinet Paper P. 4, 7 November 1916, Cab. 29/1. Robertson's paper was first submitted on 31 August.

44. "Note on the Possible Terms of Peace by the First Sea Lord of the Admiralty," Cabinet Paper P. 8, 12 October 1916, Cab. 29/1.

45. [Ralph Paget and William Tyrrell], "Suggested Basis for a Territorial Settlement in Europe," Cabinet Paper P. 5, 29 September 1916; and "The Peace Settlement in Europe: Memorandum by Mr. Balfour," Cabinet Paper P. 7, 4 October 1916, Cab. 29/1. The Paget-Tyrrell memorandum was first printed on 7 August.

46. "Suggested Basis for a Territorial Settlement in Europe." Cabinet Paper P. 5, 29 September 1916, Cab. 29/1.

47. *Pronouncements of Leading Statesmen* (LNS Publications, No. 12), London, 1917, p. 6

48. Cabinet Paper P. 18, May 1917, Cab. 29/1. Cecil's memorandum is also printed as Appendix I to his *A Great Experiment*. The first draft of Cecil's memorandum contained provisions whereby the proposed conference of powers would examine the disarmament question, but Crowe's devastating critique persuaded Cecil to delete these provisions from his final draft.

49. Viscount Cecil, *All the Way*, p. 142.

50. The role of the family in shaping Cecil's character and political values is analyzed in Hugh P. Cecil, "The Development of Lord Robert Cecil's Views on the Securing of a Lasting Peace, 1915–1919," chap. 1. See also Hugh P. Cecil, "Lord Robert Cecil: A Nineteenth-Century Upbringing."

51. Cecil to J. H. Thomas, 23 December 1918, The *Times*, 27 December 1918.

52. The conservative impetus for Cecil's proleague commitment can be seen in his *All the Way*, pp. 141–48, 159.

53. For Cecil's relationship to Grey, see P. S. Raffo, "Lord Robert Cecil and the League of Nations," pp. 6–9. See also P. S. Raffo, "The League of Nations Philosophy of Lord Robert Cecil."

54. "Notes by Sir Eyre Crowe on Lord R. Cecil's Proposals for the Maintenance of Future Peace," Cabinet Paper G. T. 404a, 12 October 1916, Cab. 24/10. See also Cabinet Paper P. 19, Cab. 29/1. The last part of Crowe's memorandum consisted of an equally incisive critique of disarmament proposals. They convinced Cecil that his

original suggestions for disarmament were unrealistic. Lloyd George summarized the memorandum in his *War Memoirs*, 5:1792–98. The *War Memoirs* referred to Crowe's memorandum as a "powerfully written document," "an accurate account of the difficulties actually experienced" (ibid., 5:1951). Crowe was in temporary eclipse in the Foreign Office having quarreled with Grey and others in his drive for war efficiency. Zara S. Steiner, *The Foreign Office and Foreign Policy, 1898–1914*, pp. 165–66.

55. Lloyd George, *War Memoirs*, 1:253.

56. For the outlines of this debate, see Rothwell, *British War Aims*, pp. 54–55, and Devlin, *Too Proud to Fight*, pp. 551–55.

57. "Memorandum by Lord Lansdowne Respecting Peace Settlement," Cabinet Paper P. 5, 13 November 1916, Cab. 29/1. See also Cab. 37/159.

58. Grey to Cabinet, 27 November 1916, Cab. 37/160. When he left office, Grey gave Balfour and Cecil a copy of the House-Grey agreement together with a covering memorandum pointing to the option of American mediation if the war could no longer be continued. Cecil sent this to the War Cabinet, but no action was taken. F. O. 800/96; F. O. 800/197; Lloyd George Papers, F/160/1/4.

59. G. Lowes Dickinson wrote to Grey upon his departure: "I hope it is not impertinent for me to say with what profound regret, I may also say with what despair for the future, I heard of your retirement from office" (Trevelyan, *Grey of Fallodon*, p. 315).

CHAPTER 3

1. U.S., Department of State, *The World War*, pp. 97–99; James Brown Scott, ed., *Official Statements of War Aims and Peace Proposals*, pp. 12–15.

2. War Cabinet Minute W.C. 16, 2, 23 December 1916, Cab. 23/1; A. J. Balfour, "Suggestion for a British Reply to the Peace Note from the President of the United States," December 1916, Cab. 37/162. For the debate on war aims at this time, see V. H. Rothwell, *British War Aims and Peace Diplomacy, 1914–1918*, pp. 59–65; and Patrick Devlin, *Too Proud to Fight*, pp. 583–92. The most detailed analysis of British policy making is in Sterling J. Kernek, *Distractions of Peace during War*, chap. 2.

3. Scott, *Official Statements*, pp. 35–38. See also Cab. 28/2/13(a).

4. F. O. 371/2806.

5. Amery, *Times* correspondent in South Africa during the Boer War, was a Unionist M.P. and fervent imperialist. Sykes negotiated the middle eastern "Sykes-Picot Agreement" of 1916 for the Foreign Office. Guinn, arguing that the "New Imperialism" repudiated by the electorate in 1906 had now "captured the citadel of power," also includes Waldorf Astor, Lionel Curtis, and John Buchan among the imperialists newly appointed (Paul Guinn, *British Strategy and Politics, 1914 to 1918*, p. 192). Beloff, analyzing the divisions among the imperialists, concludes that the theory of an imperialist takeover is "too sweeping" (Max Beloff, *Imperial Sunset*, 1:214–18). Turner dismisses the theory altogether (J. A. Turner, "The Formulation of Lloyd George's 'Garden Suburb'").

6. For the role of the Round Table movement during the war, see John E. Kendle, *The Round Table Movement and Imperial Union*, chaps. 8–9. Kendle argues that the covert influence of Round Table members in government circles was "minimal" so far as the objectives of the movement were concerned. On the other hand, Hankey, who had some contact with the Round Table group, considered it "among the most influential" of the political congeries of wartime London (Diary of Maurice Hankey, 15 August 1917, Stephen Roskill, *Hankey*, 1:422).

7. For the war-aims debate, see Rothwell, *British War Aims*, pp. 68–75.

8. Ibid., p. 73.

9. Beloff, *Imperial Sunset*, 1:220–22.

10. See A. M. Gollin, *Proconsul in Politics*, chap. 20.

11. W.C. 67, 9, Appendix I, 17 February 1917, Cab. 23/1. David Lloyd George, *War Memoirs*, 4:1790.

12. Imperial War Cabinet Minute I.W.C. 1, (Proces-verbal), 20 March 1917, Cab. 23/43. Lloyd George, *War Memoirs*, 4:1767–85.

13. Minutes and report of the Imperial War Cabinet Terms of Peace Committee (Economic and Non-Territorial Desiderata) are in Cab. 21/71. See also Keith Middlemas, ed., *Thomas Jones*, 1:32–34. For the report, see Lloyd George, *War Memoirs*, 4:1799–1800.

14. I.W.C. 12, 19, 26 April 1917, Cab. 23/40. Lloyd George, *War Memoirs*, 4:1751–53.

15. I.W.C. 13, 3, 1 May 1917, Cab. 23/40. Lloyd George, *War Memoirs*, 4:1754–55.

16. The conservative attitudes of the Imperial War Cabinet were echoed in a Foreign Office study of the proposals of the American League to Enforce Peace requested by Balfour. Cecil Hurst, the Foreign Office chief legal advisor, severely criticized the attempt to construct an elaborate, automatic system to enforce peace and instead suggested a much more flexible conference system under the control of the great powers. Hurst noted that the American plans cut directly across the Monroe Doctrine and the constitutional powers of the United States Senate. Foreign Office, "League to Enforce Peace," July 1917, F. O. 800/249; F. O. 371/3078. See also John H. Latané, ed., *Development of the League of Nations Idea*, 1:303–7.

17. For the reluctance to propagate, see Bryce to House, 26 August 1916, Keith G. Robbins, "Lord Bryce and the First World War," pp. 266, 270; and Bryce to Theodore Marburg, 7 December 1916, Latané, *The League of Nations Idea*, p. 219. As it was, the army's Department of Military Intelligence kept close tabs on the proleague groups. Cab. 17/196.

18. Bryce to House, 14 January 1917, House Papers, 3–41. Bryce explained that the president's espousal of the league cause and the Allied response to his note had now made the idea practical, "and we here can now proceed to familiarize our own people with the idea, and can consider what the main lines of such a scheme ought to be."

19. In a letter to Gilbert Murray, G. Lowes Dickinson warned that Lloyd George was probably "indifferent and the rest of the new cabinet definitely skeptical or hostile" to any scheme for a peace league. This made it "all the more important that there should be some effective and public movement." G. Lowes Dickinson to Gilbert Murray, 17 December 1916, Murray Papers.

20. League of Nations Society, *Report of Meeting, May 14, 1917* (LNS Publications, No. 2), London, 1917; *Times*, 15 May 1917, p. 10; Henry R. Winkler, *The League of Nations Movement in Great Britain, 1914–1919*, pp. 54–55.

21. Lord Buckmaster had been lord chancellor in the Asquith coalition. Hugh Cecil was Robert Cecil's High Tory, High Church brother.

22. Robbins, "Lord Bryce," p. 271. By the end of 1917 the society would have published 30 items. *Second Annual Report, March 1917–March 1918* (LNS Publications, No. 38), London, 1918.

23. For an analysis of this literature, see Winkler, *League of Nations Movement*, pp. 58–65.

24. LNS (London, 1917).

25. *Times*, 18 July 1917, p. 3. For the Church of England's support of the league cause, see Albert Marrin, *The Last Crusade*, pp. 240–44.

26. LNS, *Report of a Conference of the Legal Profession* (LNS Publications, No. 17), London, 1917.

27. Those present included W. H. Dickinson, Lord Parmoor, Aneurin Williams, Noel Buxton, G. Lowes Dickinson, Raymond Unwin, Leonard Woolf, A. E. Zimmern, and John A. Hobson. LNS, *Proceedings of the First Annual Meeting* (London, 1917), pp. 5, 11–13.

28. H. A. L. Fisher, *James Bryce*, 2:137.

29. LNS, *Second Annual Report*. See also D. H. Mills, untitled draft history of the League of Nations Union, W. H. Dickinson Papers, vol. 406.

30. Several membership lists exist in the W. H. Dickinson Papers. The League of Nations Society worried about the almost exclusively Liberal complexion of their group and tried unsuccessfully to obtain Lord Lansdowne and Lord Selborne as president. W. H. Dickinson Papers, vol. 403.

31. For a survey of the liberal press, see Winkler, *League of Nations Movement*, pp. 138–60.

32. Ray Stannard Baker and William E. Dodd, eds., *The Public Papers of Woodrow Wilson*, 4:407–14. See also Devlin, *Too Proud to Fight*, pp. 594–607.

33. Baker and Dodd, *Public Papers*, 5:6–16.

34. The important links between Wilson and British liberal and radical circles are examined in Lawrence W. Martin, *Peace Without Victory*.

35. The ideological awakening and diplomatic program of British and Allied labor is treated in Arno J. Mayer, *The Political Origins of the New Diplomacy: 1917–1918*.

36. For an account of labor conditions, see Arthur Marwick, *The Deluge*, chap. 6.

37. Mayer, *Political Origins*, p. 161.

38. Labour Party, *Report of the Sixteenth Annual Conference* (Manchester, 1917), pp. 134–135. On 26 January 1917 the Trades Union Congress also endorsed Wilson's call for a league of nations. Arthur S. Link, *Woodrow Wilson and the Progressive Era*, p. 265.

39. See Winkler, *League of Nations Movement*, pp. 176–78, for examination of the league idea in such organs as the *Herald* and the *New Statesman*.

40. Mayer, *Political Origins*, pp. 178–82.

41. Labour Party, *Report of the Seventeenth Annual Conference* (London, 1918), pp. 4–5; Mayer, *Political Origins*, p. 222; Winkler, *League of Nations Movement*, pp. 178–79; Lloyd George, *War Memoirs*, 4:chap. 58.

42. The statement is printed in the *Times*, 11 August 1917; Winkler, *League of Nations Movement*, p. 179.

43. *Daily Telegraph*, 29 November 1917; Foreign Office, "Lansdowne Peace Letter," F. O. 371/3086; Lord Newton, *Lord Lansdowne*, pp. 463–68; Harold Kurtz, "The Lansdowne Letter."

44. Henderson to War Cabinet, 19 December 1917, W.C. 302, 13, 19 December 1917, Cab. 23/4.

45. "The Labour Party and the Trades Union Congress: Memorandum on War Aims," Cabinet Paper G.T. 3167, 28 December 1917, Cab. 24/37/2; the Labour Party and the Trades Union Congress, *Memorandum on War Aims* (London, 28 December 1917). The close cooperation of Henderson, Sidney Webb, and MacDonald on the committee drawing up the memorandum illustrates how the conditions of the

war had brought the Labour party, the Fabian Society, and the Independent Labour party together by the end of 1917.

46. P. H. K[err], "Lansdowne Speech," 5 December 1917, Lloyd George Papers, F/89/1/10.

47. Lloyd George's speech of 14 December 1917 is reprinted in Scott, *Official Statements*, pp. 211–12.

48. W.C. 308A, 3, 31 December 1917, Cab. 23/13. For a detailed analysis of the situation facing the government at the end of 1917, see Kernek, *Distractions of Peace*, chap. 5.

49. "War Aims, Draft Statement by General Smuts," Cabinet Paper G.T. 3180, 1 January 1918, Cab. 24/37/2; "War Aims, Draft Statement by Lord Robert Cecil," Cabinet Paper G.T. 3181, 3 January 1918, Cab. 24/37/2; [Philip Kerr], "Statement of War Aims: Draft Statement Based on General Smuts' Draft," Cabinet Paper G.T. 3182, 3 January 1918, Cab. 24/37/2.

50. Cabinet Paper G.T. 3181. Speaking in the Commons on 19 December, Cecil asserted that he would not remain for an hour a member of any government that did not make the creation of a league of nations one of its main objects. To Cecil this was "the only thing really worth struggling for in international affairs" (Great Britain *Parliamentary Debates* (Commons), 5th ser., 100 (1917):2096–97.

51. W.C. 312, 313, and 314, 3 and 4 January 1918, Cab. 23/5.

52. Cecil and Curzon dissented, insisting on the sincerity and reasonableness of the terms as peace terms. Although Lloyd George's immediate intentions were to restore the government's image in the eyes of labor and weaken the morale of the enemy, this did not preclude making peace at the expense of Russia if the Germans offered the necessary concessions and if military victory remained improbable. See David R. Woodward, "The Origins and Intent of David Lloyd George's January 5 War Aims Speech." Lloyd George was also aware that a new definition of war aims by Wilson was imminent and wished to preempt him. Arthur Walworth, *America's Moment: 1918*, p. 3.

53. Scott, *Official Statements*, pp. 225–33; Lloyd George, *War Memoirs*, 5: 2515–27.

54. Baker and Dodd, *Public Papers*, 5:130; Scott, *Official Statements*, p. 195. Wilson, of course, was privy to some of the secret Allied war aims and suspected the rest. His instructions to House on setting up the Inquiry specifically mentioned the necessity of obtaining full information on Allied war aims and mobilizing influence against them if necessary. Ray Stannard Baker, ed., *Woodrow Wilson: Life and Letters*, 7:254. Wilson's speech was decided upon only after House failed to elicit a joint Allied statement on war aims at the inter-Allied conference in Paris of late November 1917.

55. Quotations from the text of the Fourteen Points reprinted in Baker and Dodd, *Public Papers*, 5:155–62.

CHAPTER 4

1. By November 1918 the membership figures stood at 2,230. D. H. Mills, untitled draft history of the League of Nations Union, W. H. Dickinson Papers, vol. 406.

2. The literature is analyzed in Henry R. Winkler, *The League of Nations Movement in Great Britain, 1914–1919*, chap. 3.

3. Edward, Viscount Grey, *The League of Nations*. Grey's pamphlet was discussed widely in the press and given mass circulation by the Ministry of Education. See the *Times*, 20 June 1918, and *Manchester Guardian*, 21 June 1918.

4. League of Nations Society, *League of Nations* (LNS Publications, No. 24), London, 1918.

5. W. H. Dickinson to the Archbishop of Canterbury, 30 May 1917, W. H. Dickinson Papers, vol. 403, and D. H. Mills, draft history.

6. Charles Seymour, ed., *The Intimate Papers of Colonel House*, 4:7.

7. Wiseman headed British intelligence operations in the United States and, as an agent of the Foreign Office, established intimate relations with Colonel House. See Wilton B. Fowler, *British-American Relations, 1917–1918*.

8. Cabinet Paper G.T. 2074, Cab. 24/26/2074. The memorandum began as a letter to Balfour, Cecil's cousin, 25 August 1917.

9. War Cabinet Minute W.C. 253, 17, 19 October 1917, Cab. 23/4.

10. House revealed these attitudes in conversation with Balfour's secretary, Sir Eric Drummond. "Proposed Formation of League of Nations to Secure the Maintenance of Future Peace, (Copy of Minute addressed to Mr. Balfour by Sir E. Drummond)," Cabinet Paper G.T. 2667, 15 November 1917, Cab. 24/32.

11. Cecil to Balfour, 20 November 1917, F. O. 371/3439. Balfour's comments are minuted on this letter. This file contains both a copy of the interim report of the Phillimore committee and the correspondence leading to its institution. From this correspondence, it can be seen that Lloyd George's account of the creation of the Phillimore committee is wrong both with regard to the date of establishing the committee (not January 1917) and in its exaggeration of his own role. David Lloyd George, *The Truth About the Peace Treaties*, 1:605–7.

12. Phillimore, soon to be made a law lord, had published in 1917 an analysis of past peace schemes along with a plan of his own that embodied a moderate, practical approach to the question. Baron Walter G. F. Phillimore, *Three Centuries of Treaties of Peace and Their Teaching* (London, 1917).

13. Interim Report, F. O. 371/3439.

14. The minutes of the Phillimore committee are in "League of Nations Committee: Minutes of Proceedings (Meetings 1–14 of 1918)," F. O. 371/3483.

15. Ibid., Meeting 1, 30 January 1918. See below, pp. 69–71, for an examination of Hankey's important scheme.

16. Ibid., Meeting 3, 6 February 1918.

17. Crowe's silence is especially puzzling in view of his previous criticism of Cecil's plan.

18. "Minutes of Proceedings," Meetings 6 and 7, 6 and 13 March 1918.

19. F. O. 371/3483. Cabinet Paper P. 26, 20 March 1918, Cab. 29/1. The interim report is readily available in David Hunter Miller, *The Drafting of the Covenant*, 1:3–10 and 2:3–6; and Ray Stannard Baker, *Woodrow Wilson and World Settlement*, 3:67–78.

20. States could be released from the required moratorium in certain circumstances upon application to the conference.

21. The committee recommended Versailles as a convenient seat if the league were confined to the present Allies. However, if neutrals were admitted, the seat might better be located in Holland, Switzerland, or Belgium.

22. The committee rejected the League of Nations Society's plan for a defensive union obliging collective action against attack by a nonmember because, in their opinion, this plan might provoke American opposition.

23. Winkler describes the committee's plan as "a curious attempt to reconcile the league idea with conventional diplomatic procedures and techniques" (Winkler, *League of Nations Movement*, p. 237). To A. E. Zimmern the report was "an unsatisfactory hybrid" of the chairman's international juridical inclinations and the

vague political designs of the Foreign Office members (Alfred E. Zimmern, *The League of Nations and the Rule of Law*, p. 180).

24. Diary of Maurice Hankey, 7, 21 November and 6 December 1917, Stephen Roskill, *Hankey*, 1:454, 462, 469; Hankey to Lloyd George, 12 January 1918, Lloyd George Papers, F/23/2/7; "The League of Nations, Observations by the Secretary," Cabinet Paper G.T. 3344, 16 January 1918, Cab. 24/39.

25. "Minutes of Proceedings," Meeting 1, 30 January 1918. Hankey felt the committee was "dominated by legalists and diplomatists belonging to the old gang at the Foreign Office" (Keith Middlemas, ed., *Thomas Jones*, 1:54).

26. "The Victory that Will End War," pp. 221–28, and "The Unity of Civilization," pp. 679–84. See also, John E. Kendle, *The Round Table Movement and Imperial Union*, pp. 250–53.

27. The Lords debate had begun 19 March with a resolution by Lord Parmoor and proleague speeches by Bryce and Lansdowne. Debate was adjourned due to the German spring offensive and resumed by Curzon, 26 June. Curzon's speech discouraged and disturbed league supporters in the Lords. The Bishop of Oxford "could not but feel a certain chill of the heart," while Lord Shaw, president of the League of Nations Society, warned that the government was behind both domestic opinion and its allies in consideration of the league question. Great Britain, *Parliamentary Debates* (Lords), 5th ser., 24 (1918):476–510 and 30:393–404.

28. Information on the formation of the League of Free Nations Association drawn from the Gilbert Murray Papers and the W. H. Dickinson Papers, vol. 406. See also Winkler, *League of Nations Movement*, pp. 70–72.

29. G. Lowes Dickinson described them as more "reputable," "ardent supporters of the war, and good haters of Germany" (G. Lowes Dickinson, *The Autobiography of G. Lowes Dickinson*, p. 191).

30. The objects of the League of Free Nations Association are reprinted in John H. Latané, ed., *Development of the League of Nations Idea*, 2:818–19.

31. Henry Wickham Steed, *Through Thirty Years, 1892–1922*, 2:222–24. For analysis of British economic war aims and propaganda, see V. H. Rothwell, *British War Aims and Peace Diplomacy, 1914–1918*, chap. 7.

32. *Times*, 2 August 1918.

33. Seymour, *Intimate Papers*, 4:65–66.

34. For debate in the Foreign Office on Northcliffe's propaganda, see F. O. 371/4367. In August when Eustace Percy recommended a ministerial campaign to form a wartime league and rally labor support on this program, Cecil queried: "What ministerial lamb do you destine for the sacrifice?" (F. O. 371/4365).

35. W.C. 412, 7, 15 May 1918, Cab. 23/6. The War Cabinet agreed to forward the report to Wilson, "it being made clear that the Report did not set forth the policy of the Government but was the result of the deliberations of an expert Committee."

36. F. O. 371/4365; also Cab. 24/59.

37. George Bernard Noble, *Policies and Opinions at Paris, 1919*, pp. 36, 37, 101.

38. For more information on Bourgeois's role, see Léon Bourgeois, *Le Pacte de 1919 et la Société des Nations*. Bourgeois, a former premier and foreign minister had represented the French government at the Hague peace conferences. Balfour turned the report over to the Phillimore committee for examination and comment. The committee's commentary, along with the appended "Textes Adoptés Par la Commission Française," is included in Foreign Office "Report of the Committee Appointed by the French Government: Note by Lord Phillimore's Committee," 9 August 1918, F. O. 371/4365.

39. Walters argues that the Bourgeois report was considered of little account in the Foreign Office, neglected in America, and treated with silent indifference by the Clemenceau government. Frank P. Walters, *A History of the League of Nations*, p. 23.

40. Cecil to Lloyd George, 26 June 1918, Lloyd George Papers, F/6/5/34.

41. Cecil to Wiseman, 21 July 1918, Wiseman Papers, 91–75. Cecil argued that it was unwise to leave discussion on so important a topic as the league entirely in the hands of "unguided amateurs." He was therefore proposing that the prime minister communicate the scheme to the Allies and then table it in the Commons.

42. Cecil to House, 22 July 1918, F. O. 371/4365; Cab. 24/59.

43. For the president's aversion to public debate on league schemes, see Seymour, *Intimate Papers*, 4:7, 8, 16–17.

44. Wiseman to Cecil, 18 July 1918, F. O. 800/222 and F. O. 371/4365. Reading to Foreign Office, 23 July 1918, F. O. 371/3439. Lord Reading, chief justice, headed the British embassy in Washington after the departure and death of Spring-Rice.

45. Great Britain, *Parliamentary Debates* (Commons), 5th ser., 109 (1918): 735–38.

46. W.C. 457; Imperial War Cabinet Minute I.W.C. 30, 8, 13 August 1918, Cab. 23/7. Quotations are from the "Shorthand Notes" of the meeting, which illustrate more clearly the heat generated by the debate. "Shorthand Notes," I.W.C. 30, 13 August 1918, Cab. 23/43. After the cabinet meeting, Cecil wrote to his wife that the atmosphere had been "chilly" and that Lloyd George, who had "never really cared about" the league idea, now, under the influence of Amery, Hankey, and Curzon, was "almost against it." Only Barnes, Balfour, Borden, and possibly Smuts really approved. Without the hope that the war would result in a better international system, Cecil claimed he should be a pacifist. Cecil to Lady Robert Cecil, 13 August 1918, Hugh P. Cecil, "The Development of Lord Robert Cecil's Views on the Securing of a Lasting Peace, 1915–1919," p. 133.

47. Reading to Lloyd George, 19 August 1918, Lloyd George Papers, F/43/1/14. See also Wiseman to Reading, 16 August 1918, Seymour, *Intimate Papers*, 4:52–54.

48. Lloyd George to Bonar Law, 20 August 1918, Lloyd George Papers, F/30/2/41.

49. E. A. Robert, Viscount Cecil, *All the Way*, p. 142. Wiseman showed Cecil's letter to Wilson. Fowler, *British-American Relations*, p. 217.

50. Barnes was a token labor representative and did not have the official blessing of the Labour party.

51. Inter-Allied Labour and Socialist Conference, *Memorandum on War Aims Agreed upon at the Central Hall, Westminster, London, S.W., on February 20 to 24, 1918* (London, 1918). See also Winkler, *League of Nations Movement*, pp. 181–85.

52. For the program of the League to Abolish War and correspondence, see F. O. 371/3439.

53. "Lecture by the Right Hon. G. N. Barnes," Cabinet Paper G.T. 5364, 5 August 1918, Cab. 24/60. The Foreign Office repeatedly expressed concern at the content of Barnes's speeches in view of his cabinet position. Crowe asked Balfour several times to caution Barnes but with little effect. F. O. 371/3439.

54. W.C. 481, 9, 2 October 1918, Cab. 23/8.

55. For Wilson's first draft, see Baker, *World Settlement*, 1:218–24, or Miller, *Drafting*, 2:12–15.

56. Wilson's Four Ends speech of 4 July and his Five Particulars speech of 27 September are in James Brown Scott, ed., *Official Statements of War Aims and Peace Proposals*, pp. 349–52, 399–405. The 27 September speech, particularly the

warning on economic combinations, was intended more for the Allies than the enemies.

57. Wiseman's important role through this period is analyzed in Fowler, *British-American Relations*, chap. 8.

CHAPTER 5

1. House to Wilson, 5 November 1918, Charles Seymour, ed., *The Intimate Papers of Colonel House*, 4:188.

2. War Cabinet Minute W.C. 497; Imperial War Cabinet Minute I.W.C. 36, 6, 5 November 1918, Cab. 23/8. Hughes was incensed at the lack of imperial consultation concerning the prearmistice agreement and gave vent to his feelings in the *Times*, 5 November 1918.

3. Kerr to Hankey, 13 November 1918, Lord Lothian Papers, G.D. 40/17/57.

4. For a rather extreme interpretation of House's naïveté, see Inga Floto, *Colonel House in Paris*, pp. 59–60.

5. [Sir William Wiseman], "The Attitude of the United States and of President Wilson Towards the Peace Settlement" [n.d., c. 20 October 1918], F. O. 800/214. For Wiseman's role as liason between the British and American governments as peace approached, see Wilton B. Fowler, *British-American Relations, 1917–1918*, pp. 198–235.

6. The development of "atlanticism" is analyzed in Michael G. Fry, *Illusions of Security*, chap. 1.

7. I.W.C. 38, 26 November 1918.

8. For development of Round Table views, see John E. Kendle, *The Round Table Movement and Imperial Union*, pp. 256–58.

9. "Our Policy at the Peace Conference, (Note by General Smuts), For the King and War Cabinet," Cabinet Paper P. 39, 3 December 1918, Cab. 29/2.

10. For British views, see C. Addison, "The League of Nations," 3 October 1918, F. O. 371/4356; Political Intelligence Department, "Memorandum," 21 October 1918, F. O. 371/4367; and Alfred E. Zimmern, *The League of Nations and the Rule of Law, 1918–1935*, pp. 143–59.

11. Hoover's role and American policy are documented in Suda Lorena Bane and Ralph Haswell Lutz, eds., *Organization of American Relief in Europe, 1918–1919*, chaps. 1–3.

12. I.W.C. 39, 28 November 1918, Cab. 23/42. British correspondence on this question can be found in F. O. 371/4367. The bitter infighting over relief organization would continue through December into early January 1919, the Allies getting the form of joint Allied control in the Supreme Economic Council while Hoover, as director general of relief, managed the large portion of relief as an independent American operation. Meanwhile, the Allies maintained the blockade, the major victims of this rivalry being the starving populations in various areas of Europe.

13. Lodge to Balfour, 25 November 1918, Balfour Papers, Add. Mss. 49742.

14. U.S. Congress, Senate, *Congressional Record*, 66th Cong., 1st sess., 1918, 18, pt. 1:724–28. See also Arthur Walworth, *America's Moment: 1918*, pp. 249–50.

15. Grey to House, 30 December 1918, reprinted in G. M. Trevelyan, *Grey of Fallodon*, pp. 348–49.

16. French policies are analyzed in Harold I. Nelson, *Land and Power*, chap. 2, and Jere Clemens King, *Foch Versus Clemenceau*, pp. 1–27.

17. France, *Annales de la Chambre*, 29 December 1918, p. 3328. See also George Bernard Noble, *Policies and Opinions at Paris, 1919*, pp. 85–94.

18. International Conference I.C. 97, 102, Cab. 28/5.

19. "French Proposals for the Preliminaries of Peace with Germany, communicated by the French Ambassador, November 26, 1918," Nelson, *Land and Power*, pp. 135–36. Perhaps it was a similar suggestion at the inter-Allied conference which occasioned Smuts's paper of 3 December.

20. Balfour advised Lloyd George that the proposals of Cambon, the French ambassador, were "little short of insanity" (Balfour to Lloyd George, 29 November 1918, Lloyd George Papers, F/3/3/45; also F. O. 800/199).

21. Docket note, 7 December 1918, F. O. 371/3451.

22. Imperial strategies are analyzed in Max Beloff, *Imperial Sunset*, 1:269–72, 279–85.

23. Kendle, *Round Table*, pp. 176–77, 190–209, chap. 9.

24. Beloff, *Imperial Sunset*, 1:282.

25. This information is found in Cecil's draft note, "Origins of the Covenant," Cecil Papers, Add. Mss. 51195. Those present at the meeting included Cecil, Balfour, Addison, Reading, and probably Foreign Office representatives.

26. "League of Nations: Memorandum by Lord Robert Cecil," Cabinet Paper P. 29, October 1918, Cab. 29/1.

27. "Origins of the Covenant," Cecil Papers, Add. Mss. 51195.

28. Christopher Addison, *Four and a Half Years*, 2:577–78.

29. Cecil to Gilbert Murray, 29 November 1918, Murray Papers. Cecil resigned from the government 22 November.

30. Information on events leading to amalgamation of the League of Nations Society and the League of Free Nations Association can be found in the Gilbert Murray Papers, W. H. Dickinson Papers, vol. 406, and in records of the League of Nations Union. See also Henry R. Winkler, *The League of Nations Movement in Great Britain, 1914–1919*, pp. 74–83, and Keith G. Robbins, *The Abolition of War*, pp. 169–72.

31. The meeting was written up in the *Times*, 11 October 1918.

32. League of Nations Society, *Viscount Grey on a League of Nations* (LNS Publications, No. 44), London, 1918; *Manchester Guardian*, 11 October 1918, p. 4; *Times*, 11 October 1918, p. 11.

33. The program is reproduced in Winkler, *League of Nations Movement*, p. 77.

34. League of Nations Union operations were financed mainly by David Davies. Membership figures at the time of amalgamation were 2,230 from the League of Nations Society and 987 from the League of Free Nations Association. By the end of the year the joint membership stood at 3,841. W. H. Dickinson Papers, vol. 406.

35. See Winkler, *League of Nations Movement*, pp. 78–82 for an analysis of League of Nations Union literature.

36. *Times*, 5 December 1918, p. 8.

37. *Times*, 14 December 1918, p. 12. See also *Daily News*, 14 December 1918.

38. *Times*, 28 September 1918, p. 5; 19 November 1918, p. 8; and *Daily News*, 11 December 1918. Asquith's support for the Wilsonian program, however, lacked strength and resolution. See Arno J. Mayer, *Politics and Diplomacy of Peacemaking*, p. 147.

39. Labour's election manifesto, "Labour's Call to the People," declared for a peace of reconciliation, an end to secret diplomacy and economic warfare, and demanded an international labor charter and league of free peoples as part of the peace. Labour Party, *Report of Nineteenth Annual Conference* (Southport, 1919), p. 185.

40. Fred Guest to Lloyd George, 3 August 1918, Lloyd George Papers, F/21/2/30. Perhaps the appeal of the league idea to the newly enfranchised women entered into these calculations.

41. *Times,* 13 November 1918, p. 9.
42. Ibid., 22 November 1918.
43. I.W.C. 38, 26 November 1918, Cab. 23/42.
44. See, for instance, Lloyd George's 5 December electoral manifesto, which dealt at length with the prosecution of the kaiser and war criminals, war costs, expulsion of enemy aliens, and domestic issues, but made no reference to the league of nations. *Times,* 6 December 1918, p. 9. The assertion made by Lloyd George in his memoirs that he "placed the establishment of a strong League of Nations and disarmament in the forefront of his programme of peace" is not supported by the evidence. David Lloyd George, *The Truth about the Peace Treaties,* 1:146–47.
45. For major issues in the election and the role of the "coupon," see Trevor Wilson, "The Coupon and the British General Election of 1918." See also Ronald B. McCallum, *Public Opinion and the Last Peace,* chap. 1.
46. Interview by Charles H. Grasty, 18 December 1918, David Hunter Miller Papers, 85/26. C. P. Scott, in an interview with Wilson on 29 December 1918, advised the president "not to regard the result of the election as a demonstration against the policy of a League of Nations" (Trevor Wilson, ed., *The Political Diaries of C.P. Scott, 1911–1928,* p. 336). Speaking to a mass proleague Labour rally at the Albert Hall, 2 January 1920, Arthur Henderson claimed the league project "was the one question on which all candidates were agreed" (*Times,* 3 January 1920).
47. The *Annual Register* claimed that the league project was "one of the subjects most prominent in public attention at the beginning of the new year" (*Annual Register: 1919,* pp. 1–2).
48. For treatments of the role and power of the Foreign Office, see Roberta M. Warman, "The Erosion of Foreign Policy Influence in the Making of Foreign Policy, 1916–1918"; and Gordon A. Craig, "The British Foreign Office from Grey to Austen Chamberlain," Gordon A. Craig and Felix Gilbert, eds., *The Diplomats: 1919–1939,* 1:15–25.
49. Wiseman to Arthur Murray, 4 July 1918, Fowler, *British-American Relations,* p. 164.
50. Smuts Papers, vol. 101, reel 765/46.
51. For Round Table attitudes, see [Lionel Curtis], "Windows of Freedom," pp. 1–26; and an article published anonymously by Zimmern himself, "Some Principles and Problems of the Settlement," pp. 88–113.
52. Alfred E. Zimmern, "The League of Nations," Cabinet Paper P. 68, 20 December 1918, Cab. 29/2; Lord Eustace Percy, "The League of Nations," Cabinet Paper P. 69, Cab. 29/2. Both papers were written in November and circulated to the cabinet in December. See also F. O. 371/4353. Zimmern's memorandum is reprinted in his *The League of Nations and the Rule of Law, 1918–1935,* pp. 197–209.
53. Richards to Smuts, 4 December 1918, Smuts Papers, vol. 20, reel 685/125.
54. "Europe," Cabinet Paper P. 52 (December 1918), Cab. 29/2; F. O. 371/4353.
55. See Wilson's diary entries for 22, 24 December 1918; and 22 March, 28 April, and 13 October 1919, in Major-General Sir C. E. Callwell, *Field-Marshall Sir Henry Wilson,* vol. 2.
56. L. S. Amery, *My Political Life,* 2:163–65. Amery's views on the league question can be seen at greater length in correspondence with Smuts in W. K. Hancock and Jean Van Der Poel, eds., *Selections from the Smuts Papers,* 4:docs. 866, 913, 914.
57. Stephen Roskill, *Hankey,* 2:27.
58. Churchill at Dundee, 25 November, *Times,* 27 November 1918, p. 10.
59. *Morning Post,* 21, 24 October; 1, 2 November; and 2, 3, 5, 21, 27 December 1918.

60. "Can a League of Nations Armed with the Weapon of Economic Isolation Safeguard the World's Peace?" War Office Memorandum, 20 December 1918, F. O. 371/4366, 669/253. The memorandum was composed by Major-General G. K. Cockerill together with War Office colleagues and was sent to Cecil for his information. Cockerill was subdirector of military intelligence (director of special intelligence) at the War Office.

61. *Morning Post*, 2, 3, and 5 December 1918.

62. "Memorandum by Admiralty on Naval Aspects of a League of Nations and Limitation of Armaments," Cabinet Paper P. 78, December 1918, Cab. 29/2. For admiralty views on the league, see also Stephen Roskill, *Naval Policy Between the Wars*, 1:81–82, and Arthur J. Marder, *From the Dreadnought to Scapa Flow*, 5:242–47.

63. "League of Nations: Memoranda by the Foreign Office," Cabinet Paper P. 79, 17 December 1918, Cab. 29/2. See also Zimmern, *The League of Nations*, pp. 190–209. The memorandum is reprinted in David Hunter Miller, *The Drafting of the Covenant*, 2:61–64.

64. Philip Baker (later Noel-Baker), a Quaker, joined the Foreign Office in late 1918 after finishing his work with the First British Ambulance Unit and wrote a series of memoranda on international law and arbitration in relationship to a league of nations. Cecil doubted the wisdom of this approach and advised against elaborate legal machinery that would "only add to the enormous and growing difficulties at present in our way." Cecil felt it would be "safer to have very simple provisions at first which would be elaborated later on" (F. O. 800/249). Lord Phillimore, who was responsible for drawing up the Foreign Office Handbook on the league question, stressed the importance of progress in international law and arbitration, but agreed that the main function of the league should be to ensure a moratorium on war while efforts were being made at peaceful resolution. Baron Walter G. F. Phillimore, *Schemes for Maintaining General Peace*, pp. 65–67.

65. The "functional" responsibilities of the league were charted in detail by S. P. Waterlow, who based his memorandum on Leonard Woolf's *International Government*. S. P. Waterlow, "International Government Under the League of Nations," 28 December 1918, circulated 3 January 1919, F. O. 371/4353. Waterlow argued that for the league to be a practical proposition, it must be based firmly on the existing organs of international cooperation. To build upon the current "world wave" of emotion directed towards the assurance of international justice and the prevention of war would be "folly."

66. "The Settlement," Cabinet Paper P. 53, December 1918, Cab. 29/2; F. O. 371/4353.

67. The full text of Smuts's *Practical Suggestion* is reprinted in Miller, *Drafting*, 2:23–60. See also Jan Christian Smuts, "The League of Nations: A Programme for the Peace Conference," Cabinet Paper P. 44, 16 December 1918, Cab. 29/2; and Smuts, *The League of Nations*.

68. I.W.C. 46, 24 December 1918, Cab. 23/42.

69. [Docket notes on Smuts's *Practical Suggestion*], F. O. 371/4353.

70. Cabinet Paper P. 79, 17 December 1918, Cab. 29/2.

71. I.W.C. 43, 18 December 1918, Cab. 23/42.

72. I.W.C. 46, 1, 24 December 1918, Cab. 23/42. Although Smuts's *Practical Suggestion* provided the point of reference for discussion, Smuts himself was not present due to illness.

73. Hankey and Kerr were both present at this meeting of the Imperial War Cabinet. After "vetting" the draft minutes, Hankey "dictated the P.M.'s important summing up." He was pleased that the discussion had trended "in the direction I

have always advocated" (Diary of Maurice Hankey, 24 December 1918, Roskill, *Hankey*, 2:38). Cecil was less pleased with the outcome of cabinet discussion. Writing to Bonar Law, he lamented that "the P.M. in spite of his denials has never really taken the League seriously—indeed, I doubt if he can" (Cecil to Bonar Law, 24 December 1918, Bonar Law Papers, 98/5/19).

74. Walworth, *America's Moment*, p. 149.

75. For Wilson's speeches of 28 and 30 December, see Ray Stannard Baker and William E. Dodd, eds., *The Public Papers of Woodrow Wilson*, 5:341–44, 352–56.

76. I.W.C. 47, 1, 30 December 1918, Cab. 23/42.

77. I.W.C. 48, 4, 31 December 1918, Cab. 23/42.

CHAPTER 6

1. U.S., Department of State, *The Paris Peace Conference*, 1:365–71.

2. Arthur Walworth, *Woodrow Wilson*, 2:240.

3. *The Paris Peace Conference*, 3:531–38.

4. The resolutions are reprinted in David Hunter Miller, *The Drafting of the Covenant*, 1:76.

5. The minutes of the 25 January plenary session are reprinted in Miller, *Drafting*, 2:doc. 15; *The Paris Peace Conference*, 3:178–201.

6. Miller, *Drafting*, 1:76–85; Ray Stannard Baker, *Woodrow Wilson and World Settlement*, 1:chap. 14.

7. Miller, *Drafting*, 1:76–77, 81–83; Diary of Lord Robert Cecil, 8, 9, 13 January 1919, Cecil Papers, Add. Mss., 51131. Cecil kept a daily diary through the peace conference, which throws valuable light on the inner workings of the British Empire delegation, especially on the league issue.

8. Miller long ago refuted Baker's charges that Lloyd George and Clemenceau conspired to bury the league project by referring it to a commission which they then attempted to make "as awkward and unwieldy as possible." The establishment of a commission that included small powers was necessary and wise. The original procedure favored by Wilson, that his draft should be threshed out by the British, French, and Americans in an informal committee and then submitted to a conference of Allies and neutrals, all in a fortnight, Cecil considered "fantastic" (Diary of Lord Robert Cecil, 19 January 1919, Cecil Papers). At the same time both Clemenceau and Lloyd George realized the tactical expediency of weighing down the deliberations of the League of Nations Commission while matters of greater priority to them were brought before the Council of Ten. Some idea of attitudes toward the role of the commission can be gleaned from the following exchanges of 25 January, during Leon Bourgeois's speech before the plenary session. Cecil passed a note to Balfour musing that Bourgeois's verbosity could prove ruinous in the League of Nations Commission. Balfour passed the note on to Lloyd George, who replied, "That is no doubt why Clemenceau put him on!" (Diary of Lord Robert Cecil, 25 January 1919, Cecil Papers). For Baker's charges and the subsequent debate, see Baker, *World Settlement*, 1:chap. 14; Miller, *Drafting*, 1:chap. 8; Charles Seymour, ed., *Intimate Papers of Colonel House*, 4:299–304; and *The Paris Peace Conference*, 3:178–201.

9. For the role played by Britain and the dominions in the colonial settlement, see Wm. Roger Louis, *Great Britain and Germany's Lost Colonies, 1914–1919*.

10. Miller, *Drafting*, 1:41–44.

11. *The Paris Peace Conference*, 3:749–71.

12. British Empire Delegation Minute B.E.D. 4, 27 January 1919, and B.E.D. 6, 29 January 1919, Cab. 29/28/1. House, but not Wilson, approved of this line. Seymour, *Intimate Papers*, 4:309. For Smuts's tactics, see Louis, *Germany's Lost Colonies*, p. 119.

13. Roskill gives Hankey the principal credit for "inventing" the C-type mandate. Stephen Roskill, *Hankey*, 2:37–38.

14. *The Paris Peace Conference*, 3:785–817.

15. Seymour, *Intimate Papers*, 4:310.

16. Cecil's staff included Philip Baker, Captain Frank P. Walters, J. R. M. Butler, and Lord Cranborne. Eustace Percy and Cecil Hurst served as Cecil's chief Foreign Office advisors.

17. Diary of Lord Robert Cecil, 8 January 1919, Cecil Papers.

18. Sir Eyre Crowe, "Some Notes on Compulsory Arbitration," 9 January 1919, F. O. 608/240/2.

19. Diary of Lord Robert Cecil, 8 January 1919, Cecil Papers.

20. Lord Robert Cecil, "Very secret. Record of an interview with Colonel House at Paris, Thursday, January 9, 1919," 10 January 1919, Cecil Papers, Add. Mss., 51094.

21. This memorandum, slightly revised, was again circulated to the American delegation on 18 January 1919 and is reprinted as "Draft Sketch of a League of Nations," 14 January 1919, Miller, *Drafting*, 2:doc. 6.

22. The early versions of the draft used by the league of nations section, along with other study papers, can be seen in F. O. 800/249. The records of the British league of nations section do not appear to have been preserved in one collection, but seem, rather, to be scattered through the Cecil Papers, Foreign Office files, and Cabinet Office Records.

23. The revised version of the draft convention, with changes indicated, is reprinted as "League of Nations: Draft Convention," 20 January 1919, Miller, *Drafting*, 2:doc. 10. See also Cabinet Paper W.C.P. 23, 20 January 1919, Cab. 29/7.

24. Covering note to W.C.P. 23.

25. Diary of Lord Robert Cecil, 19 January 1919, Cecil Papers.

26. Miller, *Drafting*, 2:doc. 9. The story of the shaping of American plans for the league has often been told. See particularly Miller, *Drafting*, 1:3–50; Baker, *World Settlement*, 1:213–314; Seymour, *Intimate Papers*, 4:chaps. 1, 2 and 9; and Seth P. Tillman, *Anglo-American Relations at the Paris Peace Conference of 1919*, pp. 101–17.

27. See Miller, *Drafting*, 1:51–56, for details of these exchanges.

28. Diary of Lord Robert Cecil, 22 January 1919, Cecil Papers.

29. The Cecil-Miller draft is reprinted in Miller, *Drafting*, 2:doc. 12. Changes from Wilson's 20 January draft are noted in a memorandum prepared for House by Miller. Miller, *Drafting*, 1:57–61.

30. Ibid., 1:53.

31. Ibid., 1:61.

32. See particularly Lodge to Henry White, 2 December 1918, Allan Nevins, *Henry White*, pp. 352–55. White served as the Republican on the peace commission but was much closer in his views to Wilson than to Lodge.

33. Robert L. Lansing, *The Peace Negotiations*. For Lansing's views, see also Miller, *Drafting*, 1:28–32, 77–81.

34. Lansing, *The Peace Negotiations*, pp. 78–79; David Hunter Miller, *My Diary at the Conference of Paris*, 1:51; also Miller, *Drafting*, 1:29–32.

35. For Lansing, with revolution spreading in Europe, the crying need of the world was a quick peace: "If the acceptance of an elaborate scheme for a League of Nations interferes, I would throw the scheme overboard" (Private Memoranda, 22 January 1919, Lansing Papers). Lansing's pride had been mortally wounded by the president on 10 January by the aspersions cast upon the mentality of lawyers.

36. Lansing, *The Peace Negotiations*, pp. 116–17.

37. Lansing to Wilson, 31 January 1919, Woodrow Wilson Papers, 5B/13. Since the resolution proposed by Lansing reversed his attitude on positive guarantees and included a stark guarantee of sovereign rights and territory, it is probable that the secretary was primarily interested in drawing "the fire of the opponents and critics of the League" and, thereby, confronting Wilson sooner rather than later with domestic opposition. Wilson probably saw through the ruse. The proposed resolution, but not the covering letter, is reprinted in Miller, *Drafting*, 1:80–81.

38. Diary of Lord Robert Cecil, 20 January 1919, Cecil Papers.

39. Lothian Papers, G.D. 40/17/54.

40. Diary of William Wiseman, 31 January 1919, Wiseman Papers.

41. This important meeting is reconstructed from records in the Lothian Papers and from Cecil's diary.

42. P. H. K[err], "The League of Nations," Lothian Papers, G. D. 40/17/54. This is not dated, but it was probably composed after Cecil's note to the prime minister of 29 January requesting authority to proceed on the basis of the Cecil-Miller draft. The Kerr memorandum follows directly after Cecil's note in the Lothian Papers.

43. The plan bore the heading, "P.H.K. Draft." Article 11 was added in Philip Kerr's handwriting.

44. Diary of Lord Robert Cecil, 31 January 1919, Cecil Papers.

45. Ibid. Cecil's suspicions and anger grew the next day when, visiting Bourgeois, he learned that Bourgeois had just seen Lloyd George. Diary of Lord Robert Cecil, 1 February 1919, Cecil Papers. Cecil's suspicions of a conspiracy were probably overdrawn. Nevertheless, the British and French leaders shared a common interest at this point in going slow on the league, and there may have been some collusion. Lansing may also have been involved. In his letter of 31 January to Wilson, in which he was probably playing a double game, Lansing warned that from remarks made to him by members of the Council of Ten, he had learned it was not believed or expected that a plan on the league would be ready before Wilson returned to the United States and Lloyd George departed for London. Lansing was "disposed to think that this postponement will be very acceptable to certain governments and that they will seek to delay rather than hasten an agreement." According to Lansing, the way around this was the adoption of his proposed resolution on the league, which should be done before Hankey and the British put forward their version of a resolution. Woodrow Wilson Papers, 5B/13. Wilson would be informed of Lloyd George's "desire for brevity" in drafting the covenant not by Cecil, but by Miller, who had been briefed by Hurst. Miller, *Diary*, 2 February 1919.

46. Miller, *Drafting*, 1: 65–66.

47. Diary of Lord Robert Cecil, 31 January 1919, Cecil Papers.

48. Miller, *Drafting*, 1:67.

49. For the dominions' case see Canada, *Documents on Canadian External Relations*, 2:21–22, 28, 35, 38.

50. Ibid., 2:42–50. See also F. O. 608/243. For the Canadian position, see G. P. de T. Glazebrook, *Canada at the Paris Peace Conference*, chap. 5.

51. W. Hughes, "Notes on the Draft Convention for the League of Nations," 1 February 1919, F. O. 608/243.

52. Miller, *Drafting*, 2:doc. 19, 231–37.

53. Miller, *Drafting*, 1:72; 2:doc. 14.

54. Seymour, *Intimate Papers*, 4:313–14.

55. Diary of Lord Robert Cecil, 3 February 1919, Cecil Papers. Cecil noted, "The incident is exceedingly characteristic of the great tenacity of Wilson's mind,

and his incapacity for cooperation resulting from a prolonged period of autocratic power."

56. Hankey to Lady Hankey, 5 February 1919, Roskill, *Hankey*, 2:56–57.

57. Hankey's "vision" of moving from secretary of the cabinet to secretary general of the Allies at the peace conference and then, by transition, to first secretary of the league is spelled out in Diary of Maurice Hankey, 13 October 1918, Roskill, *Hankey*, 1:612–13.

58. Hankey to Lady Hankey, 5 February 1919, Roskill, *Hankey*, 2:57.

59. Diary of Lord Robert Cecil, 5 February 1919, Cecil Papers. See also Diary of William Wiseman, 5 February 1919, Wiseman Papers.

60. Records in English of the League of Nations Commission are to be found in Miller, *Drafting*, 2:doc. 19, 229–392. See also War Cabinet Papers, W.C.P. Series, Cab. 29/7–13. Detailed secondary treatments can be found in Miller, *Drafting*; Tillman, *Anglo-American Relations*; Florence Wilson, *The Origins of the League of Nations Covenant*; and Felix Morley, *The Society of Nations*.

61. Miller, *Drafting*, 1:132–36.

62. Ibid., 1:141–48; 2:255–59.

63. Ibid., 1:158–67; 2:259–63.

64. Diary of Lord Robert Cecil, 4 February 1919, Cecil Papers.

65. Miller, *Drafting*, 1:168–70; 2:263–64.

66. Diary of Lord Robert Cecil, 1 February 1919, Cecil Papers.

67. In his diary Cecil portrayed the support of the small powers for Wilson's territorial guarantee as "singularly perverse." He was doubly amazed "to find all the foreigners quite keen for the guarantee, though almost openly expressing the view that it would not be kept, as a kind of demonstration." Furthermore, Cecil's experience of working with Wilson for a few days had resulted in a personal dislike: "I do not know quite what it is that repels me; a certain hardness, coupled with vanity and an eye for effect. He supports idealistic causes without being in the least an idealist himself, at least so I guess, though perhaps I misjudge him" (Diary of Lord Robert Cecil, 6 February 1919, Cecil Papers).

68. Miller, *Drafting*, 1:170–73; 2:264–65.

69. Ibid., 1:173–75; 2:265–66.

70. Ibid., 1:179–84; 2:268–71.

71. Ibid., 1:192–95; 2:283.

72. Ibid., 1:185–91, 197–200; 2:271–87.

73. Ibid., 1:201–11; 2:288–98.

74. Diary of Lord Robert Cecil, 11 February 1919, Cecil Papers.

75. Miller, *Drafting*, 2:296. Previously, warned by the admiralty against any loosely defined provisions in the covenant for an ad hoc international fleet "hastily collected on the outbreak of war," Cecil contemplated that there would "have to be military, naval and air sections of the permanent secretariat of the League who would act in some sort as a League Staff." Second thoughts drove Cecil away from this. Wemyss to Cecil, 28 January 1919; Cecil to Wemyss, 31 January 1919, F. O. 608/243.

76. Miller, *Drafting*, 1:213–24.

77. Diary of Lord Robert Cecil, 11 February 1919, Cecil Papers.

78. Miller, *Drafting*, 1:216–17.

79. Ibid., 1:217–20.

80. Ibid., 1:225–71; 2:298–335.

81. Ibid., 1:220.

82. Diary of Lord Robert Cecil, 13 February 1919, Cecil Papers. The procedure favored earlier by Lloyd George was that the draft covenant should be accepted

provisionally by the peace conference and then referred to the various parliaments. House, however, opposed this procedure as involving "fatal" delays and debates. Diary of William Wiseman, 7 February 1919, Wiseman Papers.

83. Miller has printed the relevant Council of Ten minutes in *Drafting*, 1: 240–42.

84. The minutes for the plenary session of 14 February are in ibid., 2:doc. 23.

CHAPTER 7

1. See especially the editorials of 1, 18, 21, and 28 January 1919.

2. *Morning Post*, 15 February 1919.

3. Ibid., 26 February 1919. The *Post*'s criticisms were echoed in racier prose by *John Bull*, 22 February 1919.

4. *Herald*, 22 February 1919; *Nation*, 22 February and 1 March 1919. UDC reactions are analyzed in Keith G. Robbins, *The Abolition of War*, p. 188. Labor attitudes on the drafting of the covenant were spelled out first at the Bern meeting of the Second International, 3–10 February 1919. See Pierre Renaudel, *L'Internationale à Berne*, and Arno J. Mayer, *Politics and Diplomacy of Peacemaking*, pp. 393–99. The criticisms of the Second International were mild compared to the vitriolic denunciations of the "League of robbery, of exploitation, and of imperialist counter-revolution" propounded by the new Comintern. See Jane Degras, ed. *The Communist International 1919–1943*, 1:19–23, 27, 35.

5. "Minutes of the Advisory Committee on International Questions 1918–1924"; "Resolutions by the Advisory Committee on International Questions Submitted to the Executive Committee, 4 March 1919," Labour Party Archives.

6. Labour Party, *Report of Nineteenth Annual Conference* (Southport, 1919), pp. 23–24.

7. *Westminster Gazette*, 3 February 1919.

8. Great Britain, *Parliamentary Debates* (Commons), 5th ser., 112 (1919): 63; 113 (1919):90.

9. See editorial and commentary in the *Westminster Gazette, Manchester Guardian*, and *Daily Chronicle* for the week following 14 February 1919. See also the special League of Nations edition of *Manchester Guardian*, 29 March 1919.

10. League of Nations Union, "The Position of the League of Nations in the Forthcoming Peace Conference: Memorandum Prepared by the Acting Executive Committee of the League of Nations Union for Submission to His Majesty's Government," [n.d., c. 10 January 1919], F. O. 371/4370. See also "Detailed Proposals for the Establishment of a League of Nations: Report by a Special Sub-Committee to the Executive of the League of Nations Union," F. O. 800/249.

11. LNU, *Proceedings of the Conference of Delegates of Allied Societies for a League of Nations Held in Paris January 26–February 3, 1919, and London, March 11–13, 1919*, W. H. Dickinson Papers.

12. LNU, "Observations on the Draft Covenant of the League of Nations, by the Research Committee of the League of Nations Union," [n.d., c. 20 February 1919], Murray Papers, LNU Folder.

13. Cecil to Eustace Percy, 27 February 1919, F. O. 371/4310.

14. LNU, *Proceedings of the Conference of Delegates of Allied Societies for a League of Nations, London, March 11–13, 1919*, Murray Papers, LNU Folder. Zimmern attended this conference and reported back to Cecil on proceedings. Alfred E. Zimmern, "Conference of Allied Societies for a League of Nations, March 11 and 12," F. O. 608/240.

15. Great Britain, *Parliamentary Debates* (Commons), 5th ser., 90 (1919):192–93.

16. Hankey to Tom Jones, 16 February 1919, Keith Middlemas, ed., *Tom Jones*, 1:77.

17. Diary of Lord Robert Cecil, 13 February 1919, Cecil Papers.

18. Major-General F. H. Sykes, Major-General W. Thwaites, and Admiral R. Wemyss, "Memorandum," 7 February 1919, F. O. 608/243.

19. "Extract from Board Minutes, Thursday, 27th of February 1919," Admiralty Office 116/1901.

20. W. H. Long, "League of Nations: Covenant," Cabinet Paper P. 109, 3 March 1919, Cab. 29/2. See also Stephen Roskill, *Naval Policy Between the Wars*, 1:84. Long became first lord of the admiralty in January 1919.

21. British Empire Delegation Minute BED 13, 1, 13 March 1919, Cab. 29/28.

22. Great Britain, *Parliamentary Debates* (Commons), 5th ser., 113 (1919): 69–90.

23. Doherty's memorandum for Borden of 22 February 1919 is in *Documents on Canadian External Relations*, 2:58–63.

24. Sir Robert Borden, "The Covenant of the League of Nations," Cabinet Paper W.C.P. 245, 13 March 1919, Cab. 29/97. See also Canada, *Documents on Canadian External Relations*, 2:73–87, 58–63.

25. *Morning Post*, 18 February 1919.

26. "League of Nations: Notes on the Draft Covenant by Rt. Hon. W. M. Hughes," Cabinet Paper W.C.P. 346, 21 March 1919, Cab. 29/9.

27. Diary of Lord Robert Cecil, 18–24 February 1919, Cecil Papers. Was Cecil's presence at the peace conference now an inconvenience for Lloyd George?

28. A comprehensive, although strongly pro-Wilson, treatment of the initial phase of the Senate fight is presented in Dana Frank Fleming, *The United States and the League of Nations, 1918–1920*, chaps. 5, 6. For the internal political dimensions of the antileague struggle, see Mayer, *Politics and Diplomacy*, p. 560.

29. U.S., Congress, Senate, *Congressional Record*, 66th Cong., 1st sess., 1919, 57:4974. The resolution was actually read after midnight in the early minutes of 4 March.

30. Fleming, *United States*, pp. 163–65; *New York Times*, 5 March 1919.

31. Hitchcock to Wilson, 4 March 1919, David Hunter Miller, *The Drafting of the Covenant*, 1:276–77.

32. Taft to Wilson, 18 March 1919, ibid., 1:277.

33. U.S., Department of State, *The Paris Peace Conference*, 3:972–79, 980–86, 1003–4.

34. Ibid., 4:108–11.

35. For Ray Stannard Baker's versions of the intrigue to divert the league in Wilson's absence, see his *Woodrow Wilson and World Settlement*, 1:289–311. The most detailed recent analysis of the tactical maneuvering at the peace conference while Wilson was away can be found in Inga Floto, *Colonel House in Paris*, chaps. 3, 4. See also Miller, *Drafting*, 1:85–100.

36. Floto, *Colonel House*, p. 163. Also George Bernard Noble, *Policies and Opinions at Paris, 1919*, p. 126.

37. Henry Wickham Steed, *Through Thirty Years, 1892–1922*, 2:281–85, 288–94.

38. Steed's editorial in the Paris *Daily Mail*, 6 March 1919, Steed, *Thirty Years*, 2:290–91.

39. *Times*, 14 March 1919.

40. Steed, *Thirty Years*, 2:283, 291.

41. House to Wilson, 28 February 1919, Wilson Papers, 5B/17/11197. House told Miller that his motive for getting the league underway immediately was to

outflank Republican opposition. David Hunter Miller, *My Diary at the Peace Conference*, 1:141–42.

42. Wilson to House, 3 March 1919, Wilson Papers, 5B/17/11518.

43. House to Wilson, 4 March 1919, Wilson Papers, 5B/18/11622.

44. Miller, *Drafting*, 1:99–100.

45. The rumors first reached Wilson, via Tumulty in America, just as the president arrived back in Europe. Tumulty to Wilson, 13 March 1919, Floto, *Colonel House*, p. 163.

46. Baker, *World Settlement*, 1:310–12.

47. Noble, *Policies and Opinions*, pp. 128–29. After American representations to Tardieu, Pichon's remarks were censored from the Paris press.

48. Steed, *Thirty Years*, 1:296–97.

49. Noble, *Policies and Opinions*, p. 103. See also Steed, *Thirty Years*, 2:296 and C. T. Thompson, *The Peace Conference Day by Day*, p. 255.

50. *The Paris Peace Conference*, 4:374–75.

51. Floto, *Colonel House*, 172–73. See also Kurt Wimer, "Woodrow Wilson's Plans to Enter the League of Nations through an Executive Agreement." Wimer's thesis, that the president planned to initiate the league by means of an executive agreement as early as November 1918, is unconvincing.

52. Miller, *Drafting*, 1:90–92; Floto, *Colonel House*, 172–73.

53. Within the British delegation, Eustace Percy, in reaction to the round robin, had advised Cecil to suggest amendments publicly that would meet the criticisms of the Senate Republicans. Wiseman, however, had cautioned Cecil to await the president's return. Miller, *Diary*, 11 March 1919, 1:162–63. See also Eustace Percy, *Some Memories*, p. 72. In America, Reading, Lindsay, and Barclay kept a close watch on events and opinions and sent detailed information back to the Foreign Office and Cecil. These reports, together with weekly summaries of press opinion, can be found in F. O. 371/4370, F. O. 608/243, and F. O. 608/244. Reports on the American situation are also to be found in the Lord Lothian Papers, Wiseman Papers, Balfour Papers, and Reading Papers (F. O. 800/222).

54. Diary of Lord Robert Cecil, 16 March 1919, Cecil Papers.

55. Miller, *Drafting*, 1:279–83. See also Miller, *Diary*, 18 March 1919, 1:177–78.

56. Miller, *Drafting*, 1:283–96; Diary of Lord Robert Cecil, 18 March 1919, Cecil Papers.

57. For the meetings with neutrals, see Miller, *Drafting*, 1:303–9; 2:doc. 25.

58. Miller, *Drafting*, 1:310–53; 2:docs. 19–20.

59. Diary of Lord Robert Cecil, 28 February 1919, Cecil Papers; Cecil to House, 8 March 1919, House Papers, 4–38; Miller, *Drafting*, 1:320–21.

60. For the relationship between revolution and peacemaking at this juncture, see Mayer, *Politics and Diplomacy*, chaps. 15–17.

61. Lord George Allardice Riddell, *Lord Riddell's Intimate Diary of the Peace Conference and After: 1918–1923*, p. 37.

62. Harold I. Nelson, *Land and Power*, p. 221.

63. For a comprehensive treatment of the many aspects of the "naval battle of Paris," see Harold and Margaret Sprout, *Towards a New Order of Sea Power*, chap. 4. See also, Roskill, *Naval Policy*, p. 91.

64. Riddell's *Intimate Diary*, p. 36.

65. Records from the Fontainebleau Conference are to be found in the Lord Lothian Papers, GD 40/17/60/61, and "Final Treaty of Peace" file in Cab. 1/28/15. See also Lord Maurice Hankey, *The Supreme Control at the Paris Peace Conference*, 1:99–103, and Stephen Roskill, *Hankey*, 2:70–73.

66. Lloyd George, "Some Considerations for the Peace Conference before They Finally Draft Their Terms," 25 March 1919. With some deletions the Fontainebleau memorandum can be found in David Lloyd George, *The Truth About the Peace Treaties*, 1:7, 404–16. Complete versions are in Great Britain, Parliamentary Papers, Cmd. 1614; and Baker, *World Settlement*, 3:449–57.

67. [Philip Kerr and Lord Hankey], "British Empire Interests," [23 March 1919], Lord Lothian Papers, GD 40/17/61, pp. 118–21.

68. "Some Considerations for the Peace Conference before They Finally Draft Their Terms," Draft of 24 March 1919, Lord Lothian Papers, GD 40/17/60, pp. 58–73.

69. Lloyd George, *Truth*, 1:410.

70. Ibid., 1:412–13.

71. Major-General Sir C. E. Callwell, *Field-Marshal Sir Henry Wilson*, 2:176.

72. [Lloyd George], "Some Considerations for the Peace Conference before They Finally Draft Their Terms," Draft of 23 March 1919, Lord Lothian Papers, GD 40/17/60, pp. 40–48.

73. [Kerr and Hankey], "British Empire Interests," [23 March 1919], Lord Lothian Papers, GD 40/17/61, pp. 118–121.

74. Paul Mantoux, *Paris Peace Conference, 1919*, pp. 2–3.

75. Diary of Lord Robert Cecil, 26 March 1919, Cecil Papers.

76. Miller, *Drafting*, 1:337; Diary of Edward House, 27 March 1919, House Papers.

77. Cecil to Lloyd George, 4 April 1919, Cecil Papers, Add. Mss. 51076.

78. Cecil to Balfour, 5 April 1919, Cecil Papers, Add. Mss. 51099. The same day Cecil also wrote to House suggesting that Wilson should submit a draft treaty to the Council of Four based strictly on his Fourteen Points and use economic leverage and a threat to return home in order to force the Allies to accept "an American peace" (Cecil to House, 5 April 1919, House Papers). See also Mayer, *Politics and Diplomacy*, pp. 585–86.

79. Diary of Lord Robert Cecil, 8 April 1919, Cecil Papers.

80. Records of the correspondence between Cecil, House, and Lloyd George leading to the 10 April 1919 agreement can be found in F. O. 800/216, Balfour Papers; House Papers, 4–38; Cecil Papers, Add. Mss. 51094. A good modern treatment of the question is Seth P. Tillman, *Anglo-American Relations at the Paris Peace Conference of 1919*, pp. 286–94.

81. House to Cecil, 8 April 1919, House Papers, 4–34.

82. [Cecil], "Memorandum," 10 April 1919, House Papers, 4–34.

83. Miller, *Drafting*, 1:439–52, 2:360–74.

84. Ibid., 1:453–72; 2:375–95.

85. See Tillman, *Anglo-American Relations*, pp. 300–304, and Paul Birdsall, *Versailles Twenty Years After*, pp. 89–115.

86. Miller, *Drafting*, 2:387–92.

87. After further detailed negotiations, Cecil was successful in obtaining the necessary amendments despite American resistance. Later, in a note of 6 May 1919 signed by Clemenceau, Wilson, and Lloyd George, Borden was given written assurance that the dominions were eligible for membership on the council under the provisons of Article 4. Miller, *Drafting*, 2:477–93. See also *Documents on Canadian External Relations*, 2:150.

88. B.E.D. 26 and 27, 21 April 1919, Cab. 29/28. See also *Documents on Canadian External Relations*, 2:120–27.

89. B.E.D. 28, 28 April 1919, Cab. 29/28.

90. [Hankey], "The League of Nations: Sketch Plan of Organization," [31 March 1919], F. O. 608/242.

91. Hankey to Esher, 10 and 16 February 1919, Hankey Papers; Esher to Hankey, 19 February 1919, Hankey Papers; Roskill, *Hankey*, 2:60–65; and Maurice V. Brett and Oliver Viscount Esher, eds., *Journals and Letters of Reginald, Viscount Esher*, 4:226–28.

92. Curzon to Hankey, [n.d., c. early April 1919], Hankey Papers.

93. Hankey, *Supreme Control*, 1:103–4.

94. Hankey to Lloyd George, 28 February 1919, Lloyd George Papers, F/23/4/27.

95. Hankey, *Supreme Control*, 1:103–4, and information conveyed by Professor Harold I. Nelson, University of Toronto, from an interview with Hankey.

96. Cecil to Hankey, 18 April 1919, Hankey, *Supreme Control*, pp. 104–5.

97. Roskill, *Hankey*, 2:80. Hankey was soon rewarded for his wartime government service with a grant of £25,000.

98. Miller, *Drafting*, 2:doc. 33, for minutes of the 28 April 1919 plenary session of the peace conference.

CHAPTER 8

1. Jan Christian Smuts, "Statement for Press," 28 June 1919, W. K. Hancock and Jean Van Der Poel, eds., *Selections from the Smuts Papers*, 4:257, doc. 1043.

2. Stephen Roskill, *Hankey*, 2:87–88.

3. Diary of Lord Robert Cecil, 3 May 1919, Cecil Papers. Cecil privately dismissed the prime minister's criticism as "somewhat belated" since the small powers had been included on the council from the time of the 14 February draft.

4. British Empire Delegation Minute, B.E.D. 30, 5 May 1919, Cab. 29/28.

5. Correspondence on this issue can be found in F. O. 371/4310 and F. O. 800/216.

6. For general treatments of this debate, see Seth P. Tillman, *Anglo-American Relations at the Paris Peace Conference of 1919*, pp. 344–56, and Harold I. Nelson, *Land and Power*, pp. 321–63.

7. Cecil to Lloyd George, 27 May 1919, Lloyd George Papers, F/6/6/47.

8. B.E.D. 33 and 34, 1 June 1919, Cab. 29/38/1.

9. Lord Robert Cecil, "The League of Nations and the German Counter Proposals," Cabinet Paper W.C.P. 916, 3 June 1919, Cab. 29/16. Cecil also argued the case for moderation at a special Paris session of the British cabinet on 31 May. Diary of Lord Robert Cecil, 31 May 1919, Cecil Papers.

10. "Reply of the Allied and Associated Powers, to the Observations of the German Delegations on the Conditions of Peace," 16 June 1919, U.S., Department of State, *The Paris Peace Conference*, 6:926–96.

11. Diary of Lord Robert Cecil, 9 June 1919, Cecil Papers.

12. Diary of C. P. Scott, 5 July 1919, Scott Papers, Add. Mss. 50905.

13. *Times*, 19 June 1919. The League of Nations Union had hoped to attract the prime minister to launch a major campaign for members and financial support, but Lloyd George advised deferring such a campaign until autumn when, hopefully, the peace treaty would be ratified. The smaller campaign launched for the summer of 1919 was viewed by the League of Nations Union as merely an interim measure to tide the union over until a major drive could be launched in the fall. League of Nations Union, *Report to First Annual Meeting of General Council held February 5, 1920* (London, 1920), p. 3.

14. LNU, "Report of Special Committee on Reorganization Adopted at a Meeting of the General Council, July 24th, 1919," Murray Papers.

15. LNU, "Memorandum on the financial position of the Union prepared by the special Organization Committee," [n.d., May 1919], Murray Papers. Murray was the author of this memorandum. Only generous donations from the private fortune of David Davies kept the union from financial distress.

16. LNU, Organizations Department, "Secretary's Report," 30 April 1919, Murray Papers. LNU, *Report to First Annual Meeting*, p. 9.

17. See especially *Manchester Guardian, Westminster Gazette*, and *Daily News*.

18. Cecil refused to chair the May reorganization committee until two Conservatives were added.

19. Labor attitudes can be seen in a manifesto, issued 11 May by the Second International and endorsed by the Labour party, and a second manifesto, issued 1 June by the Labour party and its national executive. Labour Party, *Report of the Nineteenth Annual Conference* (Stockport, 1919), pp. 212–13, and Appendix 14, p. 217.

20. *Times*, 7 November 1919.

21. Ibid., 14 October 1919.

22. LNU, *Report to First Annual Meeting*, p. 9.

23. Great Britain, Parliamentary Papers (Commons), "The Covenant of the League of Nations with a Commentary Thereon" (no. 3), Cd. 151, 1919, 685–703. This document was drafted by J. R. M. Butler and revised by senior members of the Foreign Office.

24. Great Britain, *Parliamentary Debates* (Commons), 5th ser., 117 (1919): 1125–27.

25. Ibid., 118 (1919):983–94.

26. Arthur Salter, "Note on Organisation of League of Nations," 10 May 1919, Lloyd George Papers, F/211/1/3. Reprinted in Sir Arthur Salter, *The United States of Europe and Other Papers*, pp. 14–31; Frank P. Walters, *A History of the League of Nations*, pp. 75–80. Initial planning within the secretariat can be followed in League of Nations, *Documents and Publications 1919–1946*; Minutes of the Directors Meetings, and Series 19/F/–, 19/6/–, 20/6/–, 21/6/–, 1919–21.

27. Maurice Hankey, "Towards a National Policy," 17 July 1919, Cab. 21/159.

28. Hankey nevertheless advised: "It is a calamity which statesmen who are responsible for our national safety would do well not entirely to exclude from their minds, but it is one which could never form the basis of our published policy. It could never be alluded to in public and should only be spoken of in the most secret and intimate discussions." Ibid.

29. "Post-war Naval Policy," Cabinet Paper G. T. 7975, 12 August 1919, Cab. 24/86; Adm. 116/1774. See also Kenneth MacDonald, "Lloyd George and the Search for a Post-war Naval Policy, 1919," A. J. P. Taylor, ed., *Lloyd George: Twelve Essays*, pp. 191–222.

30. Speech delivered to Oxford Summer School, 1 August 1919, Milner Papers, Box 152. See also *Times*, 2 August 1919.

31. War Cabinet Minute, W.C. 616a, 15 August 1919, Cab. 23/15.

32. Diary of Edward House, 22 August 1919, House Papers.

33. Curzon to Grey, 9 September 1919, E. L. Woodward and Rohan Butler, eds., *Documents on British Foreign Policy, 1919–1939*, 1st ser., 5:997–1000.

34. Kerr to Hankey, 21 July 1919, Lothian Papers, GD 40/17/1–7.

35. Kerr to Prime Minister, 12 July 1919, Lloyd George Papers, F/89/3/6.

36. Bryce to Smuts, 2 July 1919, Hancock and Van Der Poel, *Smuts Papers*, 4:doc. 1047, p. 261.

37. Wiseman to Balfour, 1 July 1919, Wiseman Papers, 90–65. See also Wiseman to Sir Ian Malcolm, 1 July 1919, Woodward and Butler, *Documents*, 1st ser., 5:980–81. Telegrams on the American situation can be found in F. O. 371/4245 and 4371.

38. Wiseman to Foreign Office, 18 July 1919, Wiseman Papers, 90–25. See also Woodward and Butler, *Documents*, 1st ser., 5:984–85.

39. Lindsay to Curzon, 21–29 August 1919, Woodward and Butler, *Documents*, 1st ser., 5:988–95.

40. General treatments of the struggle for the treaty and the league in America can be found in Thomas A. Bailey, *Woodrow Wilson and the Great Betrayal*; Dana Frank Fleming, *The United States and the League of Nations, 1918–1920*; and J. Chalmers Vinson, *Referendum for Isolation*. The question of Lodge's real motives and objectives is still being debated. See David Mervin, "Henry Cabot Lodge and the League of Nations," and James E. Hewes, Jr., "Henry Cabot Lodge and the League of Nations."

41. The Lodge reservations, together with subsequent revisions, are conveniently reprinted in Bailey, *Great Betrayal*, pp. 387–93.

42. The genesis of Grey's mission and the instructions he insisted upon can be studied in the Lloyd George Papers, F/12/1/30–35, F/12/2/4; Curzon Papers, F 112/211; and Diary of Edward House, 14, 24, 28 July, 7, 12 August 1919, House Papers. House returned to America in direct contradiction to Wilson's advice, having concluded that the president "was not a good pilot." At the same time the colonel was consistently denying any break with Wilson. Diary of Edward House, 22, 28 August, 4, 21, 30 September 1919, House Papers. See also Wickam Steed to Northcliffe, 19 August, 20 September 1919, Steed Papers.

43. Curzon to Lloyd George, 6 August 1919, Lloyd George Papers, F/12/1/35.

44. Curzon to Lloyd George, 17 September 1919, Lloyd George Papers, F/12/2/4.

45. Grey to Lloyd George, 5 October 1919, Lloyd George Papers, F/60/3/7.

46. Grey to Lloyd George, 6 October 1919, Woodward and Butler, *Documents*, 1st ser., 5:1003–4.

47. Ibid., pp. 1007–12.

48. Curzon to Grey, 24 October 1919, ibid., pp. 1011–12.

49. Grey to Curzon, 1 November 1919, ibid., p. 1014.

50. Grey to Curzon, 7 November 1919, ibid., pp. 1018–19, and Grey's detailed dispatch to Curzon, 7 November 1919, Curzon Papers, F 112/211.

51. P. H. Kerr to R. H. Campbell, 30 October 1919, Lloyd George Papers, F/12/2/3.

52. Untitled memorandum by C. J. B. Hurst, 2 November 1919, Lloyd George Papers, F/12/2/3. Hurst's observations were based on a summary of the American reservations printed in the *Times*, 24 October 1919.

53. Hurst to Campbell, 4 November 1919, Lloyd George Papers, F/12/2/3.

54. Note by Hardinge on Hurst's 4 November letter to Campbell. Ibid.

55. Hurst to Lord Hardinge, 5 November 1919, Lloyd George Papers, F/12/2/3.

56. Curzon to the prime minister, 7 November 1919, Lloyd George Papers, F/12/2/3.

57. [P. H. Kerr], "Memorandum on American Reservations and British Ratification of the Treaty of Peace," 10 November 1919, Lord Lothian Papers, G.D. 40/17/62. See also Lloyd George Papers, F/89/4/71.

58. *Times*, 12 November 1919, p. 20.

59. Wiseman to Tyrrell, 12 November 1919, Wiseman Papers, 90–65; Wiseman to House, 12 November 1919, House Papers, 12–41.

60. *New York Times*, 15 November 1919, p. 1; *Times* (London), 15 November 1919, p. 13.

61. Cary Travers Grayson, *Woodrow Wilson*, p. 104.

62. Kerr to prime minister, 15 November 1919, Lloyd George Papers, F/89/4/23.

63. Great Britain, *Parliamentary Debates* (Commons), 5th ser., 121 (1919): 689.

64. Arthur Willert, *Times*'s influential Washington correspondent, was now advising Steed that the time had come "to play up to the Republicans" as they were "almost certain to win the next election" (Willert to Steed, 26 November 1919, Willert Papers).

65. *New York Times*, 18 November 1919, p. 1.

66. Grey to Curzon, 17 November 1919, Woodward and Butler, *Documents*, 1st ser., 5:1022.

67. Curzon to Grey, 18 November 1919, ibid., p. 1023.

68. Ibid. In a subsequent letter to Grey, Curzon argued that Milner was very much disturbed at the attitude of the dominions who were "pressing hard, in every direction, for something that is indistinguishable from independence." According to Milner, unless the dominions were handled with the greatest discretion, a "rupture" could occur at any time. Curzon to Grey, 22 November 1919, Curzon Papers, F 11/211.

69. Grey to Curzon, 14 November 1919, Woodward and Butler, *Documents*, 1st ser., 5:1021–22.

70. Grey to Curzon, 24 November 1919, ibid., p. 1037.

71. Grey to Curzon, 26 November 1919, and Curzon's note, ibid., pp. 1038–39.

72. Details on the Crawford Stuart affair can be found in Willert, *Washington and Other Memories*, pp. 110, 136; Lansing to John Davis, 1 January 1920, Davis Papers; Diary of Edward House, 20 November, 5, 21 December 1919, House Papers; Lord Vansittart, *The Mist Procession*, p. 240; and William Phillips, *Ventures in Diplomacy*, pp. 91–92. I am indebted to James E. Hewes, Department of the Army, Center of Military History, Washington, D.C., for information on the liaisons of Baruch and Bernstorff. Perhaps Baruch was anxious to promote Crawford Stuart's early departure and therefore made sure that Mrs. Wilson was fully informed of the offense to her husband. Despite the best efforts of William Tyrrell, Willert, and Lansing, Grey refused to send his aide home. It is unclear how much Grey knew about Crawford Stuart's misdemeanors, but from his correspondence it would appear he had only partial knowledge.

73. Grey to Curzon, 2 November 1919, Curzon Papers, F 112/211.

74. Grey to Lloyd George, 11 November 1919, Lloyd George Papers, F/60/3/18.

75. Grey to Curzon, 23 November 1919, Woodward and Butler, *Documents*, 1st ser., 5:1034. See also Diary of Edward House, 23 November 1919, House Papers.

76. Curzon to Grey, 27 November 1919, Woodward and Butler, *Documents*, 1st ser., 5:1040–42.

77. Hurst's 18 November memorandum was subsequently forwarded to Grey and is printed in ibid., pp. 1024–28. Hurst also drafted Curzon's note to Grey. Kerr to Hurst, 24 November 1919, F. O. 800/158.

78. Curzon to Grey, 27 November 1919, ibid., 1st ser., 5:1042–43; Kerr to Hurst, 25 November 1919, Lothian Papers, GD 40/17/211; Polk to Lansing, 29 November 1919, *The Paris Peace Conference*, 9:675–77.

79. A similar tactic had already been suggested by Lansing. Private Memoranda, 22 October 1919, Lansing Papers.

80. Hurst's 18 November memorandum had concluded that "the existing Covenant of the League of Nations is not by any means an ideal instrument, and if, within two years it were possible to substitute an improved and simplified draft for the existing one, it would be a great advantage." Woodward and Butler, *Documents*, 1st ser., 5:1028.

81. Grey to Curzon, 28 November 1919, ibid., p. 1045. Root was secretary of war and secretary of state under former Republican administrations.

82. Curzon to Grey, 22 November 1919, Curzon Papers, F 112/211. (Sent 25 November; received c. 3 December.)

83. Grey to Curzon, [December 6, 1919], Woodward and Butler, *Documents*, 1st ser., 5:1054–55.

84. Willert to Steed, 6 December 1919, Willert Papers.

85. Diary of Edward House, 5 December 1919, House Papers.

86. Willert to Steed, 6 December 1919, Willert Papers; Grey to Steed, 29 December 1919, Steed Papers.

87. Willert to Steed, 6, 19 December 1919; Willert to Northcliffe, [c. 14 December 1919], Willert, *Other Memories*, p. 138.

88. Smuts to prime minister, 29 November 1919, included in Curzon to Grey, 8 December 1919, Woodward and Butler, *Documents*, 1st ser., 5:1056–57.

89. Eric Drummond to Raymond Fosdick, [13 December 1919], Raymond B. Fosdick, *Letters on the League of Nations*, pp. 82–83. Fosdick was the American under-secretary general of the league until his resignation in January 1920.

90. Bliss's memorandum began as "An Imaginary Letter to Two Prime Ministers," composed on 2 December after conversations with a French newspaperman close to Clemenceau. It was then given to Polk on 3 December for purposes of talks with Clemenceau and shown on 5 December to Derby, the British ambassador to France, who tried unsuccessfully to have Bliss send a copy to Curzon. After amendments it was communicated on 8 December to John Davis, the American ambassador to Britain. No copy of the memorandum appears to have been given directly to the British government by the Americans, but a copy was given to Clemenceau, probably by Polk. Bliss to Polk, 3 December 1919, Polk Papers, 74/35; Derby to Curzon, 5, 6 December, and Bliss to Derby, 6 December 1919, Curzon Papers, F 112/196; Bliss to Davis, 8 December 1919, Davis Papers, 4/170. See also Bliss Papers, Box 71, for varying drafts of his "Imaginary Letter," and Frederick Palmer, *Bliss, Peacemaker*, pp. 422–27. The memorandum, the author unidentified, is reprinted in Woodward and Butler, *Documents*, 5th ser., 2:766–70.

91. "Pour ratification américain du traité suggestion d'une declaration franco-anglais acceptant 10 ou 11 des 14 Réserves du Sénat american, à condition que les trois ou quatres réserves incompatibles avec le traité disparaissent," 9 December 1919, F. O. 371/4251. See also R. Sperling, "Memo on paper commt. by M. Clemenceau," F. O. 371/4251.

92. Hewes, "Henry Cabot Lodge and the League of Nations," p. 254.

93. According to Lodge, he had "many talks" with Grey whose stay in America had taught him that the treaty contest was not simply a matter of partisan politics but involved a "great Constitutional question" (Lodge to George Otto Trevelyan, 19 January 1920, John Arthur Garraty, *Henry Cabot Lodge*, p. 387). That Grey had discussed matters secretly with Lodge was revealed by the *New York Times*, 2 February 1920, p. 1. Grey made no explicit reference to his negotiations with Lodge even in his private correspondence with government leaders.

94. Grey's three telegrams to Curzon of 11 December 1919 were received 12 December. Woodward and Butler, *Documents*, 1st ser., 5:1059–61.

95. International Conference I.C.P. 4, 13 December 1919, Cab. 29/81. See also Woodward and Butler, *Documents*, 5th ser., 2:753–54.

96. Great Britain, *Parliamentary Debates* (Commons), 5th ser., 123 (1919): 727–28.

97. Ibid., 733–35.

98. Ibid., 769–72.

99. Kerr to Drummond, 18 December 1919, Lothian Papers, G.D. 40/17/56.

100. "Process-Verbal of the First Meeting of the Council of the League of Nations," 16 January 1920, League of Nations, *Official Journal*, No. 1, February 1920, pp. 20–22.

101. Grey's letter, generally viewed as officially inspired and signaling the Allies' willingness to tolerate American reservations, was designed primarily to put pressure on Wilson and the Democrats to compromise with the Republicans on the basis of the Lodge reservations modified slightly to remove the most objectionable features. Lodge cooperated but Wilson refused to bend. Wilson, on the contrary, bitterly resented Grey's demarche, viewing it as an Allied betrayal of the covenant despite Lloyd George's explicit disclaimers of any foreknowledge or responsibility for the letter. The letter probably did have tacit Allied sanction, although there is no proof. Grey had ample opportunity to report fully on the American situation to British and French leaders in mid-January, when Lloyd George and Curzon were in Paris for meetings of the Supreme Council and Grey attended the inauguration of the league. French newspapers close to Clemenceau supported the letter warmly on its publication, and the *Daily Chronicle*, a Lloyd George organ, advised that Grey's counsel might "weigh a little with Senator Hitchcock and his friends when they finally come to decide whether they will let the mutilated treaty go through." Grey also went over the details of his letter with Cecil and Steed, who were attempting to convince Grey to resume a political career in the hope of dishing Lloyd George. The letter probably came as no surprise to Lodge. John Hays Hammond, *The Autobiography of John Hays Hammond*, 2:649–53; Steed to Northcliffe, 16, 18 January, 10 February 1920, Steed to House, 11 February 1920, Steed Papers; *The History of The Times*, 4:1118–19; Davis to Lansing, 6 February 1920, Lansing Papers; *New York Times*, 6 February 1920; London *Times*, 6, 7 February 1920; R. S. Baker, Notebook, 3–7 February 1920, R. S. Baker Papers; Wilson Papers, microfilm reel 106; Geddes to Curzon, 29 June 1920, Lloyd George Papers, F/60/4/4; Geddes to Curzon, 1 July 1920, F.O. 800/158; *Echo de Paris, Temps, Daily Chronicle*, 2 February 1920; L. E. Boothe, "A Fettered Envoy: Lord Grey's Mission to the United States, 1919–1920"; Keith Robbins, *Sir Edward Grey*, p. 355.

102. By this time Kerr had concluded that events in America had demonstrated the fundamental flaws in the covenant's attempt to transcend the limits of national sovereignty. The truth of the matter was that the United States Senate had "expressed the real sentiment of all nations with hard-headed truthfulness." The British Empire should also assert its own freedom from the general obligations of the covenant, and "definitely denounce the idea that the League may normally enforce its opinions by military or economic pressure on recalcitrant States." A league limited to promoting free international discussion and cooperation would enjoy much greater prospects of success in attracting American participation and the support of the British Commonwealth. [Philip H. Kerr], "The British Empire, the League of Nations, and the United States," pp. 232, 246–47.

Bibliography

MANUSCRIPT SOURCES

Canada

Ottawa
  Public Archives of Canada
    Robert Borden Papers
    Loring Christie Papers
    Charles Doherty Papers
    George Foster Papers
    George Perley Papers

Great Britain

London
  Public Record Office
    Admiralty Records
    Cabinet Office Records
    Foreign Office Records
    War Office Records
London
  Transport House
    Archives of the Labour Party
London
  British Library of Economic and Political Science
    Miscellaneous records of the League of Nations Society, League
      of Free Nations Association, and the League of Nations
      Union. (Records of the League of Nations Society and the

League of Nations Union London headquarters perished
during World War II, but Council Minute Books and several
other records were deposited in the United Nations Association Library, London, and have now been transferred to the
London School of Economics and Political Science.)

London
  British Museum
    Arthur James Balfour Papers
    Robert Cecil Papers
    C. P. Scott Papers
London
  House of Lords Record Office
    Bonar Law Papers
    Lloyd George Papers
London
  India Office Library
    George Curzon Papers
London
  Archives of the *Times*
    Wickham Steed Papers
    Arthur Willert Papers
London
  J. W. Headlam-Morley Papers
    (in personal possession of Professor Agnes Headlam-Morley,
      St. Hugh's College, Oxford.)
Oxford
  Bodleian Library
    Henry Asquith Papers
    James Bryce Papers
    Willoughby H. Dickinson Papers
    Alfred Milner Papers
    Gilbert Murray Papers
Cambridge
  University Library
    Charles Hardinge Papers
    Jan Christian Smuts Papers (microfilm)
Cambridge
  Churchill College
    Maurice Hankey Papers

Cambridge
  Trinity College
    J. R. M. Butler Papers (courtesy of the late Sir J. R. M. Butler.
      This collection includes papers on the creation of the League
      of Nations donated by Philip Noel-Baker.)
Birmingham
  University Library
    Austen Chamberlain Papers
Aberystwyth
  National Library of Wales
    David Davies Papers
Edinburgh
  Scottish Record Office
    Lord Lothian Papers (Philip Kerr)

United States

Washington, D. C.
  Library of Congress
    Ray Stannard Baker Papers
    Tasker H. Bliss Papers
    Gilbert M. Hitchcock Papers
    Robert Lansing Papers
    David Hunter Miller Papers
    Woodrow Wilson Papers
New Haven
  Sterling Library, Yale University
    John Davis Papers
    Edward House Papers
    William Wiseman Papers
Boston
  Massachusetts Historical Society
    Henry Cabot Lodge Papers

GOVERNMENT DOCUMENTS

Canada

Department of External Affairs. *Documents on Canadian External
  Relations.* 8 vols. to date. Vol. 2, *The Paris Peace Conference of*

1919. Edited by R. A. McKay. Ottawa: The Queen's Printer, 1969. Vol. 3, *1919–1925*. Edited by Lovell C. Clark. Ottawa: Information Canada, 1970.

France

Assemblée Nationale. Chambre des Députés. *Annales de la Chambre, Session Ordinaire de 1919. Débats Parlementaires; Documents Parlementaires*. Paris: Imprimerie des Journaux Officiels, 1920.

Great Britain

House of Commons Debates. 5th series, vols. 65–124 (1914–19).
House of Lords Debates. 5th series, vols. 17–37 (1914–19).
Parliamentary Papers (Commons), "The Covenant of the League of Nations with a Commentary Thereon," June 1919. Miscellaneous no. 3, Cmd. 151, 1919 session, vol. 53, pp. 685–703.
Parliamentary Papers (Commons), "Some Considerations for a Peace Conference before They Finally Draft Their Terms," 25 March 1919. Cmd. 1614, 1922 session, vol. 23, pp. 643–54.
Woodward, E. L., and Butler, R., eds. *Documents on British Foreign Policy, 1919–1939*. 1st series, vol. 5, 5th series, vol. 2. London: H.M.S.O., 1948, 1954.

League of Nations

Official Journal. 1st sess., 1920.
Documents and Publications 1919–1946.
  Minutes of the Directors Meetings; and Series 19/F–, 19/6/–, 20/6/–, 21/6/–, 1919–21. New Haven, Conn.: Research Publications, [1973]. Microfilm.

United States

Congress. Senate. *Congressional Record*, 66th Cong., 1st sess., vols. 18, 57 (1918–19).
Department of State. *Papers Relating to the Foreign Relations of the United States, 1916*, Supplement, *The World War*. Washington: United States Government Printing Office, 1931.

Department of State. *Papers Relating to the Foreign Relations of the United States, 1919. The Paris Peace Conference.* 13 vols. Washington: United States Government Printing Office, 1942–47.

PARTY AND SOCIETY PUBLICATIONS

The publications of the Labour party, the Independent Labour party, the Fabian Society, and the Union of Democratic Control that fall in the period of this study are listed in the bibliographies of Austin Van der Slice, *International Labor, Diplomacy, and Peace, 1914–1919,* and Marvin Swartz, *The Union of Democratic Control in British Politics during the First World War.* Literature published by the League of Nations Society, the League of Free Nations Association, and the League of Nations Union, together with other contemporary literature on the league idea, is immense. The most significant publications are listed in the bibliography of Henry R. Winkler, *The League of Nations Movement in Great Britain, 1914–1919.*

BOOKS, ARTICLES, AND THESES

Addison, Christopher. *Four and a Half Years: A Personal Diary from June 1914 to January 1919.* 2 vols. London: Hutchinson & Co., 1934.

Ambrosius, Lloyd E. "Wilson, the Republicans, and French Security after World War I." *Journal of American History* 59 (1972): 341–52.

Amery, L. S. *My Political Life.* 3 vols. London: Hutchinson & Co., 1953–55.

Angell, Norman. *After All: The Autobiography of Norman Angell.* London: Hamish Hamilton, 1951.

———. *The Great Illusion.* London: William Heinemann, 1911.

Annual Register: A Review of Publications at Home and Abroad for the Year 1919. London: Longmans, Green & Co., 1920.

Bailey, Thomas A. *Woodrow Wilson and the Great Betrayal.* New York: Macmillan Co., 1947.

———. *Woodrow Wilson and the Lost Peace.* New York: Macmillan Co., 1944.

Baker, Ray Stannard. *Woodrow Wilson: Life and Letters*. 8 vols. New York: Doubleday, Doran & Co., 1927–39.

————. *Woodrow Wilson and World Settlement*. 3 vols. Garden City, N.Y.: Doubleday, Page, 1923.

————, and Dodd, William Edward, eds. *The Public Papers of Woodrow Wilson*. 6 vols. New York: Harper & Brothers, 1925–27.

Bane, Suda Lorena, and Lutz, Ralph Haswell, eds. *Organization of American Relief in Europe, 1918–1919*. Stanford: Stanford University Press, 1943.

Bartlett, Ruhl J. *The League to Enforce Peace*. Chapel Hill, N.C.: University of North Carolina Press, 1944.

Bartz, Peter Frederick. "The League of Nations Union Between the Wars: The Rise and Decline of a British Political Pressure Group." Ph.D. dissertation, University of Kentucky, 1964.

Beales, A. C. F. *The History of Peace*. London: G. Bell & Sons, Ltd., 1931.

Beaverbrook, Lord. *Men and Power 1917–1918*. London: Hutchinson & Co., 1956.

————. *Politicians and the War: 1914–1916*. 2 vols. London: Thornton Butterworth, 1928.

Beloff, Max. *Imperial Sunset*. 2 vols. Vol. 1. *Britain's Liberal Empire, 1897–1921*. London: Methuen & Co., 1970.

Birdsall, Paul. *Versailles Twenty Years After*. New York: Reynal & Hitchcock, 1941.

Birn, Donald S. "The League of Nations Union and Collective Security." *Journal of Contemporary History* 9 (1974):131–59.

Blake, Robert. *The Unknown Prime Minister: The Life and Times of Andrew Bonar Law, 1858–1923*. London: Eyre & Spottiswoode, 1955.

Bonsal, Stephen. *Unfinished Business*. Garden City, N.Y.: Doubleday and Co., 1944.

Boothe, Leon E. "A Fettered Envoy: Lord Grey's Mission to the United States, 1919–1920." *Review of Politics* 33 (1971):78–94.

Bourgeois, Léon. *Le Pacte de 1919 et la Société des Nations*. Paris: Bibliothèque-Charpentier, Editions Fasquella, 1919.

Brailsford, H. N. *The War of Steel and Gold: A Study of the Armed Peace*. 3rd ed. London: G. Bell and Sons, Ltd., 1915.

Brett, Maurice U., and Oliver, Viscount Esher, eds. *Journals and Letters of Reginald, Viscount Esher.* 4 vols. London: Nicholson & Watson, 1934–38.

Brock, Peter. *Pacifism in Europe to 1914.* Princeton: Princeton University Press, 1972.

———. *Twentieth Century Pacifism.* Toronto: D. Van Nostrand Co., 1970.

Bunselmeyer, Robert E. *The Cost of the War, 1914–1919: British Economic War Aims and the Origins of Reparations.* Hamden, Conn.: Shoe String Press, Archon Books, 1975.

Butler, J. R. M. *Lord Lothian (Philip Kerr), 1882–1940.* London: Macmillan & Co., 1960.

Butterfield, Herbert. "Sir Edward Grey in July, 1914." *Historical Studies* 5 (1965):1–25.

Buzenkai, D. I. "Bolsheviks, The League of Nations, and the Paris Peace Conference, 1919." *Soviet Studies* 19 (1967):257–63.

Callwell, Major-General Sir C. E. *Field-Marshal Sir Henry Wilson: His Life and Diaries.* 2 vols. London: Cassell & Co., 1927.

Carr, Edward Hallett. *The Twenty Years Crisis: An Introduction to the Study of International Relations.* London: Macmillan & Co., 1939.

Cecil of Chelwood, E. A. Robert, Viscount. *All the Way.* London: Hodder and Stoughton, 1949.

———. *A Great Experiment: An Autobiography.* London: Jonathan Cape, 1941.

Cecil, David. *The Cecils of Hatfield House: An English Ruling Family.* Boston: Houghton Mifflin Co., 1973.

Cecil, Hugh P. "The Development of Lord Robert Cecil's Views on the Securing of a Lasting Peace, 1915–1919." D. Phil. dissertation, Oxford University, 1971.

———. "Lord Robert Cecil: A Nineteenth-Century Upbringing." *History Today* 25 (1975):118–27.

Churchill, Winston S. *The World Crisis.* 6 vols. Vol. 6, *The Aftermath.* New York: Charles Scribner's Sons, 1929.

Claude, Inis L., Jr. *Power and International Relations.* New York: Random House, 1964.

———. *Swords into Plowshares: The Problems and Progress of International Organization.* 3rd ed. New York: Random House, 1964.

Clifford, John. *The War and the Churches*. London: J. Clarke & Co., 1914.

Cooper, John Milton, Jr., "British Response to the House-Grey Memorandum: New Evidence and New Questions." *Journal of American History* 59 (1973):958–71.

Craig, Gordon A., and Gilbert, Felix, eds. *The Diplomats: 1919–1939*. 2 vols. Princeton: Princeton University Press, 1953.

Crosby, Gerda Richards. *Disarmament and Peace in British Politics, 1914–1919*. Cambridge, Mass.: Harvard University Press, 1957.

Curry, George W. "Woodrow Wilson, Jan Smuts, and the Versailles Settlement." *American Historical Review* 66 (1961):968–86.

[Curtis, Lionel.] "Windows of Freedom." *Round Table* 9, no. 33 (December 1918):1–36.

Degras, Jane, ed. *The Communist International 1919–1943. Documents*. 3 vols. Vol. 1. *1919–1922*. London: Oxford University Press, 1956.

Devlin, Patrick. *Too Proud to Fight: Woodrow Wilson's Neutrality*. London, Oxford University Press, 1974.

Dickinson, G. Lowes. *The Autobiography of G. Lowes Dickinson and Other Unpublished Writings*. Edited by Dennis Proctor. London: Gerald Duckworth & Co., 1973.

————. *The International Anarchy: 1904–1914*. London: George Allen & Unwin, 1926.

————. *A Modern Symposium*. London: Brimley, Johnson and Ince, 1905.

————. "The Way Out." *War and Peace: A Norman Angell Monthly* 1, no. 12 (14 September 1914): 345–46.

D'Ombrain, Nicholas. *War Machinery and High Policy: Defence Administration in Peacetime Britain, 1902–1914*. New York: Oxford University Press, 1973.

Dubin, Martin David. "Toward the Concept of Collective Security." *International Organization* 24 (1970):288–318.

Dudden, Arthur Power, ed. *Woodrow Wilson and the World of Today*: Essays by Arthur S. Link, William L. Langer, [and] Eric F. Goldman. Philadelphia: University of Pennsylvania Press, 1957.

Dugdale, Blanche E. C. *Arthur James Balfour*. 2 vols. London: Hutchinson & Co., 1936.

Finkelstein, Marina S., and Lawrence S., eds. *Collective Security.* San Francisco: Chandler Publishing Co., 1966.

Fischer, Robert James. "Henry Cabot Lodge's Concept of Foreign Policy and the League of Nations." Ph.D. dissertation, University of Georgia, 1971.

Fisher, H. A. L. *James Bryce.* 2 vols. New York: Macmillan Co., 1927.

Fitzhardinge, L. F. "Hughes, Borden, and Dominion Representation at the Paris Peace Conference." *Canadian Historical Review* 49 (1968):160–69.

Fleming, Dana Frank. *The United States and the League of Nations, 1918–1920.* New York: G. P. Putnam's Sons, 1932.

Floto, Inga. *Colonel House in Paris: A Study of American Policy at the Paris Peace Conference, 1919.* Copenhagen: Universitetsforlaget i Århus, 1973.

Forster, E. M. *Goldsworthy Lowes Dickinson.* London: Edward Arnold & Co., 1934.

Fosdick, Raymond B. *Letters on the League of Nations from the Files of Raymond B. Fosdick.* Princeton: Princeton University Press, 1966.

Fowler, Wilton B. *British-American Relations, 1917–1918: The Role of Sir William Wiseman.* Princeton: Princeton University Press, 1969.

Fraser, Peter. *Lord Esher: A Political Biography.* London: Davis, MacGibbon, 1973.

Fry, Michael G. *Illusions of Security: North Atlantic Diplomacy 1918–22.* Toronto: University of Toronto Press, 1972.

———. "The Imperial War Cabinet, the United States and the Freedom of the Seas." *Journal of the United Royal Service Institution,* 110, no. 640 (November, 1965).

Garraty, John Arthur. *Henry Cabot Lodge: A Biography.* New York: Alfred A. Knopf, 1953.

Gelfand, Lawrence E. *The Inquiry: American Preparations for Peace 1917–1919.* New Haven: Yale University Press, 1963.

Glazebrook, G. P. de T. *Canada at the Paris Peace Conference.* Toronto: Oxford University Press, 1942.

Gollin, A. M. *Proconsul in Politics: A Study of Lord Milner in Opposition and in Power.* London: Anthony Blond, 1964.

Gooch, John. *The Plans of War: The General Staff and British Military Strategy c. 1900–1916*. New York: John Wiley & Sons, 1974.

Gottlieb, W. W. *Studies in Secret Diplomacy during the First World War*. London: George Allen & Unwin, 1957.

Gowen, Robert J. "Lord Haldane of Cloan (1856–1928), Neglected Apostle of the League of Nations." *Il Politico* 36, no. 1 (1971): 161–68.

Grayson, Cary Travers. *Woodrow Wilson: An Intimate Memoir*. New York: Holt, Rinehart, and Winston, 1960.

Gregory, Ross. *Walter Hines Page: Ambassador to the Court of St. James*. Lexington: University of Kentucky Press, 1970.

Grey of Fallodon, Edward, Viscount. *The League of Nations*. London: Humphrey Milford, 1918.

———. *Twenty Five Years, 1892–1916*. 2 vols. London: Hodder and Stoughton, 1925.

Guinn, Paul. *British Strategy and Politics: 1914 to 1918*. London: Oxford University Press, Clarendon Press, 1965.

Gwynn, Stephen, ed. *The Letters and Friendships of Sir Cecil Spring-Rice*. 2 vols. Boston: Houghton Mifflin Co., 1929.

Hammond, John Hays. *The Autobiography of John Hays Hammond*. 2 vols. New York: Farrar & Rinehart, 1935.

Hanak, H. "The Union of Democratic Control during the First World War." *Bulletin of the Institute of Historical Research* 36 (1963):168–80.

Hancock, W. K. *Smuts: The Sanguine Years, 1870–1919*. London: Cambridge University Press, 1962.

———, and Van Der Poel, Jean, eds. *Selections from the Smuts Papers*. 6 vols. London: Cambridge University Press, 1966–73.

Hankey, Sir Maurice. *Diplomacy by Conference: Studies in Public Affairs: 1920–1946*. London: Ernest Benn, 1946.

———. *The Supreme Command, 1914–1918*. 2 vols. London: George Allen and Unwin, 1961.

———. *The Supreme Control at the Paris Peace Conference, 1919: A Commentary*. London: George Allen & Unwin, 1963.

Hazlehurst, Cameron. *Politicians at War, July 1914 to Mar. 1915: A Prologue to the Triumph of Lloyd George*. New York: Alfred A. Knopf, 1971.

Headlam-Morley, James. *A Memoir of the Paris Peace Conference, 1919.* Edited by Agnes Headlam-Morley. London: Methuen & Co., 1972.

Henig, Ruth B. *The League of Nations.* New York: Harper & Row, 1973.

Herman, Sondra R. *Eleven Against War: Studies in American International Thought, 1898–1921.* Stanford: Stanford University Hoover Institute on War, Revolution and Peace, 1969.

Hewes, James E., Jr., "Henry Cabot Lodge and the League of Nations." *Proceedings of the American Philosophical Society* 114 (1970):245–55.

————. "William E. Borach and the Image of Isolation." Ph.D. dissertation, Yale University, 1955.

Hinsley, F. H. *Power and the Pursuit of Peace: Theory and Practice in the History of Relations Between States.* London: Cambridge University Press, 1963.

Hobson, John A. *Towards International Government.* London: George Allen & Unwin, Ltd., 1915.

Holbraad, Carsten. *The Concert of Europe.* London: Longmans Green & Co., 1970.

House, E. M., and Seymour, Charles, eds. *What Really Happened at Paris: The Story of the Peace Conference, 1918–1919.* London: Hodder & Stoughton, 1921.

Howard, Michael. *The Continental Commitment: The Dilemma of British Defence Policy in the Era of the Two World Wars.* London: Penguin Publishing Co., 1972.

Jacobs, Aaron Jonah. *Neutrality Versus Justice: An Essay on International Relations.* London: T. Fisher Unwin, 1917.

Jenkins, Roy. *Asquith: Portrait of a Man and an Era.* New York: Chilmark Press, 1964.

Jones, Goronwy J. *Wales and the Quest for Peace.* Cardiff: University of Wales Press, 1969.

Kendle, John E. *The Round Table Movement and Imperial Union.* Toronto: University of Toronto Press, 1975.

Kernek, Sterling J. "The British Government's Reactions to Woodrow Wilson on Questions of Peace, December 1916–November 1918." Ph.D. dissertation, Cambridge University, 1971.

————. *Distractions of Peace during War: The Lloyd George Government's Reaction to Woodrow Wilson, December, 1916–*

November, 1918, Transactions of the American Philosophical Society, vol 65, pt. 2 (1975).

[Kerr, Philip H.] "The British Empire, the League of Nations and the United States." *Round Table* 10 (March 1920):221–53.

Keynes, John Maynard. *The Economic Consequences of the Peace.* New York: Harcourt, Brace & Co., 1920.

King, Jere Clemens. *Foch Versus Clemenceau: France and German Dismemberment, 1918–1919.* Cambridge, Mass.: Harvard University Press, 1960.

Kitsikis, Dimitri. *Le Rôle des experts à la Conférence de la Paix de 1919: Gestation d'une technocratie en politique internationale.* Cahiers d'histoire de l'Université d'Ottawa, vol. 4. Ottawa: Editions de l'Université d'Ottawa, 1972.

Koss, Stephen E. *Asquith.* London: Allen Lane, 1976.

_____. *Lord Haldane: Scapegoat for Liberalism.* New York: Columbia University Press, 1969.

Kuehl, Warren F. *Seeking World Order: The United States and International Organization to 1920.* Nashville: Vanderbilt University Press, 1969.

Kurtz, Harold. "The Lansdowne Letter." *History Today* 18 (1968): 84–92.

Lansing, Robert L. *The Big Four and Others of the Peace Conference.* Boston: Houghton Mifflin, 1921.

_____. *The Peace Negotiations: A Personal Narrative.* Boston: Houghton Mifflin Co., 1921.

Larus, Joel. *From Collective Security to Preventive Diplomacy: Readings in International Organization and the Maintenance of Peace.* New York: John Wiley & Sons, 1965.

Latané, John H., ed. *Development of the League of Nations Idea: Documents and Correspondence of Theodore Marburg.* 2 vols. New York: Macmillan Co., 1932.

Levin, N. Gordon, Jr. *Woodrow Wilson and World Politics: America's Response to War and Revolution.* New York: Oxford University Press, 1968.

Link, Arthur S. *President Wilson and his English Critics: An Inaugural Lecture Delivered Before the University of Oxford on 13 May, 1959.* London: Oxford University Press, 1959.

_____. *Wilson.* 5 vols. Vol. 3, *The Struggle for Neutrality, 1914–1915.* Vol. 4, *Confusions and Crises, 1915–1916.* Vol. 5,

Campaigns for Progressivism and Peace, 1916–1917. Princeton: Princeton University Press, 1960–65.

————. *Wilson the Diplomatist: A Look at his Major Foreign Policies.* Baltimore: John Hopkins University Press, 1941.

————. *Woodrow Wilson and the Progressive Era: 1910–1917.* New York: Harper & Brothers, 1954.

————, Duroselle, Jean-Baptiste; Fraenkel, Ernst; and Nicholas, H. G. *Wilson's Diplomacy: An International Symposium.* The American Forum. Cambridge, Mass.: Schenkman Publishing Co., 1973.

Lloyd George, David. *The Truth About the Peace Treaties.* 2 vols. London: Victor Gollancz, 1938.

————. *The War Memoirs of David Lloyd George.* 6 vols. London: Ivor Nicholson & Watson, 1933–37.

Louis, Wm. Roger. *Great Britain and Germany's Lost Colonies, 1914–1919.* London: Oxford University Press, Clarendon Press, 1967.

————. "The United Kingdom and the Beginning of the Mandates System, 1919–1972." *International Organization* 23 (1969):73–96.

Lowe, C. J., and Dockrill, M. L. *The Mirage of Power.* 3 vols. Vol. 1, *1902–1914.* Vol. 2, *1914–1922.* Vol. 3, *The Documents.* London: Routledge & Kegan Paul, 1972.

Lowell, A. Lawrence. "A League to Enforce Peace." *Atlantic Monthly* 116, no. 3 (September 1915):392–400.

Luckau, Alma. *The German Delegation at the Paris Peace Conference.* New York: Columbia University Press, 1941.

MacKenzie, Norman and Jeanne. *The Time Traveller: The Life of H. G. Wells.* London: George Weidenfeld & Nicholson, 1973.

Mantoux, Paul. *Paris Peace Conference, 1919: Proceedings of the Council of Four, March 24–April 19.* Geneva: Librarie E. Droz, 1964.

Marder, Arthur J. *From the Dreadnought to Scapa Flow: The Royal Navy in the Fisher Era 1904–1919.* 5 vols. Vol. 5, *1918–1919, Victory and Aftermath.* London: Oxford University Press, 1970.

Marvin, Albert. *The Last Crusade: The Church of England in the First World War.* Durham, N.C.: Duke University Press, 1974.

Marston, F. S. *The Peace Conference of 1919: Organization and Procedure.* London: Oxford University Press, 1944.

Martin, Lawrence W. *Peace Without Victory: Woodrow Wilson and the British Liberals.* New Haven: Yale University Press, 1958.

Marwick, Arthur. *The Deluge: British Society and the First World War.* London: Bodley Head, 1965.

Mason, C. M. "British Policy on the Establishment of a League of Nations, 1914–1919." Ph.D. dissertation, Cambridge University, 1971.

May, Ernest R. *The World War and American Isolation.* Cambridge, Mass.: Harvard University Press, 1959.

Mayer, Arno J. *Political Origins of the New Diplomacy, 1917–1918.* New Haven: Yale University Press, 1959.

————. *Politics and Diplomacy of Peacemaking: Containment and Counterrevolution at Versailles, 1918–1919.* New York: Random House, 1967.

McCallum, Ronald B. *Public Opinion and the Last Peace.* London: Oxford University Press, 1944.

Mervin, David. "Henry Cabot Lodge and the League of Nations." *Journal of American Studies* 4 (1970):201–4.

Middlemas, Keith, ed. *Thomas Jones: Whitehall Diary.* 3 vols. Vol. 1, *1916–1925.* London: Oxford University Press, 1969.

Miller, David Hunter. *The Drafting of the Covenant.* 2 vols. New York: G. P. Putnam's Sons, 1928.

————. *My Diary at the Conference of Paris.* 21 vols. Privately printed. New York: Appeal Printing, 1924.

Miqeul, Pierre. *La Paix de Versailles et l'opinion publique française.* Paris: Flammarion et Cie., 1972.

Morley, Felix. *The Society of Nations: Its Organization and Constitutional Development.* Washington: Brookings Institution, 1932.

Morris, A. J. Anthony. *Radicalism Against War, 1906–1914: The Advocacy of Peace and Retrenchment.* Essex: Longmans Group, 1972.

Munch, P., ed. *Les Origines et L'Oeuvre de la Société des Nations.* 2 vols. Copenhagen: Rask-Ørstedfonden, 1923–24.

Murray, Gilbert. *The League of Nations Movement: Some Recollections of the Early Days.* London: David Davis Memorial Institute of International Studies, Annual Memorial Lecture, 1955.

Nelson, Harold I. *Land and Power: British and Allied Policy on Germany's Frontiers, 1916–1919.* Toronto: University of Toronto Press, 1963.

Nevins, Allan. *Henry White: Thirty Years of American Diplomacy.* New York: Harper & Brothers, 1930.

Newton, Lord. *Lord Lansdowne.* London: Macmillan Co., 1929.

Nicolson, Harold. *Curzon: The Last Phase 1919–1925.* London: Constable & Co., 1934.

_____. *Peacemaking 1919.* Boston: Houghton Mifflin Co., 1945.

Noble, George Bernard. *Policies and Opinions at Paris, 1919: Wilsonian Diplomacy, the Versailles Peace, and French Public Opinion.* New York: Macmillan Co., 1955.

Northedge, F. S. "1917–1919: The Implications for Britain." *Journal of Contemporary History* 4 (1968):191–209.

_____. *The Troubled Giant: Britain Among the Great Powers, 1916–1939.* London: G. Bell & Sons, 1966.

Owen, Frank. *Tempestuous Journey: Lloyd George, His Life and Times.* New York: McGraw-Hill Book Co., 1955.

Oxford and Asquith, Herbert Henry Asquith, Earl of. *Memories and Reflections: 1852–1927.* 2 vols. London: Cassell & Co., Ltd., 1927.

_____. *Speeches.* 2 vols. London: Hutchinson & Co., Ltd., 1927.

Palmer, Frederick. *Bliss, Peacemaker: The Life and Letters of General Tasker Howard Bliss.* New York: Dodd, Mead & Co., 1934.

Parrini, Carl. *Heir to Empire: United States Economic Diplomacy, 1916–1923.* Pittsburgh: University of Pittsburgh Press, 1969.

Percy, Eustace. *Some Memories.* London: Eyre & Spottiswoode, 1958.

Phillimore, Baron Walter George Frank. *Schemes For Maintaining General Peace.* London: Handbooks prepared under the direction of the Historical Section of the Foreign Office, no. 160, 1920.

_____. *Three Centuries of Treaties of Peace and Their Teaching.* London: John Murray, 1917.

Phillips, William. *Ventures in Diplomacy.* Boston: Beacon Press, 1952.

Porter, Bernard. *Critics of Empire: British Radical Attitudes to Colonialism in Africa 1895–1914.* London: Macmillan & Co., 1968.

Raffo, P. S. "The Anglo-American Preliminary Negotiations for a League of Nations." *Journal of Contemporary History* 9 (1974): 153–76.

_____. "The League of Nations Philosophy of Lord Robert Cecil." *Australian Journal of Politics and History* 20 (1974):186–96.

_____. "Lord Robert Cecil and the League of Nations." Ph.D. dissertation, University of Liverpool, 1967.

Ranshofen-Wertheimer, Egon F. *The International Secretariat: A Great Experiment in International Administration.* Washington, D.C.: Carnegie Endowment for Internal Peace, 1945.

Renaudel, Pierre. *L'Internationale à Berne: Traités et documents.* Paris: Grasset, 1919.

Riddell, George Allardice, Lord. *Lord Riddell's Intimate Diary of the Peace Conference and After: 1918–1923.* London: Victor Gollancz, 1933.

Robbins, Keith G. *The Abolition of War: The Peace Movement in Britain, 1914–1919.* Cardiff: University of Wales Press, 1976.

_____. "The Abolition of War: A Study of the Organization and Ideology of the Peace Movement, 1914–1919." D.Phil. dissertation, Oxford University, 1964.

_____. "Lord Bryce and the First World War." *Historical Journal* 10 (1967):255–77.

_____. *Sir Edward Grey: A Biography of Lord Grey of Fallodon.* London: Cassell & Co., 1971.

Roskill, Stephen. *Hankey, Man of Secrets.* 3 vols. London: Collins, 1970–74.

_____. *Naval Policy Between the Wars.* 2 vols. Vol. 1, *The Period of Anglo-American Antagonism, 1919–1929.* New York: Walker & Co., 1968.

Rothwell, V. H. *British War Aims and Peace Diplomacy, 1914–1918.* London: Oxford University Press, Clarendon Press, 1972.

Rowland, Peter. *Lloyd George.* London: Barrie & Jenkins, 1975.

Rudin, Harry. *Armistice 1918.* New Haven: Yale University Press, 1944.

Salter, J. A. *Allied Shipping Control: An Experiment in International Administration.* London: Oxford University Press, Clarendon Press, 1921.

_____. *Memoirs of a Public Servant.* London: Faber & Faber, 1961.

_____. *The United States of Europe and Other Papers.* London: George Allen & Unwin, 1933.

Scally, Robert J. *The Origins of the Lloyd George Coalition: The Politics of Social Imperialism, 1900–1918*. Princeton: Princeton University Press, 1975.

Schwabe, Klaus. "Woodrow Wilson and Germany's Membership in the League of Nations, 1918–1919." *Central European History* 8 (1975):3–22.

Scott, James Brown, ed. *Official Statements of War Aims and Peace Proposals, December 1916 to November 1918*. Washington: Carnegie Endowment for International Peace, 1921.

Semmel, Bernard. *Imperialism and Social Reform*. London: George Allen & Unwin, 1960.

Seymour, Charles, ed. *The Intimate Papers of Colonel House*. 4 vols. Boston: Houghton Mifflin Co., 1926–28.

Sharp, Alan J. "The Foreign Office in Eclipse 1919–1922." *History* 61 (1976):198–218.

Smith, Daniel M. *The Great Departure: The United States and World War I, 1914–1920*. New York: John Wiley & Sons, 1965.

Smuts, Jan Christian. *The League of Nations: A Practical Suggestion*. London: Hadder & Stoughton, 1918.

Sprout, Harold and Margaret. *Towards a New Order of Sea Power*. 2nd ed. Princeton: Princeton University Press, 1946.

Steed, Henry Wickham. *Through Thirty Years, 1892–1922*. 2 vols. London: William Heinemann, 1924.

Steiner, Zara S. *The Foreign Office and Foreign Policy, 1898–1914*. London: Cambridge University Press, 1969.

Stevenson, Frances. *Lloyd George: A Diary by Frances Stevenson*. Edited by A. J. P. Taylor. London: Hutchinson Publishing Group, 1971.

Stone, Ralph. *The Irreconcilables: The Fight against the League of Nations*. Lexington: University Press of Kentucky, 1970.

Stromberg, Roland N. *Collective Security and American Foreign Policy from the League of Nations to NATO*. New York: Frederick A. Praeger, 1963.

⸺. "The Idea of Collective Security." *Journal of the History of Ideas* 17 (1956):250–63.

⸺. "Uncertainties and Obscurities about the League of Nations." *Journal of the History of Ideas* 33 (1972):139–54.

Swartz, Marvin. *The Union of Democratic Control in British Politics during the First World War.* London: Oxford University Press, Clarendon Press, 1970.

Taylor, A. J. P., *Politics in Wartime.* London: Hamish Hamilton, 1964.

————. *The Trouble Makers: Dissent Over Foreign Policy, 1792–1939.* London: Hamish Hamilton, 1957.

————, ed. *Lloyd George: Twelve Essays.* London: Hamish Hamilton, 1971.

————, ed. *My Darling Pussy: The Letters of Lloyd George and Frances Stevenson 1913–41.* London: George Weidenfeld & Nicolson, 1975.

Temperley, H. W. V., ed. *A History of the Peace Conference of Paris.* 6 vols. London: Oxford University Press, 1920–24.

Thompson, Charles T. *The Peace Conference Day by Day: A Presidential Pilgrimage Leading to the Discovery of Europe.* New York: Brentano's, 1920.

Thompson, John M. *Russia, Bolshevism, and the Versailles Peace.* Princeton: Princeton University Press, 1966.

Thompson, Kenneth W. "Collective Security Reexamined." *American Political Science Review* 47 (1953):753–766.

Tillman, Seth P. *Anglo-American Relations at the Paris Peace Conference of 1919.* Princeton: Princeton University Press, 1961.

Times (London). *The History of the "Times."* 4 vols. Vol. 4, *The 150th Anniversary and Beyond, 1912–1948.* London: Times Publishing Co., 1952.

Toynbee, A. J., and Smith, Jean, eds. *Gilbert Murray: An Unfinished Autobiography.* London: George Allen & Unwin, 1960.

Toynbee, A. J., and Thomson, J. A. K., eds. *Essays in Honour of Gilbert Murray.* London: George Allen & Unwin, 1936.

Trask, David. *Captains and Cabinets: Anglo-American Naval Relations 1917–1918.* Columbia: University of Missouri Press, 1972.

Trevelyan, G. M. *Grey of Fallodon: Being the Life of Sir Edward Grey Afterwards Viscount Grey of Fallodon.* London: Longmans, Green & Co., 1937.

Turner, J. A. "The Formation of Lloyd George's 'Garden Suburb': 'Fabian-like Milner Penetration'?" *Historical Journal* 20 (1977):65–84.

"The Unity of Civilization." *The Round Table* 9, no. 32 (September 1918):679–84.

Vansittart, Lord. *The Mist Procession: The Autobiography of Lord Vansittart.* London: Hutchinson, 1958.

Van der Slice, Austin. *International Labor, Diplomacy, and Peace, 1914–1919.* Philadelphia: University of Pennsylvania Press, 1941.

Veatch, Richard. *Canada and the League of Nations.* Toronto: University of Toronto Press, 1975.

"The Victory That Will End War," *The Round Table* 8, no. 30 (March 1918):221–28.

Vinson, J. Chalmers. *Referendum for Isolation: Defeat of Article Ten of the League of Nations Covenant.* Athens: University of Georgia Press, 1961.

Walters, Frank P. *A History of the League of Nations.* London: Oxford University Press, 1960.

Walworth, Arthur. *America's Moment: 1918: American Diplomacy at the End of World War I.* New York: W. W. Norton & Co., 1977.

———. *Woodrow Wilson.* 2nd ed. Boston: Houghton Mifflin Co., 1971.

Warman, Roberta M. "The Erosion of Foreign Office Influence in the Making of Foreign Policy, 1916–1918." *Historical Journal* 15 (1972):133–59.

Watson, David Robin. *Georges Clemenceau: A Political Biography.* London: Eyre Methuen, 1974.

Watt, D. C. *Personalities and Policies: Studies in the Formulation of British Foreign Policy in the Twentieth Century.* Notre Dame: University of Notre Dame Press, 1965.

Weinroth, Howard S. "The British Radicals and the Balance of Power 1902–14." *Historical Journal* 13 (1970):653–82.

Willert, Arthur. *The Road to Safety.* London: Derek Verschoyle, 1952.

———. *Washington and Other Memories.* Boston: Houghton Mifflin Co., 1971.

Williamson, Samuel R., Jr. *The Politics of Grand Strategy: Britain and France Prepare for War, 1904–1914.* Cambridge, Mass.: Harvard University Press, 1970.

Wilson, Florence. *The Origins of the League of Nations Covenant: Documentary History of Its Drafting.* London: Hogarth Press, 1928.

Wilson, Trevor. "The Coupon and the British Election of 1918." *Journal of Modern History* 36 (1964):28–42.

———. *The Downfall of the Liberal Party, 1914–1935.* London: William Collins Sons & Co., 1966.

———, ed. *The Political Diaries of C. P. Scott, 1911–1928.* London: Collins, 1970.

Wimer, Kurt. "Woodrow Wilson's Plan to Enter the League of Nations Through an Executive Agreement." *Western Political Quarterly* 11 (1958):800–12.

Winkler, Henry R. "The Development of the League of Nations Idea in Great Britain, 1914–1919." *Journal of Modern History* 20 (1948):95–112.

———. "The Emergence of a Labour Foreign Policy in Great Britain, 1918–1929." *Journal of Modern History* 28 (1956):247–58.

———. *The League of Nations Movement in Great Britain: 1914–1919.* New Brunswick, N.J.: Rutgers University Press, 1952.

Woodward, David. "David Lloyd George: A Negotiated Peace with Germany and the Kuhlmann Peace Kite of September, 1917." *Canadian Journal of History* 6 (1971):74–93.

———. "The Origins and Intent of David Lloyd George's January 5 War Aims Speech." *The Historian* 34 (1971):22–39.

Woolf, Leonard. "Articles Suggested for adoption by an International Conference at the termination of the present war by the International Agreements Committee of the Fabian Research Department." *New Statesman* 5, no. 119 (17 July 1915), Special Supplement, pp. 1–8.

———. *Beginning Again: An Autobiography of the Years 1911–1918.* London: Hogarth Press, 1964.

———. "An International Authority and the Prevention of War." *New Statesman* 5, no. 118 (10 July 1915), Special Supplement, pp. 1–24.

———. *International Government: Two Reports, Prepared for the Fabian Research Department Together with a Project by a Fabian Committee for a Supernational Authority That Will Prevent War.* New York: Brentano's, 1916.

Yates, Louis A. R. *The United States and French Security: 1917–1921: A Study in American Diplomatic History*. New York: Twayne Publishers, 1957.

Zimmern, Alfred. *The League of Nations and the Rule of Law, 1918–1935*. 2nd ed. London: Macmillan & Co., 1939.

[_____.] "Some Principles and Problems of the Settlement." *Round Table* 9, no. 33 (December 1918):83–113.

NEWSPAPERS AND PERIODICALS

Daily Chronicle
Daily Mail
Daily News
Daily Telegraph
Herald (*Daily Herald* from 31 March 1919)
John Bull
Labour Leader
Manchester Guardian
Morning Post
Nation
National Review
New Europe
New Statesman
New York Times
Nineteenth Century and After
Round Table
Times (London)
War and Peace
Westminster Gazette

Index

Publication of Supplementary Volumes to *The Papers of Woodrow Wilson* is assisted from time to time by the Woodrow Wilson Foundation in order to encourage scholarly work about Woodrow Wilson and his time. All volumes have passed the review procedures of the publishers and the Editor and the Editorial Advisory Committee of *The Papers of Woodrow Wilson.* Inquiries about the Series should be addressed to The Editor, Papers of Woodrow Wilson, Firestone Library, Princeton University, Princeton, N.J. 08540.

Raymond B. Fosdick, *Letters on the League of Nations: From the Files of Raymond B. Fosdick* (Princeton University Press, 1966).

Wilton B. Fowler, *British-American Relations, 1917–1918: The Role of Sir William Wiseman* (Princeton University Press, 1969).

John M. Mulder, *Woodrow Wilson: The Years of Preparation* (Princeton University Press, 1978).

George W. Egerton, *Great Britain and the Creation of the League of Nations: Strategy, Politics, and International Organization, 1914–1919* (University of North Carolina Press, 1978).